W9-BPN-335

THE PROPHETIC FAITH

Other books by Martin Buber

THE PROPHETIC FAITH

MARTIN BUBER

COLLIER BOOKS
Macmillan Publishing Company
New York

COLLIER MACMILLAN PUBLISHERS
London

Copyright © 1949 by Macmillan Publishing Company, a division of Macmillan, Inc.

Copyright renewed 1977 by Macmillan Publishing Company, a division of Macmillan, Inc.

All rights reserved. No part of this book may be reproduced or transmitted in any form or by any means, electronic or mechanical, including photocopying, recording or by any information storage and retrieval system, without permission in writing from the Publisher.

Macmillan Publishing Company
866 Third Avenue, New York, N.Y. 10022
Collier Macmillan Canada, Inc.

Library of Congress Cataloging in Publication Data

Buber, Martin, 1878-1965.
The prophetic faith.

Translation of: Torat ha-nevi' im.
Includes index.
1. Bible. O.T.—Criticism, interpretation, etc.
I. Title.
BS1171.B7713   1985   221.6   85-7690
ISBN 0-02-084220-1

Macmillan books are available at special discounts for bulk purchases for sales promotions, premiums, fund-raising, or educational use. For details, contact:

Special Sales Director
Macmillan Publishing Company
866 Third Avenue
New York, N.Y. 10022

10 9 8 7 6 5 4 3 2

Printed in the United States of America

CONTENTS

1. INTRODUCTION

The task of this book is to describe a teaching which reached its completion in some of the writing prophets from the last decades of the Northern kingdom to the return from the Babylonian exile, and to describe it both as regards its historical process and as regards its antecedents. This is the teaching about the relation between the God of Israel and Israel. It did not begin with the first writing prophets. Generally speaking, it is not a new teaching they advance, but they fashion its form to fit the changing historical situations and their different demands, and they perfect a teaching they have received—but where is the beginning of this teaching?

We cannot begin our investigations with the primitive stages of Israel's faith, that is to say with something up to now doubtful in the eyes of many scholars. In order to find a safe starting point we must begin with the first stage at which we find evidence, the stage which no literary criticism can shake, in other words: we must begin with the question we put to a text, that, according to the common opinion of science, is the direct expression of a special age. We must ask this text, what was the faith of Israel in that age, and we must examine whether or not this faith contains the essential core of the prophetic teaching about the relation between God and Israel. If the answer is in the affirmative, we must go back step by step and find out in which earlier periods we can assume the existence of a faith possessing such characteristics as this, though of course in an earlier stage of development, and we must continue groping until we reach that stage which we may regard as the beginning. At every stage we shall discover something not only about the formation of this teaching, but also about its nature. Thus the first part of our task will be accomplished.

We shall be able then to turn to the second, the greater part of our task: we must tread the way of the history of Israel's faith from the beginning, and investigate how on this way that essential core develops until it becomes a complete teaching. Here we shall find that at every landmark the persons connected with it are designated by the term *nabi*. It is true this term came to bear witness to their character as intermediaries, bearing the word of message from heaven to earth and the word of petition from earth to heaven, as these two together are the chief work of the *nabi*. But it is clear too that apart from this there prevails a special purpose of the writing prophets, who were largely responsible for writing or arranging the stories of those men; this purpose was to bring before us the great figures of the past, whose lips from generation to generation handed down the core of the teaching at a certain stage, in their special prophetic character. But this purpose means mainly, as we shall see in our investigation, not a late alteration of the nature of that reality, but the recognition of facts in the domain of the history of the Spirit.

Now begins the historical description of the actual teaching of the prophets in its principal manifestations. This description is historical, because it places each of these manifestations in its proper place, showing how it was determined by the preceding, and how it determined the following. Our concern here is not with differentiating the single special types, but with marking the historical way of the teaching. In the second part of the book we must relate how along with the development of the powers of economy and state in the land of the settlement, this teaching advances in the midst of "the great tensions," and enters the straits of problematics within and without, and at the same time broadens and deepens increasingly in this struggle. When we reach this point we must describe the "turning to the future," that is to say prophecy in its limited sense as concerned now with the future. The rebelliousness of the hour, rebelling against the prophetic teaching, directs the heart of the prophet to the future, which will fulfil his teaching. But the connection of the *nabi* with the future is not that of one who predicts. To be a *nabi* means to set the audience, to whom the words are addressed, before the choice and decision, directly or indirectly. The future is not something already fixed in this present hour, it is dependent upon the real decision, that is to say the decision in which man takes part in this hour. When a *nabi* announces deliverance as something about to come, he presupposes *t'shubhah*, "returning," that is to say a positive and complete decision of the community, whether in this generation or in one of the generations to come. I emphasize the word "community," for even where he is mentioning individuals, the main purpose is the realisation in the whole of public life. According to the nature of things a change takes place here as in the second part: there through the formation of the state, and here, in the middle of the third and last part, through the crisis and destruction of this state: out of the depth of the community's suffering there arises the conception of God as "the God of sufferers." Just as we ascribe to the merit of the *nabi* and his teaching the change of the leader God of the semi-nomads into the God of the agrarian state, to Whose nature there clung nothing of the nature of the Canaanite gods, the local gods, so we are to ascribe to the same agency the fact that now along with His revelation as the God of sufferers nothing of His world power and His authority is lost.

In the second part one chapter leads us beyond the figures of the prophets: in the "struggle for the revelation" we can see traces of the influence of their teaching in its primitive form in the didactic story about the primeval world. And one chapter in the third part too leads us beyond prophecy: this describes how "the question," that is the question of the suffering community about the meaning of its suffering, absorbs within itself the teaching of the prophets, and how it finds its most personal expression in the didactic song and the psalm.

* * *

With regard to the use of Scriptural passages in the first and the second part we must make certain methodological observations.

The matter is made difficult because we do not possess the means of fixing the date of a great part of Scripture. Especially in the narrative books we do not know how far the chronological order of their composition corresponds with the chronological order of the things described. And this means that it is not in our power to make it clear, with accepted principles and rules of linguistic and literary history, whether or not the picture of an early religious stage bears the stamp of a nearby or a later age which has merely projected its own character or its yearning onto the background of the early time.

The attempts of modern scholarship to show each of the narrative books and especially the books of the Pentateuch, as a composite work made up of fragments from different "sources," the dates of which can to some extent be fixed, have not solved these difficulties. Such scholars have not succeeded in proving the existence of a number of complete documents, from which parts, chapters, sentences have become attached one to another. As a matter of fact they have only established one matter, namely that we have before us a number of fundamental types of the literary working out of tradition, all according to different editorial tendencies. The most important of these types are: first, a type based mainly on court prophets, a type interested in the antecedents of the kingdom of David and Solomon, appearing as those did to them as a revelation of God's will concerning this kingdom; second, a type based mainly on the free prophets, a type interested in the antecedents of the rule of God's Spirit through men seized by it; and third, a type based mainly on priests, a type interested in the antecedents of the sanctuaries, of the holy institutions and the holy customs. All of these are types and tendencies of the working out of a tradition which had already reached the written stage, types and tendencies, it is true, which, still proportionately early, have a further history. But even if we were allowed to speak of "sources" and if it were even possible to fix their dates (and also the dates of the additions and redactions), we would thereby only be able to establish layers of the *literary,* not the *religious* development, and these two need not in any way parallel one another, as it is very possible that a primitive religious element is only found in a late literary form. In order to learn something about the religious development we must look into the problem of tradition itself.

Is this scientifically possible? And if so, how?

To begin with we must fix the limits of our inquiry. The history of Israel's faith as recorded in Scripture clearly begins with the "fathers." All that preceded them can only serve us as an expression of the religious outlook of Israel, an expression of Israel's conception and picture of the beginning of the world, and its explanation of the earliest events which took place between god-head and manhood. Whereas with the wanderings of the family of Terah that part of the story begins, in connection with which we may, in fact we must, ask whether it has not in some measure the direct value of a real account of happenings in the history of faith, that is to say whether from this point on it is not advisable to take a double view of the texts and to make a double use of them. One deals with the accounts according to their character as tendencies in the working out of tradition, and therefore it is bound up with questions of dates, and one deals with them according to their narrative character independently of the question of date, if and in so far as the texts contain a tradition *near to historical events.*

In connection with this question there is no need to be afraid of the argument that "there is nothing here but legend." Historical song and legend are to a large extent—and often too in the ancient East—the natural forms of the popular oral preservation of "historical" events, that is to say events of vital importance for the tribe. They all represent a vital kind of history memorising as it happens, so long as the force of tribal life is greater than that of state control; only when the latter becomes stronger is the former obscured by the variegated history written to government order. Both kinds, the legend of the heroes (in verse or in semi-rhythmic "prose"), and the chronicles of the kings, are not intended to describe, but to glorify what took place. In the legend the practice of glorification, exaltation, and transformation grew of itself from narrator to narrator, from generation to generation of narrators, until "the fixed form" was crystallized. From now on it is made permanent and subjected to the prohibition "no addition or subtraction" (e.g., the history singers of a Negro tribe—a tribe without a script—are forbidden to make any change, and the slightest change in words or tune is even punishable by death). Is it possible then, out of such a formation, to separate a historical content, lacking as we do parallel, "objective" accounts? It is, in a special measure, first of all by examining the social-cultural background. Wherever in the narrative a definite stage in the development of economy and civilisation stands out, a stage specific to the time under description, there the historical core is not far away: the same judgement applies to the examination of geographical, political, and other data. But in particular it is possible to separate off a content from the point of view of the history of the Spirit and especially the history of religion. Here we are not concerned with the authenticity of an external event; we merely inquire whether in the period under discussion there exists the religious act or position, the religious relationship under discussion. This question can only be answered by the inner media of the history of religion. What we have to compare with here are the earlier or later stages of religious development; we have to make clear whether it is possible to understand the narrative historically, if we see in it the link in the chain of development at this point of time. But in special occurrences, which generally are of unusual significance, another criterion is to be added, only to be used, however, with great care and precision, standing as it does on the confines of knowledge, and not to be used without intuition, scientific intuition that is to say, and therefore a concern of particular scientific responsibility. I refer to the criterion expressed in all its significance in the category of the *uniqueness of the fact*. There are in the history of religion events, situations, figures, expressions, deeds, the uniqueness of which cannot be regarded as the fruit of thought or song, or as a mere fabrication, but simply and solely as a matter of fact. Only the way of speculative theory leads to a different judgement; the intuitively scientific method, that is the method that seeks after the *concreteness* at the basis of an evidence, approaches the real fact. Naturally we do not by this learn the real course of an historic event, but we do learn that in a definite age in a definite circle of tribe or people an actual relationship appeared between the believer and that in which he believes, a unique relationship and according to our perception, at a definite stage too, which also has to be designated unique, a relationship which embodies itself in a concrete event, which continues to operate concretely.

This mode of research, which I can only hint at here, must lead us in the history of Israel's faith wherever the text presents us with a tradition which we may regard legitimately as being near to the historical events. When we are confronted with such, our duty is first of all to penetrate, as far as we can, beneath the layers of different redactions of tradition and their tendencies,[1] that is to say to work from the point of view not of "source criticism" but of tradition criticism. It is true these common matters that arise from our investigation are not yet interchangeable with the unity of the tradition itself, because outside and beyond the various special tendencies, there predominates again and again under the prophetic guidance a composition tendency, a unity tendency of a religious nature, the tendency that pervades all the books in their different parts and sheds abroad one spirit, the "Biblical" spirit. It endeavours to implant one type of idea, one principle, or more correctly to restore according to its intention the first type, the latest redaction only serving as a culmination of this endeavor. It is necessary therefore to distinguish very clearly in each tradition between its fundamental unity, from which different redactions have proceeded according to different tendencies, and the unity of harmonization, fruit of the "Biblical" spirit; but we are not to see in this in any sense a late, and, from the historical point of view, utterly incorrect matter, rather we are to examine it again and again and to make it as clear as possible, whether and how far in the case of the subject under discussion there is to be found in the work of harmonization the influence of a primitive unity, preserved in the memory of generations in spite of different editorial tendencies, tendencies which in some cases had already been efficacious at the time the tradition itself came into being. And when we have come as near as possible to the tradition, we must ascertain its content from the point of view of faith, and determine its place in the development of religion.

In the account that follows I can only bring forward the results of this method; concerning the work of research itself I have written more elsewhere, and I hope to continue it.

---

[1] Cf. my essay "Samuel and the Development of Authority in Israel" (Hebrew Zion, 4th year 1f), which is part of an as yet unpublished book and some chapters of my book "Moses" (English edition, 1946).

2. THE SONG OF DEBORAH

The Song of Deborah [1] is almost universally regarded as a genuine historical song, that is to say a spontaneous poetical outbreak of the heart of man, who having taken part in a mighty historical event is now impelled to master it in rhythmical form, to grasp, to express, to transmit it. It has been rightly said of the songs of the Afghans in their revolt against England a hundred years ago, contemporaneous songs in many respects similiar to, although much inferior to the Song of Deborah, that they are a cry of history itself.[2] The singer of the Song of Deborah is not only near the event, but stands in the midst of the actual occurrence: he calls to the actors, stirring them up and encouraging them, he blesses and curses not on account of something previously done, but in the midst of the tempest of events not yet subsided. His heavily galloping rhythm he feels as a pacing in the midst of the event; the singing *nephesh,* the breath-soul, rises and falls heavily, like the step of the heavily armed man. So we are to understand that much discussed cry (v. 21) uttered the moment enthusiasm threatens to stop the singer's breath: "Tread forth, my soul, with strength." This historical song is a religious song. Here they praise and glorify a god for victory. This type of religious poetry we know from Akkadian literature: there the god Marduk is thanked for the Babylonian victory over Elam, the god Ashur for the Assyrian victory over Elam and Babylon, there are songs about "the weapons of the god" and "the army of the god." But the Song of Deborah is different from all the religious songs of victory I know in the literature of the world. Its character is apparent as soon as we look at it: a special poetic means here serves an utterly religious purpose. This means is repetition.

[1] For an explanation of the Song cf. my book "Koenigtum Gottes," 2nd ed. (1936), 161ff.
[2] James Darmesteter, Chants populaires des Afghans (1890). Intro., cxcix.

The Song of Deborah, though early, is nevertheless a song of masterful formation. The strongest of its forms is the refrain. And this form obviously is not first created because of aesthetic motives and later appointed to serve religious purposes as well but, so far as we can judge, it was born of religion. It is known that many early lyric forms spring from a magical aim such as used to set up against the hard, unbound, demonic element, one that was bound and binding: the secret of the likeness appears as something that silences and subdues. The class of Biblical forms especially noteworthy, the repetitive forms—alliteration, assonance, paranomasia, key words, key sentences, refrain etc.—has the particular purpose of emphasizing the most important aspect of the religious message, to point again and again at the fundamental idea or ideas of the belief round which the rest are grouped, and which the recipient of the message is requested to perceive as such with concentrated intention.[3] A good example of this is to be found in the refrains of the Song of Deborah.

Seven verses, including the first, end with the word Israel, and seven,[4] including the second, end with the word YHVH. Added to this there are a single refrain of a part sentence and two refrains of a whole sentence. The former, in only two verses, 3 and 5, develops the one word-refrain: "YHVH God of Israel." The two sentence-refrains stand out more clearly. The first links verse 2, that is the opening verse of the first part of the Song, with verse 9: "When locks waxed wild in Israel" (i.e., when one vowed to let the hair of the head grow wild until the enemy be conquered), "when the people willingly offered themselves, bless YHVH"— and then "My heart to the leaders of Israel! You that offered yourselves willingly among the people, bless YHVH." The second sentence-refrain links verse 13 with verse 23, that is with the final verse of the second part of the Song: "Then what escaped (i.e., what managed to avoid captivity, cf. v. 12) descended, with the nobles the people, YHVH, descend to me among the valiant"— and "Because they came not to YHVH's help, to the help of YHVH among the valiant." The last part of the Song, which leaves the field of battle and portrays two incidental events, one well known

---

[3] Cf. Buber-Rosenzweig, Die Schrift and Ihre Verdeutschung (1936), passim.

[4] The words יהוה מלאך אמר in v. 23 are an explanatory addition, interrupting the connection and disturbing the rhythm; read ארוז מרוז ארו.

to singers and hearers, and one living only in their hearts and souls, is without refrain. It ends, however, with a verse, which with the word YHVH again preserves the basic motif of the second sentence-refrain, the motif of "valor," and so truly brings the Song to its close (here of these two names we only hear the name of *God*) : "So will all Thine enemies perish, YHVH! But they that love Him are as the going forth of the sun in its valor." All the refrains of the Song work together in utter clarity and show us the motive force of the Song and the meaning of the victory of which it sings: the connection of the deity "YHVH" with the people "Israel." Following the indications of the Song this connection may be understood to comprise these points: (a) YHVH is "the God of Israel." Israel is "YHVH's people" (v. 11; with these emphatic words the first part of the Song ends). (b) If Israel acts and accomplishes itself as Israel, YHVH is to be "blessed" for "the righteous acts to His peasants in Israel." (c) YHVH leads Israel, and He Himself goes at the head of the companies of the people, as it is put in the prose version where Deborah says to Barak (4, 14) "Has not YHVH gone out before thee?" And they must "willingly" follow Him, "come to His aid." (d) The important point is to "love" YHVH.

The presupposition is that Israel is not simply an ethnological unity, but a religio-active one; yet at the same time it is a national and not an ecclesiastical unity. To Israel as YHVH's people belong those tribes that cleave to this God and willingly come to His help. The denunciation of the inactive tribes, who did not come to YHVH's aid (v. 15b–17), clearly implies the question of division and decision, as to who belongs to the Israel that cleaves to YHVH and "loves" Him, and who belongs to YHVH's enemies.

And the other presupposition is that YHVH possesses the exclusive power. All that hate Him are destroyed, whereas upon those that love Him He bestows the gifts which are bestowed upon the sun. The going forth of the sun is not a mere poetic simile, but a hint of the cosmic rule of God. He Who leads His people leads also "the stars in their courses" (v. 20). Here it is stated as clearly as was possible in accordance with the concept and idiom of the Song, that this people-God is the master of the world. There is here no expression of a "monotheistic idea," but at the same time it is made clear that in the actuality of their life there is for the men of the Song only this one god and there cannot be another. That this God comes in a storm, in the storm cloud from the south (v. 4) pouring itself upon the chariots of the enemy, does not mean that he is a "storm god" like the Syrian Hadad, but that He is god also of the storm. Neither is He a "war god" like Ashur, though He orders battle too, fighting with his enemies and conquering. He "rides on the dark clouds"—as it is put in psalm 68 (v. 5 EV 4) which in part imitates the Song of Deborah—just as in the mythical epics of Ras Shamra the rain god, Aliyan-Baal, rides upon them (the epithets are almost identical), and is no rain god, but He who brings also the rain. And he does not come, according to the accepted interpretation, from Horeb, the mount being his habitation—there is no word of this here ; he comes with the storm, and steps out of the darkness to lead the hosts of his people to battle. But this coming of YHVH appears to the poet as a new revelation, recalling the revelation from the midst of the darkness on Mount Sinai, the place where the covenant between YHVH and Israel was made. "The mountains shook before YHVH," he calls— and interrupting himself cries (this is no marginal gloss, but an essential part of the Song) : "this (i.e., Mount Tabor, cf. 4, 6) is a Sinai before YHVH, God of Israel." Again the leader-God has revealed Himself.

How may one suppose does the singer portray for himself this God, who "descends" at the head of the host, marching in the front rank of the "valiant," from Mount Tabor to the Kishon valley occupied by the Canaanite horsemen? The poet does not tell us, for this was certainly known even to the babe in Israel, and all the people that heard the Song would see the same picture in their hearts. This is the picture we know from the story of the disaster at Ebenezer (1 Sam. 4) that is undoubtedly true—no people would invent such an extreme instance of historical humiliation—"the ark of the covenant of YHVH of hosts, of Him sitting on the cherubim" (v. 4), the ark that goes at the head of the battle array. From a later song (2 Sam. 22, 10f ; Ps. 18, 10f) another picture comes before us, that of the lord, riding—as in Psalm 68 on the dark clouds—upon the highest thundercloud that is shaped like a cherub, and thick darkness under his feet. From the clouds he descends upon the waiting ark to dwell upon the wings of the golden cherubim as they touch one another, and from thence, invisible and visible to all at the same time, to lead his people to war. At the same hour the storm clouds break out at His command "from heaven" (Judges 5, 20) upon the enemies, and the charioteers, taken unawares in the twilight by the infantry of Israel, try to set in order their battle ranks in the flooded clay soil impeding all movement, while the first stars, stepping large and weird out of the scattering cloud banks, confound sight and transform retreat into wild flight and destruction.[5]

In a song slightly later than the Song of Deborah but akin to it in spirit and language, a song long afterwards connected as a frame song with the "Blessing of Moses" (Deut. 33, 2–5, 26–29), it is stated in that part of historic retrospect which corresponds to the epoch of the Tabor battle (v. 26), in a call to the people, whom the song here addresses with a glorifying name (derived from *yashar,* "upright") : "There is nothing like God, Jeshurun, riding the heavens to help thee, and the mists in His majesty." Here it is "to help thee," in the Song of Deborah it is "to YHVH's help." There is nothing like Him, like YHVH—this is the fundamental feeling of the poet inspired by the deeds of his God—Who comes to my help, to the help of Israel, and bids me, bids Israel, to come to His help, that He may lead me. And in the closing verse of the Song it is said : "Blessed art thou, Israel, who is there like thee, a people upheld by YHVH, shield of thy help, and sword of thy majesty." There is none like YHVH, and none like Israel, since they are YHVH's people. To the heavenly majesty of YHVH corresponds the earthly majesty of Israel: because YHVH is their shield and sword. And the song ends, after it has announced that Israel's enemies "shall cringe,"—as in the conclusion of the Song of Deborah YHVH's enemies "shall vanish"—with the promise to Israel, in which again there recurs a word of the Song of Deborah, a word of that call to the soul of the singer himself ("Tread forth, my soul, in strength") : "And thou wilt tread upon their high places." He who so goes his way knows that he is led.

The first part of the song (vv. 2–6) returns to the early history of this relationship between God and people. In words (v. 2) that point directly to the Song of Deborah (v. 4) the theophany at Sinai is here belauded, to which it was only compared there.

[5] For the historical event cf. Garstang, The Foundations of Bible History, Joshua, Judges (1931), 298ff.

3. ORIGINS

A. THE SHECHEM ASSEMBLY

The faith and the relationship to God of the faithful, which found expression in the Song of Deborah and became crystallised in the various acknowledgments of "YHVH God of Israel," cannot have come into being at the time of the composition of the Song itself. This does not need to be expounded. Everything points to something earlier, something long and well established. In order to understand the development of this belief, we must go back somewhat on the path of history. The first step brings us to a passage, which, it is true, differs in every respect from the Song of Deborah: while the Song is in many ways difficult to understand on account of its archaic language, this passage is written in plain language; whereas the Song is of certain date and apparently preserved for us almost without change, this passage is difficult from the point of view of its literary development, and is composed—if we may judge from a number of adaptations which have taken place in it—of two parts essentially different the one from the other. The first part is a survey of history, which for the most part can be easily recognized as a typical fragment of that Preachers' school, the later stage of which is usually designated by the name of the "Deuteronomist," and the second part is the story of a great event which belongs to a real tradition. The passage in question is the chapter about Joshua's assembly at Shechem (Josh. 24, 1–28). The historical part tells about the assembling (v. 1), about the talk with the heads of the people (14–24), preceded probably by the words of YHVH (cf. v. 27) that cannot be reconstructed, and about the making of the covenant (25–27), sealed apparently with the foundation of a central sanctuary of the tribal group at Shechem, where according to a trustworthy tradition (8, 30) Joshua had earlier built an altar "to YHVH God of Israel."

If we separate the later elements (e.g., v. 17 and 18a) from the dialogue between Joshua and the people, we are presented with a dialogical religious act of a unique character. Joshua demands of the people that they fear YHVH and serve Him "in sincerity and in faithfulness" (v. 14b is dubious), and if not—they must "to-day" decide and choose other gods, either the tribal gods of the far-off days when "the fathers" still dwelled in Mesopotamia, or the gods of Canaan around them; "As for me and my house we will serve YHVH." The people swear that they will not forsake YHVH nor serve other gods: "We too will serve YHVH, for He is our God" (v. 18). This declaration does not set Joshua at rest, and he warns them: by the way they mean to go they cannot serve YHVH, it is possible in this way to serve other gods but not Him, "for He is a holy God" (v. 19), a "zealous" God, demanding exclusive devotion and utterly consuming them who forsake Him, whether their defection be half-hearted and casual or complete. The people stand by their declaration. They are willing to be witnesses against themselves, as Joshua pronounces to them. And now he orders them to put away the foreign deities in their midst; "and turn your hearts to YHVH God of Israel" (v. 23). Only now does this refrain of the Song of Deborah appear, as it appeared at the beginning of the speech (v. 2): only now after "all the tribes of Israel" have been united to serve YHVH, is this epithet again made right. And to this the people answers finally (v. 24): "YHVH our God we will serve and hearken to His voice." Only now (v. 25) does Joshua "establish a covenant for the people" and "set a statute and ordinance for them," as it is said Moses did after the dividing of the Red Sea (Exod. 15, 25). Only in these two places in the Bible do we find this phrase "set statute and ordinance for someone," and in neither place is there any mention of the contents of that which was set. (We may conjecture that in the former case they were march rules for the wilderness journeyings, and that here they were covenant rules for the sanctuary of the Covenant, for the festivals and assemblies in connection with it.[1]) And Joshua sets up under the terebinth in the sanctuary a great stone, a pillar of witness.

What we are told here in the form of a dialogue is a historical

[1] Cf. Buber, Koenigtum Gottes, 157ff.

life decision of the people, out of which arises the formula that links together the names of YHVH and Israel "YHVH God of Israel." Are we to gather here that this was the historic hour at which in one event the tribes were linked to become Israel, and Israel linked to YHVH? Was it only here that the relationship of faith between God and people began? Some indeed have thought so, and have expressed their opinion "that Joshua's covenant was in truth the beginning, and was the first to be concluded." [2] There is, however, no basis for this view. There is nothing here of any sacramental covenant between God and people, after the manner of the story of the blood covenant at Sinai (Exod. 24, 8). We do not feel here that we are in the atmosphere of a sacred event, manifesting itself as an objective action between above and below, creating a reciprocal relation between God and people; what we find here is the spirit of collective human faith decision which does not require a special sacramental act, but only regular symbolic testimony. We are not told anything about a covenant between heaven and earth binding both sides but only about the self binding of the people towards God receiving the quality of covenant obligation. In this act Joshua is in no sense acting "as representative and in the name of the people," as some suggest; [3] the phrase "to make a covenant *for* someone" means almost always in the Bible the action of the superior party or his representative. The event here before us is just the first of those covenant renewals, the clearest example of which we see in the "covenant making" of Josiah (2 Kgs. 23, 3): the people, which had transgressed or broken the covenant, agree again to establish and perform it, whereas the deity, Who has kept the covenant faithfully, has no need to enter upon it anew. He needs only to renew it by the agency of His representative—it is the king in this case—accepting it as in force "before YHVH" (as Joshua 24, 1, "before God") and establishing it. (It is a quite different literary form used in the description of a religious political act as in 2 Kgs. 11, 17, where, as we know from ancient Arabian documents about covenant renewal, the king is to be attested as standing between god and people.)

[2] Bin Gorion, Sinai and Garizim (1926), 405.
[3] Noth, Das Buch Josua (1938), 108.

Here we must make clear our attitude to another point of view expressed by a number of important scholars.[4] According to this "the great majority of the people had hitherto no knowledge of YHVH at all, and therefore had not taken any part in the wilderness journeyings," but "remained aforetime in the land," and "only after seeing the wonderful leadership of the Moses-Joshua group, that is to say the tribe of Ephraim, did they also turn to this deity"; they now renounced, in a solemn manner "their accepted religious traditions," and chose YHVH, thus joining also the centralized covenant cult at Shechem. Only so, these critics think, is it possible to explain the fact that Israel here appears as if it had never stood at Mount Sinai, as a people, "the great part of which still serves idols," and which still "has to put away the foreign gods from their midst." Moreover amongst these gods which are to be put away are to be numbered "all the gods of the fathers of Israel": by those "other gods," which according to verses 2 and 14 the fathers formerly served, are meant their particular gods, their *elim*.

But it is not only that in the text we see nothing of any such division of the people into two (for it is not possible to attribute the saying "I and my house" to the tribes that took part in the wilderness journeyings, even if they were few in number); not only that in the speech all the answers are attributed to "the people" as such; but in the first of these answers the people declare (v. 16): "Far be it from us to *forsake* YHVH to serve other gods." So the people had continued to cling to YHVH thus far. And Joshua refers to this in his answer (v. 20), for his words "if you forsake YHVH and serve foreign gods . . ." mean: you forsake YHVH even if you serve foreign gods by the side of Him—to which the people reply: "Not (so), but YHVH (Him alone) we will serve." It will not do to regard as a later addition the verse, "Far be it from us to forsake YHVH," this being essential for the inner connection of the dialogue. It is stated here with complete clarity that "the people" had clung to YHVH already up to now *according to their consciousness,* and that as a whole. Whereas in what follows (v. 19) it is said that *in Joshua's*

[4] Cf. especially Sellin, Geschichte des israelitisch-juedischen Volks I (1924), 98f; Noth, Das System der zwoelf Staemme Israels (1930), 66ff; Steuernagel, Jahwe und die Vaetergoetter (Festschrift Georg Beer, 1935), 63ff.

eyes this service is not true service of YHVH: because it was
not exclusive, did not establish the demands of the "holy God,"
of the "zealous God." The words which they speak to Joshua
mean: we acknowledge YHVH. Whereas Joshua's words to them
mean: the acknowledgment of YHVH is not true, if one also
recognizes other powers—you must decide to whom you wish
to cleave, to them or to Him; from this moment you are not
entitled to think that you can do both together. This is not to
say, to be sure, that by "other" he means precisely *elim,* for if
this were meant, the people would not have been able to contradict so vehemently that they were thinking of other gods.
What then is the meaning? In what lay the people's sin against
the covenant, and their need to turn and renew it?

The people were not at all aware that they had served other
gods, for *as a people* they had had no other gods. As far as they
knew they had in truth had no others, for they had had no *common*
deity apart from YHVH. Indeed, no tribe had a common deity
of their own; all of them, so far as we can see, without exception
take part in the general declaration. The families, however, have
their family deities, household deities, private gods, whose existence public consciousness did not comprehend. These are objects, probably wooden masks—the epithet *taraph,* which we find
in the singular in the Ras Shamra texts and in the Bible only in
the plural, is explained apparently in later writings as something
becoming rotten—with which it is indeed easier to keep company
than with the invisible; these bestow happiness, they multiply
power, they tell the future, they may be approached at any hour
and in any mood of life, the women bring them from their father's
houses to those of their husbands. It is their nature that they
are not real gods with name, personality, myth and cult; they are
definitely subsidiary. They were subsidiary deities in the Babylonian and Syrian areas of culture, amongst those peoples through
whom Israel's way had led; they were brought from "foreign
parts"; now they have become subsidiary deities in Israel. And
just for this reason they are to be "removed." How are they to be
removed? In the tales of the fathers we find this description
(Gen. 35, 2–4): all "foreign gods" were being handed over to the
head of the family and he buried them under a sacred tree in
the neighborhood of Shechem, even the same tree apparently

under which Joshua set up the memorial stone. Here too, in the legend, the meaning of the act of removing is the beginning of a new situation. In the historical story we find a kind of concentration which bears the stamp of history. There is no fundamental distinction here between religion and politics, as is the case in general with Israel at the period when its particular qualities assumed form. Because these subsidiary private deities weaken the collection of the people around YHVH, they hinder the establishment and manifestation of a united "Israel" acting historically as such. This becomes particularly clear in a well preserved fragment (1 Sam. 7, 3)—akin in language to the oldest part of the narrative in the book of Joshua—of a tale of the time of the Philistine war, the remainder being much worked over. Here Samuel orders "the whole house of Israel" to return to YHVH with all their heart, to remove from their midst the foreign gods (the words "and the Ashtaroth" are an addition), to "prepare" their heart for YHVH and to serve Him alone. Joshua's corresponding action is the expression and outcome of his experience as leader of the people and their commander (again it is not very important whether all the tribes were subject to his rule, as the Biblical text suggests, or only a smaller group).[5] Hitherto the conquest of the land has only partly succeeded, because there was not at that time in fact any actual and vital unity of the people. The life of the tribes was restricted and wrapped up in family interests, and was devoted to the family deities. The people could not establish real historical unity, unless they all become exclusively "YHVH's people"—unless YHVH becomes "Israel's God." Around this matter everything here revolves, as it was to be later in the days of the Song of Deborah. The banding together of the tribes, which Joshua organizes, can have no center but YHVH's sanctuary, and no form of assembly but YHVH's festivals.

Joshua did not give a new deity to the tribes, nor even to a section of them. It was not he who brought together YHVH and Israel. We must take a step further backwards in history, in order to reach the roots of the matter. This brings us to the man, whose disciple and heir Joshua was according to the Biblical narrative.

[5] Cf. Alt, Josua (in the collection, Werden und Wesen des Alten Testaments 1936), 1ff.

B. MOUNT SINAI

In our examination of the Song of Deborah we found that the phrase "YHVH God of Israel" from the side of the deity implies leadership, the "going before the people," and from the side of the people the "offering themselves willingly." This offering themselves means devotion to God and to the people at once. No one can declare himself for Israel without declaring himself for YHVH. For Israel only exists as "YHVH's people," in actual fact, "coming to YHVH's help" and "blessing" Him, and he who does not belong in this sense to YHVH's people does not belong to Israel. Whosoever remains "among the sheepfolds" (Ju. 5, 16) has no part in that community called Israel. The particularism appears here as the special "enemy" of YHVH, and obviously the cry about the destruction of all YHVH's enemies is meant for the ears of those separating themselves.

From this point we have turned back to the tradition about the historical event, in which YHVH was proclaimed as the God of Israel and the radical decision demanded of the people to stand for God and against the particularism. At the Shechem assembly it was not the particularism of the *tribes* that was discussed;. Joshua's protest was directed against the particularism of the *families*, whose influence had hindered the complete entry of the tribes into the community and also their participation in "YHVH's wars," which it led. This protest was directed only against religious particularism; it attacked the *gods* of the families, as the element that had hitherto prevented the fulfilment of that covenant obligation, which Israel had accepted towards its God, so making covenant renewal a necessity. And this can only come about as a result of one of two things: either the family gods must be abolished from their houses, or all the groups remaining devoted to other gods must be banished from the people.

From this historical act of covenant *renewal* we must turn back again to the act of covenant *making*.

In chapter 24 of Exodus, which is apparently made up of traditions differing one from another in character and development, one very early tradition is preserved. Moses builds an altar beneath Mount Sinai and around it assembles twelve pillars, symbols

of the tribes. The people bring offerings. Of the blood of the
offering Moses sprinkles half on the altar, and so the part appointed for God is, so to say, touching God Himself, and half he
retains to begin with in a basin, until the people pledge themselves to observe the "book of the covenant," whereupon Moses
sprinkles the blood "upon the people," and calls out the sacramental formula: "Behold the blood of the covenant which YHVH
has made with you." After finishing this he ascends the mount
with the representatives of Israel. Here they "see the God of
Israel" (this is obviously the oldest verse, in which this concept,
"the God of Israel," is found, and its special connotation has been
acquired just by the making of the covenant). The story that
follows tells of what they really see, and its meaning is apparently: they see open before them the "kernel of heaven,"
free of all the cloud darkness (10, 11) "like a work of sapphire
stones," and they see that the heavens are "under the feet" of God.
So they visualize the godhead, and in doing this they enjoy the
sacred meal, eating and drinking.

This common vision is described as an event following the making of the covenant. The narrator knows why he represents the sev-
enty as seeing not "YHVH" but the "God of Israel." The people
pledged themselves with the words "All that YHVH has said
we will do and hear" to establish the covenant; they received
the "blood of the covenant"; the deity their representatives behold now is "the God of Israel."

This step backwards which we have taken has brought us to
the first appearance of the credal formula, "YHVH God of Israel."
But its actual origin cannot be found in a *narrative* passage but
only in a *direct* utterance. Even in a song, however, or in a dialogue
between a human leader and the people we can only grasp an
echo and not the thing itself; of necessity it must be a divine
saying handed down, a word of YHVH Himself. And if we know
of a saying that we think can be understood so, then there is a
test by which we are able to recognize whether we have understood it correctly. If it is as we understand it then we may expect
to find in it again the same fundamentals as we found in the
Song of Deborah: God's going before the people and the people's "love" for God, and that basic principle which we saw in

Joshua's speech, the "zeal" against the "service" of "other gods."
Literary criticism having gone so far that some attribute the
formation of the Decalogue to "the circle of Isaiah's disciples"[1]
or even later still to the exilic or post-exilic period,[2] cautious
critical science of our day has reached the view that we have in
chapter 20 of Exodus (after later additions have been removed)
a primitive form of the Decalogue, "the contents of which comprise nothing which forbid their connection with the generation
of Moses.[3] Verse 2 as a whole is reckoned as belonging to this
original Decalogue, and "is conceivable in the mouth of Moses,"[4]
and likewise the whole of verse 3, but the "prohibition of images"
contained in verses 4 and 5 only in an abbreviated form. The
proposed form, however, "Thou shalt not make to thyself any
graven image, thou shalt not worship *them,* nor be allowed to
serve *them,*" is from a literary point of view very improbable; the
plural can be understood only from the Biblical text. And the
second part of v. 4 is shown to be indispensable and not merely an
expansion and completion of the first part, if only we rightly
divide the sentences:[5] "Thou shalt not make to thyself a graven
image! And every shape (*temunah* does not mean in the Bible
image, but the real shape, 'the form of the species') which is in
heaven above or in earth beneath or in the waters under the
earth, thou shalt not bow down to them (i.e., to these things[6]
themselves) nor serve them." (It follows of course that in the
second part, which incidentally is longer by far than the first,
there is no word at all of the "prohibition of images," but of the
prohibition to serve any creature of the universe, and even YHVH
Himself in any created form.) It is not easy here to detach
anything. So it is with verse 5b: the sentence that has been so
much discussed, which speaks of the iniquity of the fathers to

[1] Mowinckel, Le décalogue (1927), 160; cf. Mowinckel, Zur Geschichte des
Dekalogs, Zeitschrift fuer alttestamentliche Wissenschaft, Neue Folge, XIV
(1937).

[2] So Hoelscher, Geschichte der israelitischen und juedischen Religion (1922),
129.

[3] Ludwig Koehler, Der Dekalog, Theologische Rundschau I (1929), 184.

[4] *Ibid.,* 179.

[5] Cf. Dillmann's commentary on this: the constructions in Deut. 4, 16, 25 &
5, 8 rest upon false interpretations of our verse.

[6] "To the very things found in heaven and earth" (commentary of Seforno).

be "ordained" only upon the few generations born in their life-time, is so strong a motivation for the prohibitions of verses 3–5 (the word "for" after three "no's" is early Biblical style [7]) that it cannot be far from the original nucleus.[8] And here in this verse, we find the origin of the "zealous God" in Joshua and the "lovers" of YHVH in the Song of Deborah. "Fear Him," Joshua says, and though it is not said explicitly in the Decalogue, it can be heard in verse 5 clearly enough, and in the next verse as at the end of the Song we find the words: Love Him!

The origin of Joshua's demand to renounce "other gods," the service of which is the "forsaking of YHVH," can be seen in verse 3 where the plural noun and adjective in relation to a singular verb have the meaning: any other divinity. In this is implied everything which men are liable to make into a god. What is said here to Israel as a whole, and so to each individual amongst the people,[9] is not that there *are no* other gods: to say this would be to contradict the intentional sense and connection of the passage; Israel is told, that it is *forbidden* for other gods to exist. Forbidden that *they* should have other gods: but it only concerns *them,* who are addressed, and the whole reality of the subject under discussion is that of the relationship between YHVH and Israel. It is forbidden that there should be in Israel anything that might be in the face of God (the expression "to be in someone's face" is not far removed from such strong expressions as "to dwell in someone's face," Gen. 16, 12, and "to fall in someone's face," 25, 18), nothing made by men's hands and no created being, not even a thing or being that may be regarded as a representation or manifestation of YHVH Himself. YHVH is unwilling that a figure of Himself should stand in the way of His essence. There-fore in a special, much misunderstood saying (Exod. 20, 7) He forbids men to "carry" His name "unto the delusion," that is to say unto anything fictitious, unto things of imagination (cf. Ps. 24, 5, EV 4: "who has not carried his soul unto the delusion"),

---

[7] This style is not at all Deuteronomic, so far as by this we mean the art of the Preachers' school represented in Deuteronomy; but there is in this book too a very ancient nucleus, which is sharply distinguished in style from the rest of the book.

[8] But cf. Buber, Moses, 141ff.

[9] Volz, Mose und sein Werk, 2nd edn (1932), 26.

either by giving His name to a mere appearance and nonentity, or by using it for magical purposes, for enchantment and incantation.

All this, however, springs from the first and chief saying, in which also lies the origin of the credal form "YHVH God of Israel": "I am YHVH thy God, Who brought thee out of the land of Egypt, out of the house of bondage." YHVH opens His speech to Israel with these words, which if translated from the language of address to that of assertion may run thus: "I am YHVH God of Israel." From this saying the covenant credal form develops, which we have heard in the Song of Deborah. What follows expresses the basis of the covenant: YHVH has brought Israel out. "And afterwards I brought you out," YHVH says in an apparently original verse of the Shechem address (Josh. 24, 5) to Joshua's generation. YHVH is the God, Who brings out and leads. The same thing also is expressed in the Exodus story, according to which (Exod. 13, 21) He goes before the people just as in Deborah's speech (Judges 4, 14).

And so, on our journey back through history, we have reached a beginning. Here begins the covenant between God and people, here begin the language and history of the covenant. But do we find here the beginning of the primary relationship itself, which gets here its sacramental, literary and historical embodiment? Was it in this event of the bringing forth from Egypt, which God here attributes to Himself, that these two, YHVH and Israel, first met? Did the people know nothing at all about YHVH, and was YHVH not known to them except at the hour when they heard the bringing forth and leading being announced to them and then perceived and believed it? Is everything that is said about the identity of this deity with the "God of the fathers" (Exod. 3, 6, 13, 15, 16; 6, 3f, 8) nothing but subsequent harmonisation? Whence does this deity come? And what has he to do with Israel?

This is the most important question in the history of Israel's faith. We cannot avoid it.

C. YHVH AND ISRAEL

In modern Biblical scholarship [1] the view prevails that Moses "discovered" the God YHVH at Sinai, this being in origin the God of Sinai, a mountain God of the Kenite tribe, the tribe where he was encamped and shepherded his flocks. According to this view Israel had not hitherto known the name of this God, or had heard it merely by rumor, and therefore in the pre-Mosaic period—in contradistinction to the later periods—we do not find individual names compounded with shorter forms of YHVH (Yah, Yahu), although the Yahvistic narrator continually uses this name in the book of Genesis. For the same reason, they say, YHVH did not appear to Moses in Egypt, where he would have to dwell, if Israel was truly His people from the beginning, but at the mount, where He lives and where the Kenite tribes, amongst whom Moses was sojourning, had served Him from of old. His revealing Himself to Moses as the God of the fathers does not, they say, belong to the earliest tradition, but to a later literary re-working of it : one of the narrators, whose writings are interwoven here too, the Elohist (or "the later Elohist"), put this attribute in the mouth of the God, in order that so He might be identified with the God known from the tradition of the fathers. But, they point out, the weakness of these re-workings is shown clearly when Moses asks (Exod. 3, 13) the deity's name, on the ground that the people to whom he is sent will not know it (the name of the God of the fathers!) ; and the uneasy fusion of these re-workings is shown in another passage belonging to the latest "source," to the "Priestly Document," where YHVH says to Moses (6, 3), that He had not made this name known to the fathers. And the matter becomes definitely clear, they say, when Moses' father-in-law seeks him, praises his God, the God of Midian Who had been accepted by Israel (18, 10f), and the first thank-offering of the liberated people is presented by his ministry (v. 12). And only now was the covenant ratified. Certainly, they point out, there would have been no need of this covenant, if YHVH had been Israel's God

---

[1] Cf. especially Budde, Die altisraelitische Religion (1912), 7ff; Gressmann, Mose und seine Zeit (1913), 163ff, 432ff; Galling, Die Erwaehlungs-traditionen Israels (1928), 57ff; Alt, Der Gott der Vaeter (1929), 10ff.

from the beginning; the point in question is a great "conversion" of a people, the oldest example of such known to us. The Kenites, who now join themselves to Israel, are henceforward the greatest zealots amongst the people for their primal lord (2 Kgs 10, 15f; Jer. 35). But the God Himself remains in a special measure attached to His mountain, and therefore He refuses (Exod. 33, 3) to lead the people by the way of the wilderness, and gives it up to an anxious incertitude. For this reason, according to this theory, in the Song of Deborah He comes from His resting place, and for this reason Elijah goes up to seek Him on Mount Horeb. And even one of the writing prophets, Hosea, knows no better than that YHVH first became Israel's God after the exodus from Egypt.

We cannot grasp the inner coherence of the history of Israel's faith, unless we recognize that none of these arguments stand a true unprejudiced examination.[2]

We know nothing from other sources about the existence of a Kenite mountain deity, and the little that we do know shows no resemblance to the characteristics of YHVH.

YHVH does not reside on Mount Sinai, but from time to time "dwells" there as a temporary dwelling place. (A more permanent dwelling would be expressed not by the verb used here—*shakhan* —but by *yashabh,* "to sit.") In Egypt, whither He went, according to the patriarchal story, with Jacob and his family (Gen. 46, 4) He stays as long as is required for His work there; apart from this the "Holy One" shuns the unholy land, and only from time to time descends from heaven (Exod. 3, 8). He travels with the people to Canaan; after He had pardoned them for wanting to materialize His leadership and to fashion Him in the likeness of a bull, He again walks at their head, His face turned towards the way (33, 14).[3] It is true He further reveals Himself there from time to time to one of His loved ones, as to Elijah, when he, tired after his zealous work, comes wishing to die in "the cave" (1 Kgs. 19, 9)—that is the well-known cave, where formerly (Exod. 33, 22) Moses had received the supreme revelation.

---

[2] A detailed refutation of the most important arguments is to be found in the foreword to the 2nd edition of my book, "Koenigtum Gottes," xxx–xliv. Cf. also my book "Moses," 95ff.

[3] Cf. Buber-Rosenzweig, Die Schrift und ihre Verdeutschung, 262ff.

Jethro the Kenite says (18, 11): "Now I know that YHVH is greater than all gods." Could he have said of the God, whose priest he was, that He is the greatest one? As to the offering, he does not sacrifice it at all, but he supplies it (this is the meaning of the term, cf. Lev. 12, 8) in order to be sacrificed on his behalf.

The making of the covenant comes about because the covenant lays the foundation of God's rule and order. In place of a loose cultic relationship a solid one shall come, embracing the whole life of the people. Into this relationship only a liberated, free Israel can enter. Only by acknowledging YHVH as One, Whom they are willing *to follow* in doing and hearing, do they really become His people and YHVH Israel's God. *This* is Hosea's purpose in putting again and again in YHVH's mouth (12, 10 EV 9; 13, 4): "I am YHVH thy God from the land of Egypt," and in recalling God's proclamation of adoption before the Pharaoh (Exod. 4, 22) "Israel is my firstborn son," in the saying (Hos. 11, 1): "Out of Egypt have I called my son." For a people, hitherto the possessors of a "religion"—either a religion of this deity, or a religion in which He only had a place—has become a people in real communion with its God, communing with Him as a people, as it is related of the fathers that they communed with Him as persons.

The dialogue at the burning bush, which is regarded by the critics as composed from three or four or even more sources, is shown after it has been freed from small additions to be a great structure, all of one moulding.[4] The error of division into different sources is to be seen here in an example of decisive importance. After God has told His chosen ones who He is, He informs them of the cause and purpose of the mission, on which He wishes to send them. This part of the speech begins and ends, in accordance with the compact and ingenious composition of the whole, with two verses corresponding to each other (Exod. 3, 7, 10). They repeat the central word *ammi*, "my people," and end with the name "Egypt," the name that points to the purpose of what is done: "I have indeed seen the affliction of my people, who are in Egypt," and "lead forth my people, the children of Israel, out of Egypt." Those who attribute, as is usually done, the first verse

---

[4] Concerning the changes of the divine names cf. Cassuto, *La questione della Genesi* (1934), 82ff.

to the Yahvistic (or the "later Yahvistic") source, and the second verse to the Elohistic source, miss the form and the sense of the speech. But, be the sources what they may, I cannot imagine a more powerful refutation of the theory in question, that YHVH had hitherto had no dealing with Israel, than the double "my people" at the beginning and end of the mission speech. YHVH here declares with the utmost emphasis (such repetition is the Biblical way of expressing emphasis), that Israel already now is His people, although He, YHVH, does not yet—before revealing Himself to the people—designate Himself as their God, but as God of the people's fathers. From this passage it is impossible to justify the assertion that the mention of the God of the fathers at the beginning of the divine speech (v. 6) was only introduced by the Elohistic scribe, and so is foreign to tradition. If we replace these words with words of a deity unknown to the people as an introduction to the mission, as for example, "I am the God of this mountain," or again, "I am YHVH," (as 6, 2), the message, permeated with the spirit of historic revelation and faith in history, becomes something artificial and futile.

Against this there stands a weighty objection: [5] if the deity that appeared to Moses had from the beginning designated Himself by the name God of Abraham, Isaac, and Jacob, there was no need afterwards to communicate His name; and Moses' expectation that the children of Israel would ask him about the name of the deity that sent him, if he came to them with the message "The God of your fathers has sent me unto you" (v. 13), is a contradiction in itself. The objection forces us to examine the text afresh.[6]

The people's question which Moses expects runs: *ma sh'mo?* usually translated "what is his name?" or "what is he called?" According to Biblical language, however, when the questioner asks simply for someone's name, he says: *mi atta?* "who art thou?" or even (Judges 13, 17) *mi sh'mekha?* "who is thy name?" The question introduced by "what" always asks about the nature of something; [7] "what" coupled with the word "name" points either to a meaning suggested by the pronouncing of the answer (so Gen.

[5] Alt, *op. cit.*, 12.
[6] Cf. Koenigtum Gottes, 81ff.
[7] Ewald, Lehrbuch der hebraeischen Sprache, 325.

32, 28, drawing attention to the *shameful* nature of Jacob's name—
cf. 27, 36; Hosea 12, 4; Jer. 9, 3 EV 4—a matter which shall be
effaced by a change of name), or to a mystery (so Prov. 30, 4,
where the point is not that the hearer does not know the name of
the founder of the world, but that he does not know his nature).
Moses supposes that the people will beg him to reveal and
make accessible to them the divine name, in such a manner that
they could call upon the God and conjure Him efficaciously.
This is no evidence that they have not known the name but
simply that they have not known it as a name by which the
God might be addressed. The name which came easily to their
lips, Yah or Yahu, was not made to be called upon, if reflected
in it was the primitive Semitic pronoun "Ya", that is "he," as a
"tabu-name" [8] of the deity, with which one could, so to say, hint
at the deity, but not address Him, or if it was an exclamation, an
"numinous primal sound," [9] with which also the deity could not
be addressed—and this is the reason why it was never, or hardly
ever, before this period combined with an individual name. The
answer given to Moses is obviously based upon the last phonetic
stage of development of that word or sound so that the new
form of the name appears only as condensation and not as an
alteration. The elemental word, that had an entirely oral character
and needed indeed the completion by an appropriate gesture, has
now the meaning of a verb: YHVH, that is to say He Who will
be there, He Who will be present, this is the deity's name. What
happens here is the rationalisation of the irrational exclamation.
Moses does not introduce into the history of Israel's faith a
new divine name, just as he does not introduce a new deity; the
deity becomes more intelligible, the name more explicable. The
God Himself solves the riddle of this name of His by transposing
it into the first person: *Ehyeh* ("I will be there"). But He adds
something more: *asher ehyeh* ("as I will be there"), that is to say,
in whatever appearance I will be there. It is expressed in similar
literary form in the supplement, which follows later (33, 19) and
which is to be understood according to the context as an additional

[8] Hans Bauer, Die Gottheiten von Ras Schamra, Zeitschrift fuer alttestamentliche Wissenschaft, Neue Folge x (1933), 94.

[9] Rudolf Otto, Das Gefuehl des Ueberweltlichen (1932), 203ff, 326ff; cf. Buber,
Koenigtum Gottes, 233ff, Die Schrift und ihre Verdeutschung, 190ff, Moses, 49f.

interpretation of the name: "And I will be gracious to whom I will be gracious, and I will show mercy unto whom I will show mercy." And the great narrator helps us to get out of our minds the meaning of "being" (esse) in the use of the word by repeating in accordance with Biblical style the word *ehyeh* in the sense of "being present" (adesse): he anticipates the "I will be" in question with the related "I will be with thee" (3, 12), and follows it with the related "I will be with thy mouth." Thus YHVH does not say that He exists absolutely or eternally, but—without pledging Himself to any particular way of revelation ("as I will be there"), by which He also makes it known that He cannot be bound by any conjuration—that He wants to remain with His people, to go with them, to lead them. In the same words, "I will be with thee," in the patriarchal story (Gen. 31, 3) He promises His assistance to Jacob, that He will go with him and protect him.

And so is made clear to us the other speech too (Exod. 6, 2f) which many use as a proof-text, that in the pre-Mosaic days they did not know this deity, and that this identification is nothing but a literary device. In Egypt, at the time when people, still at the beginning of their faith, were seized by doubt, the deity addresses His emissary—in words, most of which are certainly late in style, but which as far as the composition is concerned are rightly placed. The first words from the point of view of narrative logic can be spoken only now after the clarification of the name: "I am YHVH." After these words comes a verse, which in my considered judgment is at all events earlier than that which follows: "And I appeared to Abraham, to Isaac, and to Jacob as El Shaddai, but by My name YHVH I was not made known to them." It is not here stated that the deity did not make His name known to them, but that they had not acquired knowledge of the character of this name, and so its meaning was not revealed to them, the name was not yet made clear to them, and this has only been done now.[10] They already "possessed" the name, but they knew only its sound and not its sense.

Our journey backwards has brought us to the darkness of the early days, and we cannot achieve clarity here with the light of investigation, because it is not possible, as was the case with the texts previously considered, to regard those before us as im-

[10] Cf. the interpretation of Ibn Ezra.

mediate testimony of the history of faith. But because these early
days are the starting point of our way, we must try to extricate
from the problematical material a content of tradition, which will
enable us to reconstruct hypothetically some traits of this origin.

4. THE GOD OF THE FATHERS

We found at the beginning of the Decalogue all the three great articles of faith, which we met in part in the Song of Deborah and in part in Joshua's address: God's accompanying leadership, the people's "loving" devotion, and the zealous demand for decision. Are these also to be found in the stories of the fathers?

Indeed, we find them here too; but of course in the stories of the fathers these articles of faith do not appear in the life of a nation, but in personal life, life that should not be called unhistorical but may be called prehistorical in the exact sense of the word.

God takes Abraham from his house and from his land, brings him to a land, which He wants to "show" him (Gen. 12, 1) and "leading him through all the land of Canaan" (Josh. 24, 3), He promises to be "his shield" (Gen. 15, 1). So too God journeys with Jacob in all his journeyings (28, 15; 31, 3), and finally even goes down with him into Egypt (46, 4). The deity of the patriarchal tales too is a deity that leads. And the one who is led is devoted to Him in faith (15, 6), "goes" at the sound of His call (12, 4) to the final test, in which it is demanded from him to return to God what had been promised and given him, and "goes" again in silence (22, 3) to perform that which was laid upon him. Here we have an explanation of why the anonymous prophet of a late age (Is. 41, 8) returns to this phrase of the Decalogue and the Song of Deborah about the "lovers" of God, and uses it to describe Abraham. Here too in the patriarchal stories there prevails the atmosphere of decision; the main point of Joshua's speech, his command that the foreign deities should be removed (Josh. 24, 23), returns here and is repeated (Gen. 35, 2) word for word.

Do we find here some sort of "projection" of a "nomadic ideal" [1]

---

[1] Cf. Budde, The Nomadic Ideal in the Old Testament, The New World IV (1895), 726ff; Flight, The Nomadic Idea and Ideal in the Old Testament, Journal of Biblical Literature xlii (1923); McCown, The Wilderness of Judea and the

from later into earlier times in these pictures of wandering shepherds, whose deity had joined himself to them in order to escort them? Is it not rather the true original nomad faith?

But something else is here also that we have not seen there. When the patriarchs halt on their journeyings, they plant a tree or raise up a pillar or an altar, and call over them a divine name. Sometimes they call YHVH's name, and also another name composed out of the commonest Semitic name for the deity, *El,* together with a supplementary name, e.g., *El-beth-el* ("God of the God-house," 35, 7) or *El-olam* ("God of the hidden time," 21, 33). It is true we know this action also from the story of Moses, who calls (Exod. 17, 15) upon an altar *YHVH-nissi* ("YHVH my standard"), and from the story of Gideon, who calls (Judges 6, 24) on an altar *YHVH-shalom* ("YHVH-peace")—it is noticeable that we do not find such cases after this—but the epithet "El" is peculiar to the patriarchal narrative alone. Many critics see in this and in certain other similar facts the remnants of an *"El* religion," which was replaced in the days of Moses by the YHVH-faith; they maintain that "the earlier narrators of the Genesis stories knew nothing, nor wished to know anything about YHVH."²

To refute this claim we must examine the measure of historical truth in the Biblical view of the coming of "the fathers," the coming of Abraham to Canaan.

The prayer appointed for the bringing of the first-fruits to the sanctuary begins (Deut. 26, 5) with an alliterative memorial verse: "A straying Aramean was my ancestor." Here we have the language of shepherds hidden away in the midst of a prayer of land workers. The farmer, rejoicing in the blessings sent by God on the land, tells of his humble beginnings when he was a shepherd: as a sheep strays from the flock (Jer. 50, 6; Ezek. 34, 4, 16; Ps. 119, 176), so did the ancestor stray from his family. If we look at this memorial verse in itself (and it is obviously earlier than the rest of the prayer), we see that the ancestor spoken of here is not

---

Nomadic Ideal, Journal of Geography xxiii (1924), 333ff; Humbert, La logique de la perspective nomade, Marti Festschrift (1925), 158ff; Albright in Lovejoy and Boas, Primitivism and Related Ideas in Antiquity (1935), 428ff.

² Gressmann, Sage und Geschichte in den Patriarchenerzaehlungen, Zeitschrift fuer alttestamentliche Wissenschaft, Neue Folge xxx (1910), 28.

Jacob, as is implied in the remainder of the prayer, but Abraham.[3]
"Lost sheep," so the Jeremiah passage runs, "my people have been,
their shepherds have made them err." Abraham uses the same word
(Gen. 20, 13; this sentence too is a remnant left high and dry in
the midst of a story, which from the literary point of view is later)
when he speaks of his life to the Philistine king: "And it came to
pass when God *made me err* from my father's house." So he tells
how God's hand overpowered him. We recall how the first writing
prophet tells the priest (Am. 7, 15) that aforetime God had taken
him from his environment: "And YHVH took me from behind
the flock." But Abraham's speech sounds more ancient, older even
than the story of the sending forth itself (Gen. 12), not only in
language but also in content: his shepherd had led him astray.
And Abraham knows nevertheless that this causing to err is also
a leading; he trusts (15, 6), and in his trust he hears the saying:
"I am YHVH Who brought thee out from Ur." [4] The saying, which
apparently originates from a very old section of the story, reflects
the opening of the Decalogue, except that in the Abraham story
the emphatic word "thy God" is lacking, and in place of the
emphatic "I" (*anokhi*) with which YHVH in the Decalogue
opens His direct contact with the people, here the unemphatic
pronoun (*ani*) is used, continuing close contact. Just as the command to Jacob to remove the foreign gods anticipates the command
to the people by Joshua, the personal form preceding the collective,
so here the revelation to the individual anticipates the revelation
to Israel. Here YHVH expresses something which apparently is
foreign to the traditions bound up in the narrative up to this point:
namely that not only the second, independent journey from Haran
to Canaan, but also the first, that of the whole family from Ur to
Haran, was His work. The *whole* of Abraham's Hegira is a "religious" act.

[3] Cf. the commentary of Rashbam.

[4] The word "Chaldeans" is in my opinion a later addition from the time after
the coming of the Chaldeans to Ur. A later editor apparently felt the epithet "Ur
of the Chaldees" in the mouth of God an anachronism, and corrected the text
"from the land of the Chaldeans," which was before the translators of the Septuagint (therefore they translated 11, 28, 31, 50 in the same way). In spite of the
arguments, which have been heard down the ages, there is no reason to doubt the
identification of this Ur with the city in S. Babylonia, known to us from the
excavations.

What hypothesis can we make concerning the historical content of all this, its content in the history of religion? Has it any? Can it have any? If so, what approximately is its nature?

Here we are dependent on a groping kind of investigation. But that which we come across in this way has definite material form.

As one wave of the Semitic migration that occurred at the end of the third millennium and the beginning of the second millennium B.C.E. northwards and westwards over the Syrian steppes, we see the family of the sons of Terah with their companions travelling, numerically probably like a small tribe, from Ur, center of South Babylonian culture, to Haran in northern Mesopotamia. Semi-nomads they travel with their flocks and herds, pitch and strike their tents from pasturage to pasturage, in between whiles making a temporary stay, tilling the ground year in, year out, but also exchanging goods with the city dwellers, and sometimes encamping near the gates. Men of peace, they are nevertheless ready for battle as one man, as is the accepted custom with this economically superior type, in which there is a fusion of pastoral and military virtues.[5] The sons of Terah journey from one center of culture to another, near which they settle.

The two cities, Ur and Haran, are the centers of the Babylo-Syrian moon cult. The name Haran, where Terah died, means *way*, also *caravan*, and denotes probably "the place where caravans meet, and from which they set out on their journeys." [6] The moon god of Haran was also called Bel-Haran, and we are entitled to understand this as meaning lord of the way. In hymnology the moon god is designated by the name "the leader." He it is who "points out the way of the caravan, who illuminates its way as it goes, in order to avoid the blaze of the sun all through the night over the steppes," the "god of the Mesopotamian nomads." [7] On the banks of the Nile it was apparently the sun god Amon, who was regarded as god of of the way, and who transmitted to his emissaries an image called "Amon of the way" as a heavenly deputy; [8] on the banks of the Euphrates it was the moon god, who enjoyed this position. It may

[5] Toynbee, A Study of History III (1934), 14.

[6] Schrader, Die Keilinschriften und das Alte Testament, 3rd edn. (1903), 29.

[7] Dhorme, Abraham dans le cadre de l'histoire. Revue biblique xxxvii, 509.

[8] Erman, Die Literatur der Aegypter (1923), 225f, 235.

be conjectured that this god had among the multitude of the gods of Babylon certain assistants, at all events we hear [9] from Ur of a small goddess, whose special function it was to protect the wanderers in the desert.

It seems to me a singular phenomenon in the history of religion, that one day in the distant past a certain wandering Aramean—Biblical tradition calls him Abram—forsook the faith he had received from his environment, the faith in "the planet of way for the wayfaring Semitic race," [10] and acquired instead a faith in One, Who was no "nature god." This was a guardian deity; not a family fetish, but a great guardian deity, hidden and yet manifest, a guardian deity not of all the sons of Terah, but of his own, Abram's, and of his new "straying" family, and of all those attached and joined to him. A God, Who goes with those He guards, not only on moonlit nights, but also on the nights without moonlight, and on winter days too, at that period of the year, when Mesopotamian steppe wanderers prefer to make their way by day. A God, Whose light will not be extinguished. A God, Whom men trust, because He addresses them by word and calls them. He is a God that *tells* a man He is leading him.

But whither is He leading him? Not to the place whither the man wished to come. The God guards as He Himself wills, and He leads man whither He wills. He leads man whither He sends him. He brings Abraham safely to Haran. Here the man settles, desiring to remain, but the God wills otherwise, He sends the man further, leads him further—from the father's house to a foreign land, to the foreign land, which He promised him. He makes this man a nomad of faith.

If we wish to fix in the history of faith the hour of the *revelation* to Abraham, we cannot say that it took place in Haran, but earlier than this, as is suggested by God's call in the old story—the fundamental kernel of Genesis 15—about the covenant of the Pieces (v. 7). But the hour of the *decision* occurs at Haran. Only here does this God reveal Himself as One Who brings forth, when He orders the separation from the world of the fathers. The prophets from Moses to Jeremiah recognized Him afterwards in this way. Here too, however, we have nothing to do with the "projection"

9 Woolley, Abraham (1936), 104, 226.
10 Doughty, Travels in Arabia Deserta I, ch. 13.

of later prophetic experience, but rather with its simple, early beginning. The bringing forth belongs to the nature of this God as well as the leading.

The whole Hegira of Abraham is a "religious" event, but the second stage is so in a special sense. The faith becomes something established by necessitating the *separation*.[11] The God Who goes forth with these men goes not with the sons of Terah, but with His *chosen* one, who also chose Him. He separates him from them, and sets him in His presence as He is going with him. The God, Who at the beginning was a guardian deity of a man, will become deity of a community of men, afterwards deity of a people, and finally deity of the peoples; this God, Who at the beginning was the deity of a personal, private biography, will become the deity of history; but this combination, this "correlation" of guidance and devotion, revelation and decision, God's love for man and man's love for God, this unconditional relation between Him and man remains.

In contemporary Biblical scholarship it is more and more understood that the fathers have "reached their position in the tradition of Israelite history especially in virtue of their work as recipients of a revelation and founders of a cult." [12] In particular, Abraham is recognized as "initiator" and "precursor" of a religious movement (but I would not have described it as "spiritualistic-monotheistic") "which arose in connection with the great popular migration in the first half of the second millennium." [13] Scholars are beginning to take into consideration again the traces of a community with faith and cult, which are preserved in the Bible in spite of the powerful tendency to attach to the subject a family character only: "the souls which they had acquired in Haran" (12, 5) may be linked with that company of the "initiated men" (14, 14).[14] The gathering and sanctifying of the primitive community appears as the work of the founder.

What is the name of the God of this community? We cannot decide from the Bible by which of His names and titles Abraham

[11] Cf. Winckler, Abraham als Babylonier (1903), 25f.

[12] Alt, Der Gott der Vaeter, 52.

[13] Boehl, Das Zeitalter Abrahams (1931), 42.

[14] Yahuda, Die Sprache des Pentateuchs I (1929), 282, connects the "hanikhim" with the three confederates of Abraham mentioned in v. 13; but it is not likely that the word "wayareq" (and he emptied) was used of confederates; neither does the Samaritan variant "wayadeq" (and he scrutinized) suit confederates.

addressed Him. Perhaps by *"Eli"* (my *el*) ; for this deity was certainly *his* deity, the deity Who revealed Himself to *him*, and led *him*. Perhaps it was *"Elohai"* (my *Elohim*), for only by means of this plural-singular combination, in which the Semites "condensed the sum of all divinity," [15] could he express what was in his heart : "Thou Who art everything that is divine for me." It is almost certain that Abraham in speaking of his God used the phrase *"El Shaddai,"* the etymology of which we do not know (some now think that its meaning is "the inhabitant of the mountains," but it may also mean "the exalted one"),[16] but apparently it contains some hint of a mystery of the relation between the deity and the family, for in all the verses in Genesis the name is linked with the multiplication of the family by the deity. It may be supposed that the man used the epithet *"shaddai,"* because it is found in a verse of the Blessing of Jacob (49, 25), which is certainly ancient. And we are justified in supposing that at the time when he wished to point to Him, so to say, with his voice, to proclaim Him in an enthusiastic manner, he used that "tabu word," [17] that "god-cry," [18] that "stammering," [19] *"Yah"* or *"Yahu"* or *"Yahuvah,"* [20] that is "He!" or "This One!" or "This is it," or "Oh he!" This elemental sound was apparently common to the west Semitic tribes, who hinted by it in a mysterious and enthusiastic way to the deity whose name could not be designated; we find it in this sense still in the mysticism of Islam.[21] It was impossible to call the deity by this sound when they addressed Him directly, because it referred to the third person, but it was possible to use it when proclaiming Him.[22] It is

---

[15] Dhorme, L'évolution religieuse d'Israel I (1937), 360.

[16] But there are also those who resort again to the meaning "essence of power." Cf. Nyberg, Studien zum Religionskampf im Alten Testament, Archiv fuer Religionswissenschaft xxxv (1938), 350.

[17] Bauer, Die Gottheiten von Ras Schamra, 84. Cf. also Hehn, Die biblische und die babylonische Gottesidee (1913), 248.

[18] Rosenzweig, Der Ewige, in Buber-Rosenzweig, Die Schrift und ihre Verdeutschung, 207. Cf. G. R. Driver, The Original Form of the Name Jahweh, Zeitschrift fuer alttestamentliche Wissenschaft, Neue Folge v (1928), 24.

[19] Schleiff, Der Gottesname Jahu, Zeitschrift der Deutschen Morgenlaendischen Gesellschaft xc (1936), 700.

[20] Cf. Fried. Delitzsch, Wo lag das Paradies? (1881), 166; Koenig, Ja-u und Jahu, Zeitschrift fuer alttestamentliche Wissenschaft xxx (1915), 45, and also the statements of Mowinckel in R. Otto, Das Gefuehl des Ueberweltlichen, 236.

[21] Cf. e.g., Nicholson, Selected Poems from the Divani Shamsi Tabriz (1898), 127, 282.

[22] Cf. Koenigtum Gottes, 237–53.

of such proclamation (and not of prayer) that the story is thinking, which tells how the fathers call upon the name of YHVH (the narrator here uses the same expression as YHVH Himself uses, Exod. 33, 19; 34, 5), after they had built an altar or planted a holy tree (Gen. 12, 8; 13, 4; 21, 33; 26, 25). The recipients of the revelation walk "before" the God, announcing His coming (17, 1; 24, 40; 48, 15), just as the herald walks and calls before the approaching king (cf. 1 Sam. 2, 35).

In the third of these proclamations the name YHVH is linked with the epithet *"El olam,"* which is to be understood as indicating "God of the ancient time," or better, "God of the duration," [23] an epithet suited to the end of the story about the oath of the covenant sworn with the neighbouring king. At all events the name YHVH here is no later addition : there is to be found here something of the nature of *identification,* that is to say, not only is the speaker's God, the God Whom the man brought with him, Who goes with him, equated with the familiar *El* of this place, the *El,* which he found in it, but there is a suggestion here that the power of the deity of the place is swallowed up and absorbed, so to say, in the power of the coming deity, and this is accomplished by calling the deity by the tabu-word. That the power and authority over this place is his and has been his from everlasting, although in a strange form—this is the proclamation.

The identification becomes still clearer in the story, the essence of which is certainly ancient (especially in the verses of blessing and swearing), where Melchi-zedek, King of Salem and priest of El-Elyon, "the most high God," "brings forth" in "the valley of the king" bread and wine for Abram, praising and blessing him with the name of El-Elyon, "founder of heaven and earth." And Abram replies (in the text before us he addresses the king of Sodom, but in the original text he certainly addressed Melchizedek, the end of the original speech being lost), "I have lifted up my hand to YHVH, El-Elyon, founder of heaven and earth" (apparently to be completed like the answer to Melchizedek's speech, "Blessed be YHVH, El-Elyon": that is to say, Abram lifted up his hand for the sake of this blessing). By this is meant : He, whom I serve, is also thy god, but apart from this he is "He"

---

[23] In the Ras Shamra texts the most high god is called "king, father of the years."

(*"Yahu"*)! That this mutual sacred act is preserved for us in the form of an incidental story is certainly to be attributed to tendencies connected with the house of David to prove the merit of Jerusalem to be cultic center of the world,[24] but the tradition appears absolutely trustworthy from the point of view of the history of religion. The concept of creator of heaven and earth is known to us from ancient oriental and other faiths as an *early* one. And this word "founder" or "author," occurs in a sexual sense (cf. Gen. 4, 1)[25] in one of the Ras Shamra texts as an epithet of Asherat, wife of the most high god, called "authoress of the gods," that is to say, progenitress of the gods, and in the light of this the later Greek accounts of the Phoenician Elyun as father of heaven and earth appear to be reliable. "The generations of heaven and earth," which according to the Canaanites are real generations, are heard of again in the Biblical story of creation (Gen. 2, 4), the sexual content having been removed, and I think we are entitled to see in the saying, "these are the generations of heaven and earth: their being created," a sort of polemic against the sexual cosmogony of the Canaanites.

The meaning becomes even clearer in the story we have in a curiously circumstantial form (16, 13) of Hagar; after the "messenger of YHVH" (i.e., a primitive hypostasis of the divine interference) has spoken to her, she calls "the name of YHVH Who spoke to her: Thou art *El Roi*." It had to be expressed so in order that the identification, which is crucial here, might be recognized. The narrator here by no means brings YHVH into a tale told of a deity in "pre-Mosaic *El* religion," as some think, but YHVH, so to say, annexes the *El*. By His own appearing and acting He shows this "God of seeing" to be identical with Himself, the deity Who wanders and goes out with the fleeing Egyptian maid, a member of His community, into the desert, and lets

[24] Die Schrift und ihre Verdeutschung, 235. It is irrelevant whether or not the narrator, responsible for the tradition itself, meant already Jerusalem by "Salem"; if the identification expressed by Ps. 76, 3, EV 2, comes from a later tendency, this can scarcely be other than the Davidic one.

[25] We find this verb in a sexual sense in the Bible not only in so early a passage as this, but also in one as late as Deut. 32, 6, where there is no doubt that the author no longer felt the sexual sense of the word. It may be assumed that the sexual meaning of the verb was the procreation of the child by its parents, in contradistinction to the verbs that express either the bearing alone or the begetting alone.

Himself be seen by her. The designation *"El-Roi"* points to a primitive divinity connected with a kind of "incubation": whosoever lay down to rest by the well of God "saw" a vision. The revelation story shows how the guardian deity here reveals Himself as such. As soon as such a story circulates, all previous tradition is absorbed and swallowed up in the new tradition, which is fixed in time, and henceforward the well is the well of the coming God.

We know from Babylonian and Egyptian religion the inclination to emphasize belief in the supremacy of a god to such an extent that all the rest of the gods are understood as His manifestations. But in the immense pantheon there has been no attempt to actualize this in full earnest, indeed no such attempt could be made. Only in the atmosphere of faith in a solitary, exclusive, zealous God, leading His believers and demanding their devotion outside the pantheon, could the identification become real. A *coming* deity like this could not acknowledge any domain in the universe or life, on which he set foot, remaining outside His sway; whoever had possession of the place and sphere was forcibly put down from his throne, or was clearly shown to be the substitute of the coming deity, or even to be identified with this very deity. The Semitic *El* is not generally sharply individualized. Among Eastern Semites the form of the *El* becomes so indistinct that it comes near to being a "heavenly being in general." Among Western Semites the *El* becomes condensed and develops from a formless, dispersed, yet powerful substance into a powerful yet not sharply defined personal essence.[26] He appears wherever a power holds sway (his most personal form, the somewhat indolent Phoenician *El,* lord of the gods, as we know him from the Ras Shamra tablets, the "father of mankind," apparently lies outside this historical sphere). This indefinite godhead was content to be subdued by a coming El, Who was wholly personal, and Who to His worshippers was the one divine personality, being always "with them." There was no need of a war between Him and the gods. It was only with the *Baalim,* or "the Baal,"

[26] Brockelmann, Allah und die Goetzen, Archiv fuer Religionswissenschaft xxi (1922), 120f, sees the pre-Islamic Allah too as essentially identical "with that godhead which emerges in Israel's tradition in the shape of the *El Olam* and the *El Elyon* of the patriarchal stories."

that a long and bitter struggle did break out; over against the single deity coming to Canaan without a spouse stood here a wilful sexuality, which according to its whole nature opposed His leadership.

From the tendency towards identification—and it is to be regarded as a matter of tradition itself and not in any sense as a literary device—we find also an explanation of the strange verse (31, 53) long the subject of different opinions, in which Laban confirms the covenant of peace he makes with Jacob: "May the God of Abraham and the God of Nahor judge between us, the God of their fathers!" The last words are no later addition based on opposition to the "paganism" of the context, but mean that the Aramean acknowledges at least—since he could not be supposed to accept for himself the religion of YHVH—that the two gods, designated by different names, are in fact one, the deity Whom the father of the family had already indicated. Some scholars in their investigations wrongly find here hints of the theological subtlety of later days; it is a particular kind of early religious thought. How the form of such a primitive "universalism" was transformed by a great theologian and great poet in a late age's atmosphere of longing for renewal, the book of Jonah shows.

Albrecht Alt in his book "The God of the Patriarchs" has compared the epithets God of Abraham, God of Isaac, and God of Jacob, with similar divine epithets in Transjordanian inscriptions of the Nabataean age, and has concluded that the meaning of the epithet "god of so and so" is one and the same in both places: the deity this man was the first to worship, the god formerly unknown who revealed himself to this man, and therefore is designated among this man's adherents as his god. Alt rightly stresses [27] that here "there sprouts into growth the first bud of a totally different phenomenon from that which we find in the local and nature deities: no attachment of the divine being to a small or large parcel of earth, but its alliance to human life, at first to an individual, and later through this to a whole group." He rightly emphasizes [28] "the relation of this deity to groups genealogically linked together, families and tribes," and cn this

[27] Alt, *op. cit.*, 41.
[28] *Ibid.*

point he [29] indicates that "the trend towards the social and the historical" corresponds to the living conditions of nomadic tribes. But he is wrong when he says that we must recognize in the three epithets peculiar to each of the patriarchs—shield of Abraham, fear of Isaac, and paladin of Jacob—three gods, gods of three revelations. When Laban in the story (adduced also by Alt) mentions beside the God of Abraham the God of Nahor, this does not mean that Nahor too was the recipient of a revelation of a new deity. Two essentially different kinds of divine epithet have the same form: the designation after the first recipient, and the designation after one who, possessing a tradition about this god, expresses by a new epithet his personal relation to him as a relation of the utmost importance for himself and his companions. Alt produces in his book a tomb inscription of the fourth century C.E., in which a man of the name of Abedrapsas proclaims his belief in a deity, which he designates by the name of "god of Arkesilaos," but which also appears to him himself. A description "god of Arkesilaos and god of Abedrapsas" would not have been inappropriate in the mouth of one of a later generation. Isaac proclaims his faith in the God of Abraham, Who is also his own God in a special manner based on life experience, and therefore He is so called, and so on. Hence it may be said: they are not three gods, but one, a great deity of the road, who goes with his believers on their life way before He will go with "His people" on its life way. The God, Who will later be proclaimed by the name "YHVH" (i.e., He Who is there), He is the deity now indicated by the elemental sound "He!": He does not dwell upon Mount Sinai and wait, but already He now goes, leads, is present.

[29] *Ibid.*, 46.

5. HOLY EVENT

We know nothing of Israel's religious situation in the Egyptian age, and we can only conjecture on the basis of scattered disconnected phrases (e.g., Ezek. 20, 7f), that it was out of a state of religious decay that Moses stirred them up. We can proceed only by putting the period of the Exodus alongside that of the fathers.

When we pass from the atmosphere of the patriarchal tradition, as we have tried to picture it hypothetically, and enter the atmosphere of the Exodus tradition, we are confronted at the first glance with something new. But it is quickly manifest that this does not mean a change in the deity, but a change in men. We have already seen that the deity is in essence no other than the primitive deity. Against this the human partner is essentially changed; therefore, the situation common to the two is entirely different; and with this the sphere in which the deity acts is so different that one may easily think the very character of this activity to be changed, and one does not recognize the identity of the agent. The new thing from the human side is that here we have "people," not "a people" in the strictest sense, but at all events the element, people. That is to say, this collection of men is no more a company assembled around the recipients of revelation and their kinsmen as in the patriarchal age, but a something that is called "Israel" and which the deity can acknowledge to be "His people"—again it is not of decisive importance whether this people comprises all the tribes of Israel, or only some of them, the rest having been left in Canaan or having returned thither before this. We do not know whether "Israel" originally was the name of a people or the name of a "holy confederacy," to which the tribes were gathered together by the leadership of Moses,[1] and gave

[1] Sachsse, Die Bedeutung des Namens Israel (1922), 91; cf. Noth, Das System der zwoelf Staemme, 90ff.

themselves, after their sacred call, the name "Israel," the meaning of which probably is not "God strives," but "God rules." [2]

But if this is the original explanation of "Israel," then this community has already, in consequence of the special historical conditions, reached, at the moment of the exodus—i.e., at the moment when we are able to perceive them historically—that stage of self-evident unitedness, so that we are justified in applying to them the name "people," even though they do not yet possess all the marks reckoned as belonging to this concept. And if "Israel" was already in origin the name of a people, then it is only at this point, at the exodus from Egypt, not in Egypt itself, that the people comes into actual existence, and only at this point is the name "Israel" perfectly manifest as "the visible programme of God's sovereignty." [3] And the deity now acts historically upon this people seen by Him as an absolute unity, the same deity Whom the fathers discovered as the guardian God accompanying them. The change which we think we perceive in Him as we now advance in time is nothing but the transformation of the situation into a historical one, and the greatness of Moses consists in the fact that he accepts the situation and exhausts its possibilities. No external influence is to be found here. Indeed it is vain to attempt to find here a Kenite ingredient; YHVH has taken over nothing from the Egyptian god Aton, who is brought into the picture as "monotheistic"; and other things which may have approached Him have not touched His nature. This God has become manifest as a God of history, because He became the God of Israel, this Israel that only now came into being, that only now He was able to "find" (Hos. 9, 10), and because this Israel only now has entered the realm of history. He reveals Himself to it: what was hidden in prehistoric time is made historically manifest. Our path in the history of faith is not a path from one kind of deity to another, but in fact a path from the "God Who hides Himself" (Is. 45, 15) to the One that reveals Himself.

If we look at the first of the writing prophets, Amos, and examine the traditions which he handles concerning this activity of YHVH, and ask: what are the reminiscences that he knows to

---

[2] Noth, Die israelitischen Personennamen (1929), 207f; Buber, Koenigtum Gottes, 193, 252f, Moses, 113f.

[3] Volz, Mose, 88.

be common to all his hearers, these two appear before us: the leading from Egypt through the desert (Am. 2, 10; 3, 1; 9, 7), and the appropriation which the deity expresses in a word reminiscent of the marriage union (Gen. 4, 1), but later uses to indicate the primal mission of the prophet (Jer. 1, 5), "you have I known" (Am. 3, 2). The first of these two, talked over by everyone and thought to be understood by all—"I have brought you up" (2, 10) —Amos shows (9, 7) to be something that is in no way peculiar to Israel, but the fundamental fact of the historic contact of this leader God with the peoples. It is with set purpose that record is here kept of the names of the two neighboring peoples who fought most mightily with all Israel or Judah, the one in early times, the other in the immediate past. In these instances, very painful as they are to you—this is the force of the prophet's words —you see that this God of yours, of Whose historic dealing with you you boast, deals historically with other peoples as with you, leading each of them on its wanderings and singling out its lot. The second thing, not familiar to the people as to its expression and sense, but corresponding in the people's memory to the events of revelation and covenant making, he lays bare as the *suprahistorical election* to be bound absolutely, peculiar "only" to Israel alone among all the peoples: "therefore"—and now comes the iron word from the Decalogue—"I will ordain upon you all your iniquities." YHVH has not revealed Himself to any other family of "the families of the earth" save only to this Israel, and to them He has revealed Himself really as the "zealous God." And in the mouth of Amos' contemporary, Hosea, who presupposes no general thought or teaching, but expresses directly the things of the heart, YHVH illustrates His zealousness by His experience with Israel in the desert: I loved (11, 1) and they betrayed me (9, 10; 11, 2; 13, 6).

Those Semitic peoples who call their tribal deities by the name *malk,* meaning originally counsellor, arbitrator, leader, and only afterwards receiving the meaning of king, appear to have expressed by this name not the oracle power of the settlement but the leadership in primitive wanderings and conquest. These are nomad gods, leader gods of the tribe which, through the political change of meaning of the word, become afterwards "kings"; the type of this tribal god, although not the name, we find in the message of

Jephthah to the king of the "Ammonites" (or more correctly the king of Moab), where he tells him that Chemosh his god "disinherited" other peoples even as YHVH had done, in order to give a land to the people led by him (Ju. 11, 23f). Amos' saying about the bringing up of the Aramaeans disposes of such a notion: the peoples do not know who is their liberator, they each call him by a different name, each one thinks to have one of its own, whereas we know the One, because He "has known" us. This is the *national* universalism of the prophetic faith.

The Mosaic age does not possess this religious view of the history of peoples, but it does have the fundamental religious experience which opens the door to this view. What is preserved for us here is to be regarded not as the "historization" of a myth or of a cult drama, nor is it to be explained as the transposition of something originally beyond time into historical time:[4] a great history-faith does not come into the world through interpretation of the extra-historical as historical, but by receiving an occurrence experienced as a "wonder," that is as an event which cannot be grasped except as an act of God. Something happens to us, the cause of which we cannot ascribe to our world; the event has taken place just now, we cannot understand it, we can only believe it (Ex. 14, 31). It is a holy event. We acknowledge the performer (15, 1, 21): "I will sing unto YHVH, for He has verily risen, the horse and its rider He has cast into the sea."[5]

In this undeniably contemporary song the deliverance is asserted as a holy event. A later song, which nevertheless is very ancient in form, vocabulary, and sentence construction, the song framing "the Blessing of Moses," praises in its first half (the second half tells of the conquest of the land) a series of divine appearances in the wilderness,[6] beginning with the appearance at Mount Sinai. From the difficult text it can be understood that the "holy ones" of the people collect round YHVH, when they camp "at His feet" (cf. Ex. 24, 10); that later the people receive from the divine words the "instruction" (*torah*) which Moses "commands"; that so "the congregation of Jacob" becomes YHVH's "inher-

---

[4] Cf. Koenigtum Gottes, 119ff (against Mowinckel, Psalmenstudien II).

[5] Cf. Moses, 74ff.

[6] The view connecting these words with the Shechem assembly is without foundation; nothing in the Joshua story fits this hymn of a great theophany.

itance"; and that finally the heads of the tribes gather together and proclaim YHVH to be king over them. What is recorded here of the holy event can only be reconstructed incompletely out of the exodus story. The fact that the proclamation is lacking here is probably to be explained by the fear which they felt for the influence, combatted by the prophets, of the *melekh* cult of the neighboring peoples, that is to say, for the penetration of child sacrifice into Israel. Isaiah is the first (6, 5) directly to give YHVH the title *melekh,* king, after forcibly demonstrating the uncleanness of the people over against Him. But we still have preserved for us another echo of the proclamation, namely the last verse of the Song of the Sea (Ex. 15, 18), which although it is not so near in time to the event as the opening of the Song, yet clearly is "not long after the event about which it tells." [7] Here proclamation is made triumphantly that the divine kingdom will stand forever. This is to be understood not in the light of the state concept of kingship, nor on the basis of the later idea of a cosmic-cultic kingdom of the God, but only as the recognition by wandering tribes of their divine leader: the sovereignty of this leader over his people is proclaimed.

Thus over against the two sayings of Amos we have before us two series of events. The first comprises the deliverance from Egypt and the leading through the wilderness to Canaan, the second comprises the revelation, the making of the covenant and the setting up of an order of the people by the leadership of the divine *melekh.* That is to say, the first series exists for the sake of the second. So we are to understand the words "unto me" in the first Sinai message (Ex. 19, 4), which still precedes the revelation in the thunderstorm.[8] YHVH bears the people, as the eagle from time to time bears one of its young on its wing (a late form of the picture is found in Deut. 32, 11), to the place of revelation: if the people hearken to the voice that now speaks to them, they will become for YHVH, Whose is all the earth, a "peculiar treasure" among all the peoples that are His: they will become for

[7] Sellin, Einleitung in das Alte Testament (1935), 22. The view that this is a late psalm (so e.g., H. Schmidt, Das Meerlied, Zeitschrift fuer alttestamentliche Wissenschaft, Neue Folge viii, 1931, 59ff), cannot be supported from the fact that there is hardly any more mention in it of the dividing of the Red Sea than in other psalms; no other psalm is so built upon the one event and its effects.

[8] Cf. Moses, 101ff.

Him, the king, a "king's realm" (cf. 2 Sam. 3, 28), surrounding Him near at hand and serving Him directly, a circle of *kohanim*, that is "foremost ones at the king's hand" (so 1 Chron. 18, 17 calls the office, while 2 Sam. 8, 18 gives it the name *kohanim*, meaning those who minister to the king), a "holy" (i.e., hallowed, set apart for Him) *goy* (i.e., body of people). The saying dates apparently from the time before the division of the Israelite kingdom,[9] and it is already influenced by the political changes of meaning in the concept *melekh;* but it is clear that a traditional basic view of the meaning of the events, the exodus and the making of the covenant, became crystallized in it. YHVH acts as *melekh* in the sense of sovereign. So through a holy event there comes into existence this category decisive from the point of view of the history of faith, of the "holy people," the hallowed body of people, as image and claim; at a later time, after the people had broken the covenant again and again, this category changed and was replaced by the Messianic promise and hope.

Both series of events are blended together in a most noteworthy way in the great holy object, indeed the greatest of all holy objects created by the "nomadic faith," the faith of a people seeking a land and believing in the divine leader, Who brings them to it, namely the ark.[10] It clearly cannot be dated any later; for there is to be found in it all the incentive and motive force of the holy adventure, all its symbol-begetting power. And in spite of the many parallels in the history of religion to one or other aspect of the ark,[11] it can hardly be maintained that the ark is borrowed from anywhere, for its nature lies precisely in the unity of these different aspects. It carries the cherub throne of the Lord Who, seated thereon, guides the wandering and the battle (here both are still absolutely interconnected the one with the other); and together with this is the ark proper containing the tablets. These are called "the testimony," because it is by

---

[9] The saying is later elaborated many times homiletically (cf. Deut. 4, 20; 7, 6; 14, 2; 26, 19; 1 Kgs. 8, 53); but it differs completely from these in its concentrated style. Its presentation of the deity, to whom the whole earth belongs and who can choose to himself one people out of all, is *earlier* in the history of faith than the universal liberator deity of Amos.

[10] Cf. Eerdmans, De godsdienst van Israel (1930), I, 56ff; Volz, Mose, 100ff; Klamroth, Lade und Tempel (1933), 30ff; Sellin, Alttestamentliche Theologie (1933), I, 30ff; Buber, Koenigtum Gottes, 228ff, Moses, 147ff.

[11] Cf. M. Dibelius, Die Lade Jahves (1906).

them that the covenant is always attested anew, and so the ark is also called "the ark of the covenant." Neither of the two could be wanting. This holy object is a visible unity of the two divine activities: the activity of the leader, Who now, in the historic situation, has become also "a man of war" (Ex. 15, 3), and the activity of the revealer, Whose revelation, once it had taken place, is never more to be concealed and hidden, but must remain carved on stone or written on a scroll. At the same time even this characteristically is not attached to a place: the tablets are fixed in the ark, but the ark is by nature mobile, moving in the tent and outside it, for it is forbidden to remove the poles (25, 15). Even after the ark stands compact in the temple in Jerusalem, they are not removed (1 Kgs. 8, 8) ; but this means only reverence for tradition and symbolism, and not any longer a direct notion of the leader deity. The double call, originating in the wilderness (Num. 10, 35f), to the Lord of the ark, Who travels and halts with the camp, "rise up YHVH" and "return YHVH" and the *"melekh* shout" because Israel's God is "with him" (23, 21), is no more heard. His special name "YHVH of hosts" (i.e., the host of the people and the host of heaven, concerning both of which the Song of Deborah speaks) is still in the mouth of the people, but its real meaning is no longer really known—until Amos comes and expounds it again.

The paradox on which the sanctity of the ark is based (every "holy" thing is founded on a paradox) is this, that an invisible deity becomes perceptible as One Who comes and goes. According to tradition, as far as we can still recognize it, the ark must be brought into the "tent of meeting"—not the tent which is described in all its parts in Scripture, and which really cannot be conceived in the wilderness, but the tent of the leader ("the tent" of Ex. 33, 7ff)—after atonement for sin had been made. The image of the steer, which has no other design than to be a likeness of that very God, "Who brought you up from the land of Egypt," (32, 4), was put up to make the leadership permanently perceptible. In the hour of forgiveness God grants (33, 14, 17) that His "face" will go with the people. The meaning of this is that a visibleness is conceded which in fact is none; that is to say, not the visibleness of an "image" or a "shape" (20, 4), but as in the vision of the ancients (24, 10) the visibleness of a *place*. This is the hour in which the holy object is born. Later, men attempted to render the principle, that could no longer be reconstructed in its reality, more conceivable by means of a concept of the *kabhod,* that is the fiery "weight" or "majesty" of the God radiating from the invisible, which now "fills" again and again the "dwelling" of the tent (40, 34), just as it had "taken dwelling" upon the mount (24, 16). In truth this idea of a filling of the tent, so that Moses "cannot come into the tent of meeting" (40, 35), contradicts its character and purpose. The true tent—formerly Moses' leader tent, and now that of the leader deity—is characterized by just this that Moses enters it for the sake of "meeting" the deity, and that "everyone who seeks YHVH" (33, 7) can hand over his petition to Moses who will talk it over with the deity. It is of the essence of the leadership that there is the divine word in dialogue: informative and initiative speaking. The informative function passes afterwards from the divine speech to the oracle vessels called *Urim and Thummim,* and from the *nabi*—for as such the former writing prophets know Moses from tradition (Hos. 12, 13)—to the priest. Whereas the initiative speech, the genuine speech of the leader which is no answer but a commission and a command, is henceforth also spoken only to the *nabi,* whom "the hand" seizes and sends. Kings rule, priests minister in their office, while the man of the Spirit, without power or office, hears the word of his Leader.

Besides the moveable divine abode, yet another feature of the nomadic period has entered into the life of the settled community and so deeply, that it persisted long after the age of the settlement and shared the subsequent wanderings of the people in all ages and generations, becoming almost a perpetual renewal of the first event: the feast of the Passover.[12] A nomadic feast, as it certainly was in primitive times, it was transformed by the holy event into a feast of history; but that which recurs in the festival is the act of going forth, the beginning of the journeyings; the nomadic feast, without any historical character, becomes the historical feast. With loins girt, with feet shod and with staff in

[12] Cf. especially Pedersen, Passahfest und Passahlegende, Zeitschrift fuer alttestamentliche Wissenschaft, Neue Folge XI (1934), 161ff; and my book "Moses," 69ff.

hand, in the haste of departure they eat the sacrifice (Ex. 12, 11). The Israelites do what was done formerly, not only performing the action, but in the performance doing it. Through the length and breadth of history, in every new home in a strange land, on this night the stimulus of the God-guided wanderings is active again, and history happens. The Israelites recount the story of the feast, this story which "cannot be the literary product of a later source," but which "contains facts," "solid tradition, springing from the ground of historic events." [13] But it is not the purpose to recount only what happened there and then. In the night of the Passover "the assembled company is fused together in every year and in all the world with the first cult confederates and attains that unity, which existed formerly at the first occasion in Egypt." [14] As they who keep the covenant in life know it to be the covenant which "YHVH our God made with us in Horeb," "not with our fathers," but "with us our very selves here this day, all of us being alive" (Deut. 5, 2f), so telling the story of God's leading they experience His historic deed as occurring to themselves. In His footsteps they are wakeful through the night, which was a night of watching for YHVH and is now a night of watching for all the children of Israel in their generations (Ex. 12, 42).

Berith, covenant, between YHVH and Israel denotes an expansion of the leadership and the following so as to cover every department of the people's life. The fundamental relationship represented perceptibly, that the deity—and it is the same in whatever form (pillar of fire, etc.) or even in no form (ark, "face") —goes before the company of wanderers and they follow after Him, and know in their heart that His way is the right way, this relationship is now taken as an all-embracing relationship founded as an everlasting bond in the making of the covenant. Here the mutual character of this relationship is announced, but the people feel already that a covenant with such a deity as this means no legal agreement, but a surrender to the divine power and grace. The most sublime expression of this is given in two sayings of YHVH (3, 14 and 33, 19), which by their sentence structure are

[13] Pedersen, *op. cit.*, 168.
[14] Hempel, Das Ethos des Alten Testaments (1938), 43.

shown to belong to each other (two similar verbal forms linked by the word *asher,* meaning "whoever," "whomever"). The first says that indeed the deity is always present but in every given hour in the appearance that pleases Him, that is to say He does not allow Himself to be limited to any form of revelation and He does not limit Himself to any of them; and the second says that He bestows His grace and mercy on whom He will, and lets no one order a criterion for Him nor Himself orders any. But connected with this is that element called YHVH's "demonism," [15] the dread of which overcomes us whenever we read about YHVH meeting Moses, His chosen and sent one, and "seeking to kill him" (4, 24). This is no survival, no "primitive fiend" which has entered, as it were, by mistake from earlier polydemonism into this purer sphere, but it is of the essential stuff of early Biblical piety, and without it the later form cannot be understood. The deity claims the chosen one or his dearest possession, falls upon him in order to set him free afterwards as a "blood bridegroom," as a man betrothed and set apart for Him by his blood. This is the most ancient revelation of grace: the true grace is the grace of death, a gracing; man owes himself to the deity from the beginning. And here too as with Jacob (Gen. 32) the event is significantly linked with a journey ordered earlier: the wanderer has to go through the dangerous meeting, in order to attain the final grace of the leader-God.

The idea of following the deity raises itself—no longer in the Mosaic but still in an early Biblical age—to the idea of imitating the deity, notably in the interpretation of the greatest institution set up by Moses, the Sabbath. It appears that the Sabbath too was not created *ex nihilo,* although its origin is not yet clear.[16] It is certain that the material used for this institution was adopted by a mighty force of faith, recast and molded into an indestructible creation of the life of the faithful. It is impossible to think of an age, later than that of Moses, in which this could have happened. Many think the "ethical Decalogue" (Ex. 20) to be later than the "cultic" (34), but the latter with its harvest and pilgrimage feasts presupposes an agricultural usage, whereas the former is yet "timeless," not yet stamped with any particular

[15] Volz, Das Daemonische in Jahwe (1924), and my "Moses," 56ff.
[16] Cf. Moses, 80ff.

organized form of human society; [17] the "cultic" is seen after detailed examination to be a "secondary mixture," whereas the "ethical" in its fundamental core is known to have a primary, "apodictic" character.[18] The Sabbath ordinance contained in it, in the original shorter version—beginning apparently with the word "remember" and continuing as far as "thy God"—is the ordinance of setting apart the seventh day for YHVH (that is to say, a day not ordered for cultic reasons, but freed of all authority of command except that of the one Lord). On this day men do not do, as on other days, "any work"; the meaning of this for the nomad shepherd, for the shepherd who cannot neglect his flock, is that he puts off all "jobs which he can do today or leave to tomorrow," that he interrupts the cultivation of land in the oasis, that he does not journey to new places of pasture, and so on.[19] It is only in the age of the settlement that the Sabbath becomes a strict day of rest. Among the established and illustrative sayings that come up for consideration (we find in the Pentateuch seven variants of the ordinance) two are of special importance, Ex. 23, 12, and 31, 12ff. It is customary to connect them with different "sources" from different periods, but a very rare verb (which is only found elsewhere in the Bible once, in the apparently contemporaneous story of Absalom, 2 Sam. 16, 14), meaning "to draw one's breath," links the two, the "social" and the "religious" motives, in true Biblical repetitive style, referring to one another and explaining one another. The one says that the purpose of the Sabbath ordinance was that the beast might rest and that men, whose work is obligatory, that is to say the slave and the hireling sojourner, who *must needs* work all the week, might draw breath. The other passage, which sets out the Sabbath ordinance in the most solemn form and imposes the death penalty upon those who transgress it, belongs in the original core of its first part (v. 13–15 in a shorter version) to the species of ordinances in the "apodictical style" of which Alt writes.[20] Having examined them fundamentally in their typical difference from all the rest of the

---

[17] Oesterley and Robinson, A History of Israel I (1932), 96; and my "Moses," 119ff.

[18] Alt, Die Urspruenge des israelitischen Rechts (1934), 52.

[19] R. Kittel, Geschichte des Volkes Israel I, Supplement I.

[20] Alt, *op. cit.*, 69. For an examination of the types of ordinance style, cf. Jirku, Das weltliche Recht im Alten Testament (1927).

later Canaanite influenced "casuistical" forms, he rightly says, "that the rise of this species was possible when the bond-relationship to YHVH and the resulting institution of making and renewing the covenant with Him came into being." But to this part of the ordinance is added a second, obviously a later expansion, in which the Sabbath is designated as an "everlasting covenant" and a "sign for ever," "for in six days YHVH made the heaven and the earth, and on the seventh day He rested and drew breath." The crass anthropomorphism binds together the deity and the tired, exhausted slave, and with words arousing the soul calls the attention of the free man's indolent heart to the slave; but at the same time it sets up before the community the loftiest sense of following the leader. Everyone that belongs to the essence of Israel—and the servants, the sojourners included, belong to it—shall be able to imitate YHVH without hindrance.

"The sayings in the apodictic form," says Alt,[21] "mostly have to do with things with which casuistic law did not deal at all, and by its secular nature could not deal. For the question is here on the one hand the sacred sphere of the contact with the divine world . . . and on the other hand holy realms in men's life together . . . religion, morals, and law are here still unseparated together." And again,[22] "in Israel's apodictic law an aggressive, as yet quite unbroken force operates, a force which subjects every realm of life to the absolute authority claim of YHVH's will for His people, and therefore cannot recognise any secular or neutral zone." These words fit our view that YHVH as "God of Israel" does not become the lord of a cultic order of faith, shut up within itself, but the lord of an order of people including all spheres of life, that is to say a *melekh,* and a *melekh* taking his authority seriously—unlike the gods of other tribes. I do not at all mean to go too far beyond Alt's carefully weighed thesis and to connect with Sinai the whole series of these sayings, rhythmically constructed in order to engrave them upon the memory of the people, among which there recurs again and again the "I" of the speaking God, and the "thou" of the hearing Israel; but in those too that bear the distinct scent of the field about them, we feel that the

[21] Alt, *op. cit.,* 47.
[22] *Ibid.,* 70.

fiery breath of Sinai has yet blown upon them. They are fragments of a people's order subject to the divine sovereignty.

As with the term "divine sovereignty" the meaning here is not a specialized religious authority but a sovereignty operating on all the reality of the community life, so with the term "people's order" the meaning is not the order of an indefinite society but of a completely definite people. To what is called in the Song of Deborah and in other ancient passages of Scripture "people of YHVH" a secular concept can approximate, namely that of "a true people," that is a people that realizes in its life the basic meaning of the concept *am*, "people," of living one *im*, "with," another; it approximates to it though, to be sure, it does not actually reach it. The "social" element in the apodictic laws is to be understood not on the basis of the task of bettering the living conditions of society, but on the basis of establishing a true people, as the covenant partner of the *melekh*, according as the tribes are a people as yet only by God's act and not by their own. If for example it is ordered (Ex. 22, 21 EV 22) not to afflict the widow and orphan, or (22, 20 EV 21; 23, 9) not to oppress the sojourner—here there is word about individuals dependent on others, lacking security, subject to the might of the mighty, but the aim of such commands is not the single person, but the "people of YHVH," this people which shall rise, but cannot rise so long as the social distance loosens the connections of the members of the people and decomposes their direct contact with one another. The *melekh* YHVH does not want to rule a crowd, but a community. There is already recognizable here, as in a network of roots, the widespread prophetic demand for social righteousness, which reached its highest peak in the promise of the union of the peoples in a confederacy of mankind through the mediation of the "servant" from Israel (Is. 42, 6).

Hence we see that the agricultural statute with its ordinances for the periodical interruption of the families' privilege of eating the fruits of their alloted ground, the remission of debts in the Sabbatical year, and the levelling of all possessions in the year of Jubilee, is only late with regard to the literary setting before us (Lev. 25), whereas with regard to its contents it presents "a transposition of the patriarchal conditions of the wilderness age to the agricultural conditions of Palestine," and is designed so that "the absolute coherence of the people" will live on in the consciousness of the common possession of land.[23] This common ownership is by its nature God's property, as we know from ancient Arabic parallels,[24] and the undeniably early saying, "Mine is the land, for you are sojourners and settlers with me" (v. 23), expresses the ancient claim of the divine leader on the ways of land-seeking and land-conquest, His claim to all the land of settlement.[25] We have already seen above how in the patriarchal story the divine name was called as of their true owner upon the places occupied beforehand in Canaan, as the names of their owners are called upon the great estates (Ps. 49, 12 EV 11). The divine ownership of the ground and the whole people's possession of it originate in a unity meant to last forever, whereas the rights of the individual are only conditional and temporary.

Within the ancient people's order, as we can deduce it from the apodictic laws, we find the sacred sphere of contact with the divine world substantially "only in the sense of keeping away all practices directed to gods or spirits other than YHVH, or implying a misuse of things belonging to Him and therefore holy, as for example His name or the Sabbath." [26] Only a single short sacrificial statute (Ex. 20, 24ff) can be cited here in its original form, purified of additions.[27] The words, "in every place, where I cause My name to be remembered, I will come unto thee and bless thee," come from the true character of the ancient nomad deity Who does not allow Himself to be kept to any mountain or temple. Sacrifices were apparently not customary in the wilderness apart from the nomadic offering of the firstborn of the flock (13, 12; 34, 19), except in extraordinary situations (the joining of Kenites, the ratifi-

---

[23] Jirku, Das israelitische Jobeljahr (Seeberg-Festschrift, 1929), 178. Cf. Alt, *op. cit.*, 65f; but he ascribes only the statutes about the Sabbatical year to an early age, and conjectures that in this year there was a complete new allotment of field plots to families, somewhat like that which is to be found amongst semi-nomads in our time; cf. also Kennett, Ancient Hebrew Social Life and Custom (1933), 77.

[24] Cf. Koenigtum Gottes, 56ff.

[25] Cf. Eerdmans, Alttestamentliche Studien IV (1912), 121ff; Kugler, Von Moses bis Paulus (1922), 49ff; Ramsay, Asianic Elements in Greek Civilization (1927), 49f.

[26] Alt, *op. cit.*, 47.

[27] Such an addition is to be seen in the mention of the two kinds of sacrifice in verse 24.

cation of the Sinai covenant). And there appears to have been no fixed sacrificial cult with special sacrificial rules; Amos was probably following a reliable tradition in this connection (5, 25), although he gave it an extreme interpretation.

But there is one more feature belonging to this *melekh* covenant between God and people, this leading and following, and that is the person of the mediator. The revelation, the making of the covenant, the giving of the statutes, was performed by the "translating" utterance of a mortal man; the queries and requests of the people are presented by the internal or external words of this person; the species of man that bears the word from above downwards and from below upwards is called *nabi*, announcer. So Hosea (12, 14 EV 13) calls Moses. In the earlier parts of the Pentateuch Moses is not so designated directly; in a remarkable story (Num. 12) an ancient verse inserted in it (v. 6b–8a) sets Moses apparently above the *nebiim*: for they only know the deity by visions, whereas to Moses, "His servant," He speaks "mouth to mouth" (not mouth to ear, but really mouth to mouth "inspiring"; cf. also Ex. 33, 11, "face to face as when a man speaks to his neighbor"), and moreover not in riddles, which a man must still explain, but so that the hearing of the utterance is itself a "sight" of the intention. And this just fits the concept of the *nabi*, known also in a later verse of the Pentateuch (Ex. 7, 1; cf. 4, 16), where the "god" who speaks into a person is, so to say, dependent on the *nabi* who speaks out. It is relatively unimportant when this term came into existence, but it is important that the thing is as old as Israel. In the story, composed out of the saga material in a strictly consistent form, we are told in a particularly manifold repetition of the roots *ra'ah, hazah* (to see) (Gen. 12, 1, 7; 13, 14, 15; 15, 1; 17, 1; 18, 1, 2a, 2b), of the series of visions Abraham saw, until he became the mediator between below and above, an undismayed mediator, pleading with God (18, 25), Who now declares him to be a *nabi* (20, 7); in this story the prevailing view in prophetic circles of the antiquity of prophecy is obviously expressed. The temporary order seer-prophet recalls an ancient note on word changes, which tells us more than mere word history (1 Sam. 9, 9). At all events no age in the history of early Israelite faith can be understood historically, without considering as active therein this species of man with his mission and function, his declaration and mediation.

Whatever else Moses is and does, his prophecy, his ministry of
the word, is the crystal center of his nature and work. It is true,
he does not "prophesy," the prophetic mission in the strict sense
belonging to a later and different situation between God and
people, but he does everything a prophet should in this early
situation: he represents the Lord, he enunciates the message, and
commands in His name.

Here we meet a problem, which historically, both in the spiritual
and the political sense, is singularly important.[28] The divine *melekh*
leads the *qahal,* the assembly of the men,[29] by means of the
one favored and called by Him, the bearer of the "charismatic"
power, the power of grace. This power, however, is not based, as
with oriental kings, upon the myth of divine birth or adoption,
but upon the utterly unmythical secret of the personal election
and vocation, and is not hereditary. After the man's death it is
necessary to wait until the *ruah,* the stormy breath ("spirit") of
the deity, rushes into another man. (Of the transmission of the
visible charisma, the "splendor," or part of it, to a man "in whom
there is spirit" Scripture speaks only once, that is concerning
the transmission by Moses to "his servant" Joshua, Num. 27, 15ff.
The doubtful character of this passage increased later consid-
erably with the insertion of the Urim as a determining power of
leadership, v. 21f). Because of this, the commission and therefore the actual leadership discontinues, a break which in the time
of the conquest served the semi-nomads ill, for even without
this they were given to unlimited family and tribal particularism,
loosening the YHVH confederation and weakening "Israel's"
power of action. Joshua's attempt to secure the continued unity
of the people by getting rid of the family idols and by founding
a tribal amphictyony [30] around a cult-directed center only, succeeded but partially as can be seen from the Song of Deborah. The
divine *melekh,* Who wishes to determine the whole life of the community, is not content to be substituted by a cult deity, to whom
it is sufficient to offer sacrifice at the yearly pilgrimages. The
Sinai enthusiasm for the absolute God grows again and expresses

[28] Cf. Koenigtum Gottes, 143ff.
[29] Cf. Rost, Die Vorstufen von Kirche und Synagoge im Alten Testament
(1938), 7f.
[30] Cf. Koenigtum Gottes, 157f, 287f.

itself in the activity and song of the Deborah circle. But the increasing difficulties of accomplishing the as yet incomplete conquest and of strengthening a position against the hostile neighbors arouse in opposition to this theopolitical ardor a "realist-political" movement, aimed at establishing the hereditary charisma known to Israel from the great powers, the dynastic securing of continuity. The opposition of the faithful to the *melekh* arises especially strongly in the days of Gideon, whose refusal to accept the royal crown may be regarded as historically true.[31] But already his son Abimelech stands in the opposite camp. And a national catastrophe, which the people may be inclined to see as a defeat of the leader God Himself, occurs; on the battlefield of Ebenezer the victorious Philistines capture the ark of the covenant which went at the head of the Israelite host. This hour represents the turning point in the history of Israelite faith.

[31] *Ibid.,* 3ff.

6. THE GREAT TENSIONS

A. THE RULE OF GOD AND THE RULE OF MAN

The period between Moses and Samuel is noteworthy from the point of view of religious history particularly for the fact that in time of war YHVH not only marches at the head of the army above the ark, but also time and again Himself chooses the commander and empowers him. His stormy breath, "YHVH's *ruah*," rushes upon His elect, seizes him, "puts him on" (Judges 6, 34), and his sword is henceforth the sword of YHVH Himself (this is the meaning of the cry of Gideon's men "sword of YHVH and Gideon," 7, 20, that is to say, the two have one sword), as his warfare is the warfare of YHVH Himself against "His enemies" (cf. 1 Sam. 18, 17; 25, 28). In place of this type of "great judge," who in the beginning "procures for the people its right," that is to say overcomes the invader, and also later restores from within the tottering order of justice (the two are designated by the same verb), there comes at the time of the Philistine oppression the Nazirite warrior, already known to us from the Song of Deborah, volunteering for YHVH's war [1]—the man, whom the *ruah* "pushes on" (Ju. 13, 25) and equips for wonderful deeds of might, as the story lovingly pictures in the person of Samson. But when the Danite guerrilla warfare failed before the military and technical superiority of the Philistines, when the tribe of Dan was compelled to leave its inheritance and the danger threatening all Israel became noticeable—then the only existing central institution, which had hitherto been chiefly connected with the cult alone, namely the Shiloh priesthood, attempts (apparently by preserving the form of the ancient judges' office) to materialize the divine sovereignty apart from the inspiration of the Spirit, as hierocracy, to unite the tribes more closely by using the accepted oracle authority and the

[1] Cf. Schwally, Semitische Kriegsaltertuemer (1901), 69.

fighting power of the ark, so as to lead all the people against the Philistines. The disaster of Ebenezer, the historicity of which there is no reason to doubt (no people would invent such a thing), put an end, with the capture of the ark, to all the priestly enterprise and to the whole basis of a priestly policy; the *kabhod*, the radiation of the "divine weight" from above the ark, had gone into exile (1 Sam. 4, 21f). From that time the *ruah* impulse begins to operate again in a new form. In the text, as it is before us, the person of Samuel [2] has about it something variable and indefinite; but if instead of distributing the story between the sources, we deal with it as a homogeneous account and detach from it later additions, we arrive at the indeed somewhat mutilated image of a remarkable religious personality.

Samuel, "minister" of the ark (3, 1, 3), as Joshua was "minister" in the tent (Ex. 33, 11), came from no priestly family. Unlike Joshua he was called by YHVH Himself in the hall of the ark and in days when the passion of faith in the reception of the Spirit had given place to the permanent sovereignty of the priestly oracle— "and the word of YHVH was precious" for "no vision broke through" (1 Sam. 3, 1). This undoubtedly ancient verse indicates a turning point in the history of Israel's faith; expressions such as this may be used of the pains of a new birth. YHVH overcomes the sterility of the oracle by a new initiative, announcing the coming catastrophe of the ark. It is only in this sense that we can understand verse 11 ("I will do a thing in Israel . . ."), which is also unmistakably early; the Lord of the ark declares from the outset that the ark will go into exile and be desecrated, and Samuel is chosen by Him to utter the divine word as a free *nabi* in the days without the ark, replacing the priesthood though without its oracular ephod. It may be asked, why does not Samuel restore the ark—even if it seems likely it was emptied of its contents—some time after the disaster, when it could have been obtained again? We sense that which the narrator dared not say: Samuel does not want to do this. YHVH Himself allowed His ark to be captured: now He has brought it out of the hands of the Philistines, but still He does not wish to restore it to the people of Israel, for He does

---

[2] In what follows about the age of Samuel I have introduced some conclusions from my as yet unpublished book (see Introduction, note 1). There I explain the literary and exegetical basis of my interpretation.

not wish them to use Him instead of serving Him. The leader-God wishes only that they should hearken to His voice. The saying "to hearken is better than sacrifice" (15, 22) has the ring of a genuine Samuel saying. God's leadership without the ark, that is Samuel's "idea" and that is what he proclaims in the hour of disaster. It is Jeremiah's idea, but this is the hour of its birth, not four hundred years later. The priesthood, which brought the disaster upon the people, must be eliminated. Samuel has no contact with it, and assigns it no function. The ark had resided in a sanctuary super-vised by priests; as its "minister" the young Samuel used to sleep in its "great-hall" (*hekhal*), but it was just here that the break-down was announced to him. No ark—that is to say, the offering of the community, hitherto supposedly bound up with the priestly center, is withdrawn from it: in hours of distress Samuel himself offers great sacrifices (7, 9), in all the other cases he hands the sac-rificial cult not to a Levite, but to a "slaughterer" specially appointed for this function, an appointment we find only at this time (9, 23). No ark—that is to say, no more pilgrimages to the material oracle; from now on there is the man of God, wandering about from place to place, to whom YHVH speaks, and who can declare what the will of the leader is.[3] There can be no forcing YHVH's hand, even against the Philistines; the duration of their supremacy is a concern of His acting and planning for Israel. The Israelites have sinned against Him, and so they are under obliga-tion to make confession and to pray, and this they are allowed to do. This is the background of the original core of the much worked-over chapter 7; Samuel intervenes, in the true manner of the *nabi*, as a mediator between people and God (v. 5). He himself, the "one entrusted as a *nabi*" (*ne'eman l'nabi* 3, 20), he is the one to whom is directed the epithet "trusted priest" (*kohen ne'eman*, 2, 35) in the prophecy about Eli's children, an epithet the meaning of which is confused by later accretions. The true *nabi*—this is the intention of the early narrator—is the true priest.[4]

Samuel attained authority after the catastrophe—the double catastrophe of Israel and of the faith—first of all by virtue of his

---

[3] The incident of the casting of lots (10, 20ff) does not belong to the oldest tradition of the story; but even so no priest takes part.

[4] Only in the text of the story before us, which has been influenced by a ten-dentious completion, does the word appear to refer to a new dynasty of priests, replacing the old, i.e., the dynasty of the Zadokites.

religious idea, that enabled him to strengthen the despairing hearts and to fix them again on YHVH. Added to this apparently was the assistance given him by a circle, about which we do not hear anything here, but which we are permitted to identify with those early *nebiim,* which Amos, although he did not feel very warmly disposed towards the *nebiim* of his own time (Am. 7, 14), mentions alongside the Nazirite warriors as a great gift of God from former days (2, 11f), as the species of men, which later generations silenced (that is to say, compelled them to be silent about affairs of public life) and so corrupted. These early *nebiim* come from the movement of faith, which in the period after Joshua opposed the merely cultic centralization of the tribes as an Amphictyonic covenant,[5] and demanded a militant devotion to "YHVH God of Israel" and to "Israel the people of YHVH" in the whole domain of public life—a sentiment we have seen expressed in the Song of Deborah. Only so can we see in its right light that "band" of *nebiim* indisputably linked with Samuel (1 Sam. 10, 5), which comes down from the holy high place with the playing of lutes and pipes (the *bamoth,* the high places, are here characteristically not the sphere of the priests but of the *nebiim*). What the company of *nebiim* is doing to the sound of music, what the meaning here is of *hithnabbe,* to behave or act as a *nabi,* should not be understood as disorderly movements and inarticulate sounds without any connection or coherence. War enthusiasm is not stirred up in a people of early culture by such acts as these, but by an enthusiastic singing of monotonous songs. Truly such singing is ecstatic and lays claim to man's whole being, but it is also bound up with a strict rhythm and is accompanied by rhythmical movements of all the members. It is true that such singing is sometimes contagious like some primitive communal dances, but it does not drag into utter frenzy, rather taking the form of a musical fusion of declaratory and proclamatory gesture, declaratory and proclamatory sound, a rhythmically adjuring fusion. It passes with the growth of the rapture into a rhythmically controlled prelude to the holy war itself. It is easy to understand how powerfully such a circle was able to carry away the *nabi* Samuel.

Indeed the noun *nabi* in the singular has not the same meaning as in the plural; but fundamentally Samuel the *nabi* and

[5] Cf. Koenigtum Gottes, 157ff, 287f.

the "band" of *nebiim* have this in common: both are in a special
way under YHVH's influence. With the priest, as with the counter
type, the sorcerer and the conjurer, the *decisive* movement goes
out from the human person towards the realm of the deity (or
of the spirits and powers), whereas with the *nabi* something descends from the divine sphere upon man: *dabhar* or *ruah, logos*
or *pneuma,* word or spirit. These two are not sharply distinguished.
Dabhar does not displace *ruah,* but joins with it. According to
the Biblical view he to whom full power is given first experiences
the *ruah,* and afterwards receives the *dabhar.* In the one case
one receives the stimulus, in the other the content. Where the
nebiim appear in a company, the *ruah* rules alone, as in the story
of the outpouring of the Spirit on the elders (Num. 11). *Nabi* is
originally the attribute not of a class or profession, but of a
condition, that is to say mainly of a collective condition, which
from time to time seizes the men exposed to the *ruah,* gathering
them and driving them over the land. But this cannot mean a
qualitative distinction between the *nebiim* in the band and the
individual *nabi.*[6] He, too, the single *nabi,* when he is called not
to "declare" his message, but to "perform" it, is subject to the
influence of the power that precedes the word. On the other hand
the *dabhar* is not strange to the bands of *nebiim.* It is true, the
new word is not released to them, which in order to be heard
chooses and "denudes" (1 Sam. 9, 15) the ear of a person; but
what they say or sing to musical accompaniment is nowhere
characterised as shouting or glossolaly. They are words, and we
may suppose that they arise not in glossolalic confusion, but in
a *remembered* formation: most of what they speak or sing in
constant ecstatic form is certainly ancient *dabhar,* faithfully preserved by word of mouth in its original form. These men of the
pneuma also minister to the Logos. Only on the basis of this joint
activity of *nabi* and *nebiim* in the hour of the catastrophe can we
find an explanation of the fact that Samuel suppresses the mis-
carrying priesthood, and replaces the priestly with a prophetic
guidance, instituting free announcement in place of the oracle
fettered by sanctuary tradition, and apparently also congregational
sacrifice moving about from high place to high place instead of the
one which was tied to the priestly sites.

[6] This view is expressed in particular by Jepsen, Nabi (1934).

In spite of this joint activity the turning point in the history of faith which might be called after Samuel's name acquired no permanent historical form; Samuel's primitive reform of the cult failed, his leadership became merely an historical episode. The longing of the "realist politicians" to secure the community by setting up a royal dynasty grew stronger, until Samuel and his men were compelled to abandon their opposition and to establish a king of flesh and blood (this is not from a late "source," but belongs to the essence of the story). This withdrawal of Samuel and his men is to be explained by the fact that they were able to accomplish nothing decisive against the Philistines, and obtained only a slight and partial success, which in the text before us appears very exaggerated.[7] Victory has not been granted to Samuel's prayer, and certainly he was not a charismatic warrior in the sense of the early tribal heroes, the "great judges."

Having removed from chapter 8 of 1 Samuel the additional matter, which contains sufficient to twist the sense of the whole, we read in the beginning that all the elders came to Samuel in Ramah and asked him: "Appoint us a king to judge us, like all the nations." From the renewed and more exactly reasoned demand in v. 20 it is clear that the word "to judge" here is used in its ancient sense, that of procuring for someone his right, helping him to attain his right, fighting for his right and winning it. If we wish to understand this demand in its full significance in the development of religious history, we do well to set over against it the words of Deborah (Ju. 4, 14). "Has not YHVH gone forth before thee (*yatsa l'phanekha*)?"—so Deborah speaks to Barak; "Nay but there shall be a king over us, and so shall we too be as all the nations, and our king shall judge us and go forth before us (*w'yatsa l'phanenu*), and fight our battle"[8]—so the elders of Israel speak to Samuel. In his first reply to their demand he gives them YHVH's word: they want to dethrone Him, Who has been their *melekh* until now, to "reject Him from reigning over them," but He will grant them their demand, "only that" they are to be told of the legal obligation attaching to the king who will rule

[7] Verses 13f do not agree with the situation prevailing at the beginning of ch. 13. They are an addition originally intended simply to interpret the "so far" in v. 12 in a manner anticipating the victories of Saul (v. 13) and David (v. 14).

[8] The *scriptio defectiva* suggests that the original intention was to refer only to the present battle against the Philistines.

over them, his "ordinance." [9] The reference is not to what follows
in verses 11–18 (this is a later addition apparently taken—as well
as Deut. 17, 16f—from a pamphlet of Solomon's time or there-
after), but to the statute read in the ears of the congregation, 10,
25, set up to bind the anointed one in YHVH's name as *nagid*
(10, 1), that is to say set at the head, representative of sovereignty,
deputy responsible above (cf. Jer. 20, 1), that can be "rejected
from being king" from above (1 Sam. 15, 23). So finally the
conceded kingdom is not as those of "all the nations," and the
designation *melekh* means only the true king's viceroy or representative. The elders of the people, however, do not understand
what is said to them, and repeat their demand more exactly. The
nature of their call can only be understood on the basis of the
historical situation. There is in it some living reminiscence of the
catastrophe of the ark and the Israelite army led by it, and of the
fruitlessness of the hard struggles for freedom since then; behind
it stands the disappointment of the people over the sanctuaries
and the men of God where it concerns the war against the Philistines. They were disappointed of the ark and they were
disappointed of the *ruah*. The people call for a charismatical
commander, for one graced with permanent heavenly favor. He
must not be a temporary commander as were the "great judges."
With their death there had always been an interregnum. The
people call for security from above against death and interregnum,
and for a succession which would not suffer interruption with its
consequent dangers; they call for hereditary heavenly favor like
"all the nations" have. Only in such a bodily, biologically established manifestation of power, contained in the continuity of a
ruling dynasty, can the people look for deliverance by the grace
of heaven.

YHVH's *ruah* government had brought about a state of disorder
within and powerlessness without, because Israel was not in truth
"YHVH's people." But now the second instrument, the representative "kingship," is set up by holy anointing, that is by
empowering and imposition of permanent duties (sacramental
anointing means preservation of a special substance or power).
Just as in the ancient East we have instances of a covenant between

[9] Cf. Num. 9, 14, the "ordinance" for the celebration of Passover.

God and people,[10] but it is only in Israel that we find the venture to treat it seriously, so while in Egypt, in Babylon, and in S. Arabia, we come across the concept of the king as deputy of the deity,[11] it is only in Israel that we meet the venture to understand this in its full reality as something life-determining and imposing genuine responsibilities. In the first period it was required of the *am* that they should be a true *am,* and in the second period it was required of the *nagid* that he should be a true *nagid.* These two things did not come about by the exposition of the writing prophets, but with the setting up of the instrument itself, with the foundation of the people, with the foundation of the kingship. The exposition of the prophets is not a basic action, but a re-action to the fact that the people and kings did not in their lives and deeds realize the goal implicit in the nature of the kingdom. The prophecy of the early writing prophets, of Amos and Hosea, marks the *maturity* of the protest. It is not a beginning, it remembers the beginning and pleads with the generation concerning what was intended there. If we regard this prophecy as the outcome of what may be called airy roots, of conceptions lacking a real basis, and not rather as a growth from well-grounded roots, we have something which we term prophecy, but which is in truth nothing but religious literature.

The image that we see throughout the Israelite kingdom, the image of the prophet pleading with the king, is not properly understandable on the basis of general religious or special historical conditions, even though these exercise an influence upon it. We can only grasp its essential content, if we recognize the *theopolitical supposition* of this prophetic standpoint, a supposition which for the most part is not openly expressed and does not need any such expression: the commission of YHVH's representative which is not fulfilled by the kings in Israel. Indeed, "the ordinance of the kingship" which is bound up with the election and anointing of Saul, and engages the king to obey his divine Lord, his commissioner and authorizer, is not found any longer in subsequent days, but stands at the inception of the kingdom as a symbol, so to speak, and all the subsequent things, the literary criticism

[10] Cf. Koenigtum Gottes, 124.
[11] Cf. *ibid.,* 49f.

of the historian and the politico-factual criticism of the prophets, must be examined in the light of this basic fact, that this kingship in the hour of its foundation is bound up with God's will and declared to be responsible to Him. It has been rightly said [12] that there is no reason to doubt the historical basis of the view, according to which the king is considered "as the executor of the divine will and Samuel as the prophet and guardian of it." If so, we are further right in supposing that this fundamental relationship was accepted as the root principle of Israel's kingdom by the conscience of the men who, in the time of the state, represented YHVH's absolute claim, formerly revealed in the wilderness, that all community rule was in His hand, and who now demanded that all state rule should be subject to His power. So these men, the prophets, who mostly have no appointment but only a mission—nevertheless it is related of them that they were the ones who anointed all the kings in Israel (except Omri) acting on divine authority, a fact the influence of which was still recognized in postexilic times (Neh. 6, 6f)—they stand and summon to justice the representatives on the royal throne for their treachery against YHVH and His commandments. One after the other they repeat God's word, "I have anointed thee to be *melekh*," or "I have appointed thee *nagid*": Samuel to Saul (1 Sam. 15, 17), Nathan to David (2 Sam. 12, 7), Ahijah to Jeroboam (1 Kgs. 14, 7). For four hundred years they come one after the other and take their stand before the prince and reprove him because of the violated covenant, and finally Jeremiah (22, 6ff), some time before the disaster, announces destruction for the king's house which had not been just, and therefore was no more justified. What here appears as the meaning of that bond between the king and his divine Lord, Who lays the duty upon him and bestows upon him the power, is already expressed long before this in a most important document, the antiquity of which cannot be doubted because of its genuine and not sham archaic character, the so-called "Last words of David" (2 Sam. 23, 1–7). Out of the mouth of God's "anointed" "YHVH's *ruah*" speaks. "The God of Israel said: to me (the rock of Israel speaks) is a ruler over man, righteous, a

[12] Weiser, 1 Samuel 15, Zeitschrift fuer alttestamentliche Wissenschaft, Neue Folge XIII (1936), 22f; cf. also Alt, Die Staatenbildung der Israeliten in Palestina (1930).

ruler in God's fear, and he shines forth as the light of morning, the sun of a morning without clouds because of the brightness." "To me . . . ," Israel's God says: such a ruler He "has," He intends him.[13] Here the Messianic idea breaks through out of its historic covering.

David brought the ark, which Samuel had not wanted to return, "in joy" to Jerusalem (6, 12). But by this not only the wanderings of the ark came to an end, but also its leadership. Some time before David had experienced the leadership directly without the ark: YHVH had said to him (5, 24), repeating Deborah's words to Barak, that He should go forth before him against the Philistines rushing through the tops of the balsam trees. Now when YHVH "had given him rest round about from all his enemies" (7, 1) the leadership had come to an end. We hear about battles fought, but no more about leadership. "YHVH's war," which is "a warring for Israel," begun at the exodus from Egypt (Ex. 14, 14, 25) and felt as a cosmic act in the battles of the conquest (Josh. 10, 14; Ju. 5, 20), has come to an end now with the securing of the promised land. Only in the far-off future, in the time of the new beginning after the return from Babylonian exile, are we to hear again and for the last time the saying "our God will fight for us" (Neh. 4, 14 EV 20). In the message YHVH sends David by Nathan after the return of the ark, He recalls the time (2 Sam. 7, 6) when He was with the people "walking in tent and dwelling place." He recalls (v. 8) how He took him "from following the flock"—as formerly Moses, and later Amos—to be a ruler over His people, over Israel, and how from that time "He was with him" wherever he went (v. 9). But now "he has planted" Israel (v. 10), now the people cannot any longer be oppressed as in the days, when He commanded judges over the people, now "He has given rest" to David and wills "to make him a house" (v. 11). That is the speech to which "the Last Words" allude, as to the making of an everlasting covenant. Clearly David did not mean himself when he used the phrase "righteous ruler," and the writer cannot have been referring to himself. The "rest" is there, and the "house" is there, but that kingdom of righteousness is lacking, which is described in the instruction tract for princes, transposed into the Psalms (72) with the title "To Solomon" or "Of Solomon." Con-

[13] This interpretation of A. Klostermann has not been surpassed.

cerning the ordinance binding the king there is no further whisper in the history of Solomon—as opposed to David, who confessed and repented. This history concludes with YHVH "raising up" against him "adversary" after "adversary" (1 Kgs. 11, 14, 23) and later (v. 29) sending a prophet to empower the rebel to rend the kingdom of Israel in two. The story by its arrangement of things and presentation of events expresses every criticism that had to be expressed.

From Moses to Samuel is only a step in the history of faith, whereas from Samuel to Solomon, the son of his protégé, is a long way. The self-assurance that is manifest in the saying at the dedication of the temple (1 Kgs. 8, 12f), that Solomon boasts to have built "for an everlasting abode," the house in which the ark was now brought to rest, threatens to hide the appearance of the leader-God Himself, of Him Who remembers the wanderings of His tent.

But from another quarter too a shadow seems to approach His image.

B. YHVH AND THE BAAL

The old controversy among scholars, whether the Hebrews who wandered from Egypt to Canaan were "polytheists" or "monotheists," or whether they are to be given some other scholastic designation, is an unreal business. These Hebrews were devoted to YHVH, Who was their liberator and leader of their journeyings. Certainly not all were equally devoted, but a part of the people reached the stage of passionate exclusivism; everything in which they were able to see the finger of the God, Who went at their head, they accepted as His gift. But wherever and whenever they met anything noteworthy, which had apparently not been brought or sent them by their guardian deity, something which had existed previously in this place, such as a bush of strange formation, or an unusually steep rock, they were impressed by after the common Semite manner (even though this is nothing but a special residue of the ways of primitive man in general); they saw a force breaking out in this place and blessed it, the *El* of this particular appearance. Or when anyone, without having sinned against YHVH, was attacked by a strange fever with the cruel suddenness of the desert storm, and began to be consumed by it, he saw in this a "demonic" force that had descended upon him, and proceeded to utter incantations against the *shed*. (I say "saw," because what is here described is not in any sense simply a manner of *interpreting* things and events, but a manner of *seeing* them, something really primary and self-evident). But when they proceeded to travel away from that place, or when that evil passed from them, they turned their attention away from that occurrence, and were at once ready to *forget* that strange being, whether friendly or hostile, which had crossed their path. In addition to this there were all kinds of fetishes or amulets, which were only remembered when the wearer needed them, and apart from this were not thought of at all. Set faith and worship existed only where there was continuity, where the divine person perceived endured and contact was possible with him without interruption. Only after surmounting, time and again, many natural stumbling blocks do these men, who experience every unusual event with violent feeling, learn to recognize their God and His activity also in the spheres which seemed necessarily foreign to Him. The extension of YHVH's power and influence to cover all departments of life was solemnly proclaimed at the time of the covenant revelation in the stormily anticipating decision of the people, but the actual accomplishment of this process takes place slowly, step by step, retreating and advancing, until the life of the congregation accepts the authority of the "living God in their midst" (Josh. 3, 10).

There is, however, in the new status of life, the status of the settlement, *one* sphere which by its very nature is opposed to the nature of the God coming to Canaan. This is the central sphere in the existence of the primitive peasant: the secret of the fertility of the ground, the astonishing phenomenon, from the discovery of which the invention of agriculture springs. A marvel fills the hearts of those who are confronted by the blessings of plant increase, an increase not to be understood as cattle procreation is from the well known event of pairing: apparently it is in the depth of the ground that the cause of this increase lies hid. For there, they say, male and female powers, Baal and Baalath, "lord" and "lady" copulate, countless pairs of deities, mostly only distinguished by place names: the pouring forth of water—rain or spring or underground waters—makes the soil fruitful and a rich growth results; [1] still in the Talmud, and even in late Arab legal language, the field that needs no artificial irrigation (in Arabic only the field that drinks underground or spring water) is called the field or the house of the Baal. This is not to be taken as the interpretation of the natural process, but as the innate manner of preserving it. Man, however, is not merely a passive witness of the nuptials of powers; by an act of sacral pairing, in which man and woman imitate the deities, identifying them with themselves so to speak, man is able directly to enhance the force and the working of the divine fecundity. Such fertility powers, connected with a locality, are widespread in the agricultural stage of Canaan at the time of Israel's entry into the land; but we see in the more developed Syrian culture, how the *baalim,* spirits lacking individuality, tend to unite into a personal god called Baal. This Baal is likely to appear in the form of a town deity in a well-watered land, or in the likeness of a rain-giving deity dwelling in the clouds of heaven. We have learned about the second kind from the mythological Ras Shamra texts; this god of the Phoenicians, Baal or Aliyan, has been identified with the storm god Hadad, already known in this land before the advent of the Phoenicians. We read in these texts how the god who, as Aliyan, is called "lord of the deep springs," and dwells in the depths of the earth, "opens" as Baal of the heavens "the sluices of the clouds," and how he, assuming like his father *El* the shape of a bull, "loves" a goddess in the shape of a cow on the pasture land, and engenders a bull calf.

The Hebrew nomads who burst into the land of Canaan found these *baalim* not only in the imagination of the aborigines, but, as it were, in bodily reality: they needed only a slight suggestion, penetrating this great oasis, in order to see too "under every luxuriant tree" the divine pairs. And these they did not forget, as they forgot the deities of the desert wanderings, it was impossible to forget them: for they were already there where they settled, they were indeed "owners" (*baalim*) of this soil, which men woo by ploughing, and one's labor would not be blessed unless he served them according to their will. In this they mean to depart

---

[1] Cf. Koenigtum Gottes, 65f, 205ff. To the literature mentioned there add especially Dalman, Arbeit und Sitte in Palestina II (1932), 31f.

in no way from YHVH, and in the hour of adversity and hostile attack they turn to Him and devote themselves to His well-tried leadership, but in matters of peasants' secrets and charms ·they cannot of course turn to the ancient nomad deity.

According to the Biblical story (Num. 25, 1ff), which Hosea (9, 10) corroborates, the people while still outside the land of Canaan were enticed by the daughters of Moab into worshipping Baal Peor, the "Baal of the sprawling chasm," "and they became abominations like the object of their affections." But the weaving of sexual ceremonies into the rhythm of agriculture they learn only from the people of Canaan, son of Ham, that same Canaan who is mentioned again and again in the story of Noah's drunkenness (Gen. 9, 18ff), although he himself had nothing to do with it,[2] and finally is cursed with a threefold curse, although he did no wrong. It concerns not the man, but the people, and the theme words "the nakedness of the father," three times repeated, we find again in the legal chapters (Lev. 18 and 20), in which the introductory command of God is that they should not do "after the manner of the land of Canaan, whither I bring you." These are the statutes dealing with unchastity and the first prohibition (18, 7) begins with the words "the nakedness of thy father" (a combination of words only found in these two places). The verses in Genesis and Leviticus are interrelated by paranomasia, and we can read between the lines a warning concerning the sexual promiscuity of the Canaanite cult; this is obviously what is meant by the phrase "the iniquity of the Amorite" (Gen. 15, 16), which still recurs in later traditions (Testament of Judah 12) as "the custom of the Amorite," through which "the land became defiled" (Lev. 18, 25, 27) and "spued out its inhabitants" (v. 25); Israel must be careful lest the land spue them out too (v. 28). This is one of the pieces of evidence showing how deeply interwoven into the *composition* of the Hebrew Bible—the work on which began not in post-exilic times but in the period of the kings—is the protest against the worship of the Baal. No mention is ever made of the sexual rites except by implication; the word "high places" is used to indicate what goes on there; use is made of strange, so to speak, technical expressions, as for example, "yoking oneself

---

[2] On the following cf. Buber-Rosenzweig, Die Schrift und ihre Verdeutschung, 58ff. Cf. also my "Moses," 193f.

to the Baal" meaning a pair joined together by common function, as a pair of oxen, and so serving the Baal, or of a conventional phrase, as for example that used of the daughters of Canaan (Ex. 34, 16), who are said to have "made thy sons go a whoring after their gods." The sacred orgies of Syrian temple prostitution are mentioned explicitly in the statutes of the Torah only in a passing hint (Deut. 23, 18), and in the Biblical narrative we learn of it only in the account of Josiah's reforms (2 Kgs. 23, 7) fifty years before the downfall: we read that in the days of his predecessor Manasseh, they even penetrated to YHVH's temple with their sacred male and female paramours.

This extreme "syncretism," it must be admitted, has more of the court character than the popular about it; but wherever the kings established the worship of the great Phoenician Baal, as Ahab and his successors did, they thought—rightly or wrongly— they could use for their own ends the popular leaning toward the small local *baalim*. Before Ahab, indeed, we do not find any trace of Baalism acquiring a place and a station beside the YHVH cult. The *baalim* were accepted by the people as a fact, but treated as the indispensable religious requisites for the successful fertilization of the soil, for which YHVH, the wanderer and warrior, was not competent. Even now they wished to *acknowledge as a people* YHVH only; whereas the fertility deities they *knew* only, and this in a private and intimate manner. These local deities that had been, so to speak, found on the spot, offered themselves for such a division of life as the old family idols, which the Israelites had brought to the land, had in their time. As everyone knew simply his local deity, they did not come within the general knowledge of the people as such. The community on the whole was able to regard itself as remaining the congregation of YHVH.

For those who were with all their heart faithful to YHVH it was very difficult to fight against this mode of life, for it was indeed only a mode of life and became in no sense a confession of faith. When the enemy oppressed, they had only to throw down the altars of the local *baalim* (Ju. 6, 28), and thereby the requirements of the hour were accomplished. As soon as the war of liberation is proclaimed, there is in reality none but YHVH, and immediately the *baalim* are forgotten, just as formerly in nomad days the gods of the moment were at once forgotten. But when peace returns and the regular life of soil-cultivation is re-established, it is difficult for YHVH to stand up against the small nameless powers, swarming everywhere without special forms. He, YHVH, cannot remain really the Lord of the people, the God of Israel in the old absolute sense, unless He brings under his rule the domain of the new, agricultural form of life. But how is this to be done without perverting His own nature? The Canaanite soil cultivation is linked with apparently unbreakable bonds of tradition to sexual myths and rites; whereas YHVH by His uncompromising nature is altogether above sex, and cannot tolerate it that sex, which like all natural life needs hallowing by Him, should seem to be declared holy by its own natural power. There is no place here for compromise. Whoever baalizes YHVH introduces Astarte into the sanctuary. In Jerusalem of the seventh century B.C.E., we meet with a goddess Anath,[3] "queen of heaven" (essentially identical with Astarte), as YHVH's rival, still strange to the sanctuary and known only in the private cult of the women (Jer. 44, 17ff). But in the Jewish colony of Elephantiné in the fifth century—in many ways recalling the situation in Jerusalem before Josiah's reformation—we find her as official partner of the god "Yaho," who has shrunk into a *baal*. The really faithful YHVH worshippers recognize the incompatibility between the nature of YHVH and the nature of the Baal. At first YHVH is addressed by the name Baal as the only true lord of the country, both in Saul's house and in David's, as the proper names we find there testify; but apparently this custom was not long lived, although Hosea seems to have been the first to sound a public alarm against the grave danger involved in such a fusion.

We find that the rallying cry, "YHVH versus Baal," is necessarily intended to shake the religious foundation of West-Semitic agriculture: the sexual basis of the fertility mystery, hidden in the meeting of water and earth, must be abolished. The natural irrigation is not the work of the union of a streaming-in male element and a receiving female element, but the gift of the deity Who gives, the Lord of all fertility. This—if translated from the language of *faith* itself into the language of the *history* of faith

[3] Cf. especially A. Vincent, La religion des Judéo-Araméens d'Éléphantine (1937), 622ff.

—is in essence the core of the testimony of the story about Elijah the Tishbite, who lived a hundred years after David and a hundred years before Hosea. The second, and positive part of the sentence, from which the first follows, is indeed handed down from the days of David in Jacob's blessing of Joseph (Gen. 49, 25), which ascribes natural fertility to the divine *berakhah*, "blessings of heaven above, blessings of the deep below, blessings of the breasts and womb." To estimate the significance of this passage we must note that in a later fragment, in ch. 28 of Deuteronomy (v. 4, cf. v. 18 and 51) the writer says: "Blessed is the fruit of thy womb, and the fruit of thy ground, and the fruit of thy cattle, the off-spring of thy kine, and the 'Ashtaroth' of thy sheep," and by this term "Ashtaroth," which is undoubtedly a familiar expression, is meant, of course, the pregnancy which in Canaan was customarily regarded as Astarte's gift.

As Solomon set up a cult of the Sidonian Astarte for his Sidonian wife (1. Kgs. 11, 1, 5, 8), so Ahab set up for his Tyrian wife a cult of the Tyrian Baal, locally called Melkart, that is "city king," the only difference being that, unlike Solomon, Ahab himself wor-shipped the foreign deity (16, 31)—even though he gave his sons names that testified to his worship of YHVH—and thereby be-trayed his duty as the anointed of Israel's God. Formerly critics used to distinguish between this Phoenician Baal and the Ca-naanite fertility gods, seeing in it something characteristically and essentially different; but recently he has been recognized in the Ras Shamra texts, as their true, although incomparably greater and more powerful brother, and the narrator himself confuses him with them (18, 18) intentionally as it seems; here too the attachment to Baal is identified with those "doings of the Amorite" (21, 26). It was this concentration of numberless small local deities in the "Lord of the earth," mighty in flood and fertility, which made possible the frontal assault on Baalism.

Elijah, son of the Transjordanian desert, is perceptible through the veil of legend as a great historical character, though he appears without a parental name and disappears without a grave. He passes through the midst of the city culture with all its degenera-tion as the zealous and inflexible nomad, long-haired, wrapped in a hairy garment, with a leather girdle, reminiscent of the Babylo-nian hero Enkidu of the Gilgamesh epic, except that Enkidu is enticed by the temple whore, whereas Elijah never has any contact with Baal seductions. All the stories about him have to do with going, wandering; God's voice, angel voices again and again bid him rise and go; YHVH's stormy breath carries him away, no one knows where (18, 12), YHVH's hand comes upon him and urges him to run (v. 46). His life is connected with Israel's journeyings in the wilderness and with the revelation at Mount Sinai: when (19, 4) under "one" (that is, a solitary) juniper tree he is overcome by the wish to die, and an angel feeds him, he goes forty days and nights according to the forty years of Israel's wanderings in the wilderness, returns so to speak, on Israel's tracks to the mount of revelation, and there he receives the revelation, a form of which, though not its content, tells that the zealous Sinai God does not appear in storm or fire, but in "the voice of a slender silence." He "hears" the voice, although it was not a whisper nor a rustle, but silence indeed (v. 13); and this too goes over into a mission. Through the veil of the legend we recognize the man of holy unrest, hanging between the fulfilment of his mission and his search for God out of despair about the world. But later the veil is rent, and in the clear light of history the man stands over against Ahab (21, 17ff) in the right historical position of YHVH's prophet before "Israel's king" (v. 18), and pleads with Him concerning the great iniquity he had done, and in the name of the true ruler and in the name of the obligations laid upon His royal representative he curses the faithless one. Here the stern theopolitical facts in all their fulness stand opposed to every attempt of tradition to resort to legendary transfiguration.

Not so in the story of the drought, the battle on Mount Carmel, and the deluge of rain (ch. 17f), with which the string of stories about Elijah begins (once apparently a book, the beginning of which was lost). The language of this is that of legend, but it is possible to reconstruct without difficulty the content of the story from the point of view of religious history, if we remove from it the purely legendary passages, and arrange the rest of the chief events according to their real significance. Its concern is to prove that the *baalim* have no authority over the waters of the firmament nor over the fertility of the land. In his first speech to Ahab Elijah announces (17, 1) a long drought, and only by YHVH's word in his mouth will dew or rain again appear. After a protracted drought he announces to the king (18, 1) that the drought would cease, but to the people the prophet calls (v. 21) that they shall think no longer they could hop on two branches (the figure refers to the bird that hops along a bough up to the point at which it forks into two branches, and then puts one foot on one branch and one foot on the other, and imagines it will be able to go on in such a manner). Only one of the two can be true: either YHVH is "God" or the Baal; only one of the two can possess the power (what power is self-evident in an agricultural land after a long drought); whoever should prove his power, him they should follow. And now after the prophets of the Baal had exerted in vain their magic arts, Elijah "repairs the broken down altar of YHVH" (v. 30), offers sacrifice,[4] calls on the name of his God, goes aside and sits bowed, his head between his knees, not repeating his cry until "a great rain" breaks forth (v. 45) and the people fall on their faces and cry: "YHVH is the Godhead!" The leader-God of early days, Whose zeal Elijah imitates by his own (19, 10, 14) and Whom he serves in all his goings and runnings, is proved and declared to be the God of heaven, that is pouring forth water, and of earth that is refreshed and "brings forth" every plant (Gen. 1, 12). Hereby is also fulfilled what Elijah expressed in a symbol, when for building the altar he took twelve stones (1 Kgs. 18, 31) "according to the number of the tribes of Jacob's sons, unto whom the word of YHVH had come saying: Israel shall be thy name," and after this prays in an emphatic refrain (v. 36): "YHVH God of Abraham, Isaac, and *Israel*, let it be known this day that Thou art God in *Israel*." Because the people are united around YHVH, the tribes now again become a single Israel, as the stones became a single altar: only now is there again a people Israel. There is no Israel and there can be none except as YHVH's people.

The mystery of the soil is wrested from the Baal's grasp, and the people acknowledge the sovereignty of their true Lord, the nomad deity, Who is become an agricultural deity while re-

---

[4] It is noteworthy that the expression "to stand before YHVH," which Elijah, and after him Elisha, uses to describe his office, is elsewhere only used (generally in conjunction with the word "to serve Him") in relation to the priesthood, and also to Jeremiah, who came of priestly stock. We may compare Samuel's rights in the matter of offering public sacrifice: in such times, times of crisis, the prophet stands in the place of the priest.

maining what He was before; what Hosea was to say (2, 10 EV
8)—that the fruitfulness of the plants came not as the product
of baalistic unions, but as a gift of the one giver—is here already
manifested. The people in acknowledging the sole lordship of
YHVH thereby acknowledge that the power of sexual magic
is broken. From now on there remain faithful to the Baal only
the king's court and household, a small number, as the later
story proves, which relates how at the command of the rebel
Jehu, anointed king by Elijah (this is obviously the original tradition, cf. 1 Kgs. 19, 16), they were all gathered together to a
"great sacrificial feast" in the "house of the Baal," and were
slaughtered at his command (2 Kgs. 10, 18ff)—a slaughter, which
later legend ascribed to Elijah (1 Kgs. 18, 40). In Judah too the
Baal cult was soon eradicated (2 Kgs. 11, 18).

Jehu's companion in the work of extermination is Jonadab, the
son of Rechab (10, 15, 23), a Kenite, the man who, according to
a precious communication out of the later history of the kingdom
of Judah (Jer. 35, 6f), orders his sons not to build houses, nor to
sow seeds, nor to plant vineyards, but "to 'sojourn' in tents all
over the land." (This is obviously an old tradition of the nomad
tribe, wrapped up with Israel since the days of the station on
Mount Sinai, and they have recast it into an "everlasting" legacy).
From their ancestor's part in Jehu's rebellion we learn the religious basis of this tradition of a community, which can be described both as "reactionary" [5] and "revolutionary" [6] according to
the viewpoint: YHVH in the eyes of this community is the God
of the wilderness, and He cannot be served truly except by the way
of life of free nomads. This "nomadic ideal"—which in fact in no
way contradicts the view of the nature of the *baalim* as fertilisers
of the soil, except in so far as it is a duty to keep far from their
seductions—is foreign to Elijah, as it is to be foreign to Hosea
in his time. By the driving of the people into the wilderness,
which Hosea prophesied, he did not mean a return to the golden
age, but a chastisement, and only after true repentance the renewal
of the covenant. The Rechabites wished to reduce YHVH's lordship to its primeval limits; He is a nomad deity, and therefore
the settlement is essentially evil; He is a nomad deity, and there-

---

[5] Ed. Meyer, Die Israeliten und ihre Nachbarstaemme (1906), 136ff.
[6] Oesterley and Robinson, A History of Israel I, 350.

fore must remain such. Elijah serves his God as a nomad, but he
has no nomadic ideal. He demonstrates the futility of the Baal,
who merely usurps the sovereignty of the settlement. He demonstrates that the waters above are in YHVH's hand. Not the
Baal, but YHVH is "Lord of the earth"; not the Baal; but YHVH
is "the rider upon the clouds." [7] Just as Abraham walking before
God as His herald, when he calls His name upon altars, seizes
the land for Him as His agent, so Elijah in the name of his
Lord, for Whom he "is zealous," seizes the fruitful earth and the
fructifying heavens above. The great nomad serves his God by
occupation of land for Him.

C. THE STRUGGLE FOR THE REVELATION

We have seen that the faith in YHVH, which throughout the
period of the wanderings and the conquest of Canaan remained
essentially unimpaired in spite of all the deviations and aberra-
tions, was forced to come to grips with the weighty questions
raised by the growing consolidation of economic and political
conditions of life. On the one side, through the establishment
of the kingdom, the great *melekh* idea gradually lost its original
form, its realism, its power of embracing the whole life of the
people. But in place of it there appears at this time the engage-
ment of the man appointed as God's representative to his
lord and His constitution. On the other side, a rivalry grew
up out of the basic conceptions and imagery of Canaanite
agriculture, which the new settlers receive together with the
rules and customs of land cultivation, not as something belonging to a creed, but as something wholly natural and self-
evident. This rivalry is hardly to be fought just because of the
absence of the unifying personality of a rival, until a union takes
place for political reasons under a foreign flag. Now a struggle of
far-reaching importance breaks out. On both sides apparently the
problematic situation is overcome; the first at the very beginning
of the foundation of the state, the second only in the days of king
Jehu of Israel and king Joash of Judah. But the rent opens again

---

[7] The same term is used in the Ras Shamra texts for the Baal, and in Ps. 68, 5
EV 4 for YHVH.

after these temporary triumphs, it deepens and becomes an abyss, from which there issues a new stage in the battle for YHVH, the battling by the word as such: militant script and militant speech.

We must begin by considering the first of these two phenomena in the history of faith.

The newly established kingdom resists the seriousness of the deputy's duty and responsibility as laid upon it. It is prepared to accept the symbolic sense of the charge and authorisation from on high, implied in the act of anointing, but it resists the realism, according to which orders can be given to the king and an account of his activities can be demanded. Already at its inception the kingdom attempts to grasp the power to dispose of the sacred sphere of public life, as is shown in the story of Saul's rejection. It is particularly unwilling that war should be dependent upon the prophetic revelations of God's will; war is solely an affair of the king, and YHVH has no part in it except through the priestly institution (1 Sam. 14, 3, 18) : the king offers himself the common sacrifice in Samuel's place (13, 9; 14, 35), and refuses to let his decisions be influenced by the sacred ban (15, 9). Not only does Samuel announce Saul's rejection by YHVH, but he also offers the community sacrifice before the anointing of David (thus 16, 5, is meant with all seriousness and not as a kind of pretext), and thereby declares that his right to it stands. This act, if it is his-torical—we do not know whether all these events truly happened thus, but there can hardly be imagined a more representative ex-ample of the historical process—was the last independent religio-political act of the prophet. From Samuel to Elijah repairing the altar we hear of no prophet offering the community sacrifice, and so far as we know no prophet after Elijah did so. David offers the sacrifice himself (2 Sam. 6, 17), when the ark is brought up to Jerusalem, Solomon (1 Kgs. 8, 62f) at the dedication of the temple, Jeroboam I (12, 32) when he set up the rival sanctuary. After that we do not again hear of the offering of the community sacrifice, and there is no reference to it, but only because the priesthood, adapted to the monarchical system, arranges it regularly. There is an occasional rebellion, it is true (2 Kgs. 11), but obviously only in order to enforce the worship of YHVH against the Baal cult, and not in order to censure God's deputy for failing to guide the state in accordance with God's justice. From now on no one censures the king except the prophet, the man without appointment. The prophets consider royalty truly responsible for its activity, and sometimes they are not afraid to demand responsibility from it in very deed—a fact which the kingship naturally regards as a potential revolution. The early kingdom strives to neutralize the prophets by giving them an official status in the form of a court office. It accepts them, whether it introduces them individually, as David who introduced Nathan the prophet—although Nathan, officially appointed as he was, did not bow down before his master (only Solomon apparently knew how to make him subservient)—or whether it introduces them collectively, as Ahab did with his "four hundred" prophets of YHVH (1 Kgs. 22, 6). But over against them again there stands the unsubdued one, fearlessly plastering the king's face with his word (v. 17), and it is not enough for him to proclaim the rejection of a single king, as Samuel spoke to Saul, but he ventures to declare the kingdom as such to be rejected and annulled for the time being—a word which even Hosea will not be able to surpass: "I saw all Israel scattered to the mountains as sheep which have no shepherd, and YHVH spake: these have no longer a ruler."

Let us consider more carefully the way from Solomon to this contemporary of Elijah.

In Solomon's saying at the consecration of the temple (1 Kgs. 8, 12f) we meet the unreserved expression of the aim of the early kingdom to confine YHVH's sovereignty within the cultic sphere alone—an aim that had been checked by David through his intense personal faith, but now the restriction was removed. The saying is apparently preserved more perfectly in the Septuagint, where it begins with the words "YHVH has made manifest the sun in the heavens." If we penetrate through to the sense of the archaic wording, it tells us that God put the sun in the heavens for the sake of manifestation, whereas He Himself said (the order of words is influenced by the rhythm, and should be taken: *amar ba-araphel li-sh'kon*) formerly in the thick darkness above Mount Sinai (Ex. 20, 21), that He wished "to make His dwelling," that is to say His earthly dwelling, "in the midst of the children of Israel" (29, 45, cf. I Kgs. 6, 13), and now Solomon has built Him the "lofty house" as "a sitting place for ever." But YHVH did not say, either on Sinai or at any other time, that He wanted a permanent abode, but only that He wished *to make His dwelling,* that is to say to come down from time to time to the cherubim on the ark. It has been rightly said,[1] that in the polar relation of the ark (the movable) and the temple (the stationary) conceptions we meet a classic expression of the tensions between the free God of history and the fettered deity of natural things. More precisely put: there is here an acknowledgment of the Lord of the heavens and of the Lord of the cult too, but there remains no place for God as the leader of the people, and indeed Solomon did not need this. The functions of YHVH are to be reduced so that they *do not bind* the king: the cosmic spheres are left in His control, as is the Holy of Holies, whereas for the government of Israel full power has been given to His anointed one, and with this YHVH, so to speak, surrendered His influence in this domain. Now, after the failure of the prophetic attempt to seize power in the days of Samuel, there is no one else to assert YHVH's right to the leadership in the common life save only the prophet, albeit bereft of power. This is the significance of the reply made to Solomon's reduction of YHVH's authority many generations later by that irrepressible fearless man, Michaiah the son of Imlah, speaking to the two kings of Israel and Judah, who sit upon two thrones at the threshing floor of the gate in Samaria. The God, Whom Elijah had shown to be the real, unlimited ruler of heaven and earth, this same God Michaiah sees sitting upon His royal throne in heaven attended on the right hand and on the left by all the host of heaven. This heavenly deity, however, is the God of history. He does not perform cosmic acts before the seer, but sends one of his spirits, the spirit of wind (the word *ha-ruah,* 22, 21, means simply "the wind," a genuine Biblical play on words), in order to fill the court prophets of Ahab with wind instead of the prophetic spirit and to entice Ahab by their words to his destruction. The paradox of the matter is that Michaiah at the express command of his God (vv. 14 and 19) reveals this to the king—at first indirectly by branding the prophecy of safety with mockery, and finally directly and without any restraint. YHVH "entices" (v. 20), but He does not deceive: the one enticed hears from Him that it is enticement, that the Spirit sent to him and in which he trusts is a false spirit; so the decision lies after all with the man. This is the true prophetic situation. The clear prophetic

[1] Klamroth, Lade und Tempel, 60.

type, seen a hundred years later in the writing prophets, already stands before us in this vision, the wording of which seems to me no less genuine than that of the spiritually related inaugural vision of Isaiah.

But we have to ask whether even before this there has not been a reply to Solomon's policy of reduction. As I have already hinted above, there appears to have been no lack of protests, declaring in the "sultan's" hearing the king's obligation, which he had not fulfilled. In my opinion the Deuteronomic legislation about the kingdom (Deut. 17, 14–17) springs from an anti-Solomonic manifesto: only in the history of Solomon do we find again all the elements of this criticism. There appear again the "horses," the "wives," the "silver and gold"; and it is in those days too that the alliance with Egypt begins, that alliance which is here censured; and after Rehoboam, son of the Ammonitess, there is no other king in Judah, who on his mother's side can be called a "foreigner" (v. 15). The Deuteronomic royal ordinance repeats the people's demand mentioned in the book of Samuel: like all the nations, and in agreement with the standpoint of Samuel (1 Sam. 10, 24) this ordinance speaks of the *choice* of the king by YHVH as an absolute condition of Israel's kingdom, an element of faith not found elsewhere in the historical records except in relation to Saul and David. The critical saying about the privileges the king will adjudge to himself, inserted in the eighth chapter of 1 Samuel (v. 11–17), a saying closely resembling in language a fragment of the story of Saul and David (cf. 8, 12, 14 with 22, 7), apparently also comes from kindred circles. And it may be noted further that akin in spirit to this aspiration is a certain part of the original kernel of the worked-over divine speech addressed to David by Nathan (2 Sam. 7, 5ff), the original part (12–15) of the verses about his "seed" (personified as in Gen. 4, 25; cf. also the explanatory addition 1 Chr. 17, 11) with which YHVH undertakes to deal as with His son, chastising him as His son. Over against the kings, who boast themselves to be sons of God to whom full power is given in accordance with the ancient Eastern conception of the king as adopted by the deity (cf. Ps. 2, 7), we have these words declaring that this sonship is meant as responsibility to the father, who time and again calls his son to account. As in the report on the establishment of the kingdom, the people's demand is not rejected, but the granting changes the nature of its purpose, so it is here with the demand of David's house. The divine sovereignty, the commission contained in the appointment, the duty to render account of the fulfilment of this commission to the appointing lord—these are the basic principles of the relationship of the prophets to the king, the relationship expressed here. The world of faith, the foundations of which are fixed in the wholeness of a community life subservient to God, naturally guards against the division into two realms, the realm of myth and cult, heaven and the temple, subject to religion, and the civic and economic realm, the reality of everyday public life, subject to special laws of politics, civic politics and economic politics. The leader-God, Who "was then walking in tent and tabernacle," does not wish to be shut up in a "house of cedar," in other words, he wants to root out of men's hearts the notion that it is possible to satisfy Him merely with worship and cult. We may compare the lofty free language of the main part of this speech with the dull phraseology of the sayings sanctioning Solomon's temple (1 Kgs. 6, 12f; 9, 3ff), and we are left in no further doubt as to what is genuine testimony about the struggle for the revelation and the covenant and what is theological literature written by order of the royal court.

The struggle for the revelation, however, is not at all restricted to protests against the resistance of the kingdom to the sovereignty of God. This opposition of the kingdom is supported by a negative tendency common in the history of faith, a tendency with a certain productive influence, to be sure, in the domain of religious culture. This tendency, as I have already hinted above, claims to take from God's actual leadership and from man's actual response their character of reality, by fostering the mythico-cultic sphere independently of individual and public ways of life. The cosmic extension of the concept of God, the growth of the idea that the guardian deity accompanying the people on their journeyings is no other than the mighty God of heaven Himself—this extension brings about a limitation: the authority of God loses much of its actuality. He is the great Lord of heaven, wrapped in the mantel of ancient oriental cosmic myth [2] as in a gorgeous coronation robe; it is not Marduk, but He Who slew the primordial chaos dragon. But at the same time the distance between heaven

[2] Cf. especially Gunkel, Schoepfung und Chaos (1895).

and earth is understood as though it were permissible to be satisfied—this too is in accordance with ancient oriental culture—with a mere symbolic imitation of the heavenly order, as for instance the temple below corresponding to a temple above, and apart from this the king is to be endowed as the earthly representative of the sovereignty of heaven. And the account which the king has to render before the God Who commissions him they are certainly prepared to interpret symbolically, as was done in Babylon, where on New Year's day the king was symbolically judged; obviously the priest, whose duty was there to censure and to humble the king symbolically, would not dare the day following the feast to reprove him for a wrong done—but this exactly was the appointment of those prophets of Israel, who had no appointment in state and society.

Add to this the matter of the offering. Its primeval meaning was that man wants to offer himself to the deity, but he is given permission to redeem himself by an animal (from this the custom developed—known also among the Hittites [3]—of a man laying his hand upon the head of the victim, that is to identify himself with it).[4] Later on the offering developed more and more into a complicated cult, by which even without any intention of self-oblation on the part of the individual offerer it was possible to annul man's guilt against YHVH: by offering up "that which goes up" (this is the meaning of the *olah*, the holocaust) in smoke to heaven, according to the precepts, atonement is accomplished, and thereby man has adjusted his relationship to God for the present. And naturally the king's offering is the most powerful of all.

From this we understand the acute nature of the prophetic struggle against the sacrificial cult, and also why the older texts, including the early writing prophets, completely neglect the cosmic myth, which in early times had certainly attached itself to YHVH, being indeed eminently qualified to express YHVH's conquest over all the forces of chaos. Isaiah is the first to adopt this myth,

---

[3] Friedrichs, Aus dem hethitischen Schriftum, II (Der Alte Orient, 1925), 11f; Gustavs, Kultische Symbolik bei den Hethitern, Zeitschrift fuer alttestamentliche Wissenschaft, Neue Folge IV (1927), 139f; cf. also Pettazzoni, La confessione dei peccati II (1935), 214ff.

[4] Cf. Koenigtum Gottes, 100f, 247ff.

at a time when there was certainly no more need to fear its negative effect.

But the struggle against this very tendency to reduce the actuality of the divine authority in day-to-day public and political life, also begins early in a book of immense importance from the point of view of religious history, the composition of which cannot be dated later than Solomon's time. I refer to the original version of the history of primitive times from the story of the creation of man to the story of the attempted sacrifice of Isaac, for here only is it permissible to break the line which stretches from the beginning; here only has the narrator reached the first objective, receiving and transmitting the first answer to the question "For what reason?"

This book is not composed, as most critics are accustomed to maintain, from three "sources." Scholars are beginning to recognize that the critical dogma of a whole period of thought does not fit either linguistic and stylistic facts, or facts of literary composition, or spiritual facts, especially in the book of Genesis,[5] which was the starting point of criticism. What is here usually named the Yahvist is a document very much more comprehensive than had been supposed. If we restrict ourselves to the book of which we are here speaking (the sequel has partly a looser character, and one much less founded on correspondences, ingenious repetitions, symmetrical structures, and partly, in the story of Joseph, belonging to a quite different type of epic), we have a consistent account. True, there are to be found, on the one hand, a number of somewhat later narrative additions, most of which have a different tendency (these additions belong to a spiritual-literary type, corresponding to what is customarily called the "Elohistic" source, but possess no unity of composition), and on the other hand, frequent portions of another kind, not narrative or semi-narrative, for instance expositions, genealogies, legal arguments (these belong to the type associated with what is called the "Priestly book," but these too have no unity in their make-

---

[5] Cf. especially Volz-Rudolph, Der Elohist als Erzaehler (1933) ; B. Jacob, Das erste Buch der Tora (1934) ; Cassuto, La questione della Genesi; cf. also Buber, Genesisprobleme, Monatsschrift fuer Geschichte und Wissenschaft des Judentums (1936), 81f.

up). The narrative sets out to tell of the election and probation of Abraham, that is to say the original election and probation of Israel, in connection with the story of their antecedents. We see here some selection, arrangement, completion, adaptation, and composition of traditional material in different stages of development, material which apparently already in Samuel's day was associated with prophetic circles, which sang the words, linking them to epic, orally preserved passages, and all of this editing was done under the influence of the dominant prophetic purpose. The whole work serves a single intention: to stretch a long line from "Eden" to "Moriah," a line every single point of which has its precise place and value. And this intention is determined by the huge task of anchoring in the origin mystery the unalienable right of revelation and its irreducible sense against the claims of a myth and a ritual that had become independent, that is to say to prove that every creation, foundation, blessing, commandment, judgement, punishment, election, assistance and covenant-making in early history is a kind of revelation. According to the intention this cannot be done by laying down certain theological propositions over against which other contradictory propositions can be set up; the teaching must be nothing other than narrative history. With the success of the unknown author's intention Israel's history-faith acquired its most important documentation. His work became the basis of a narrative system of faith.

All these stories point to Abraham, first father of Israel, that the narrator addresses in his story, and to Abraham's call for the sake of Israel and his fulfilment of it after many ups and downs —unlike the Israel which in later days failed to fulfil its mission. The establishment of a humanity, the blessing of God, man's failing, the decree of destruction, the preservation of a second mankind, and again God's blessing, man's failing, the decree of division, all this was a prelude to the election of Abraham. And this second election is different from the first which took place before the Flood: the first had chosen one family for deliverance, whereas the second, which takes place after the division, in the world of nations, is the election of a new *people*, not yet existing, a people that must yet be generated. The man who was fetched out of the world of nations receives the third blessing, which differs from the former two; those, the blessing of Adam and the blessing of Noah, were natural, bestowing natural gifts, promising fertility alone, whereas this third blessing is dialogic, promising and demanding at the same time: promising the formation of a people and imposing the obligation of a people, addressing the people in the person of its father and demanding in his person from it, to "become a blessing" (Gen. 12, 2), a blessing for the world of nations. This narrator is the first to set before the people the demand and the obligation which had not been fulfilled, but for this purpose he does not add any word that goes outside the confines of the story. In future days the prophets were to return to this saying, but not in the form of a demand: one (Is. 19, 24), with the eye of a person looking from a high tower into the midst of world history, returns to it in the form of a Messianic promise, another (Zech. 8, 13), with the unbroken courage of the believer, whose faith had not been weakened by the adversities of history, returns to it in the form of Messianic comfort. For the narrator the saying is the turning of his story: after describing the way of early mankind to its collapse, he tells of the way of the chosen one until he reaches the final stage of the utmost devotion to his God and there is extended to him the latest blessing which embraces and confirms all (Gen. 22, 17f).

So there arises in this book over against the cosmogonies of the nations, inseparably linked as they are to theogonies, a cosmogony without any mixture of theogony and by nature nothing but an anthropogeny, more exactly: a history of the rise of the *believing* man. The life of this man together with his cosmogenic antecedents the narrator sets up before royal court and patriciate, which strive to pervert the relationship to God into the purely mythical and cultic and to remove man's obligation from it.

From this we can also understand the narrator's image of the godhead, an image which is also fashioned by narrative means alone.

Before the narrative there is the chapter about the creation, in its original content an ancient composition, although in its literary form much less so, a chapter that may indeed be designated by the name "Priestly" and possibly to be regarded, as the Babylonian epic of creation, as a New Year cultic reading. It concludes with that remarkable verse (2, 4a), which appears to be an ironic counterblast to all the sexual cosmogonies: "These are the generations of heaven and earth: their being created." And now comes the opening of our story, linked now in an intuitive way to the preceding lection, the order being reversed: "On the day YHVH, God, created earth and heaven . . ." The earth here precedes the heaven, because here it is the central factor, the earth and man placed upon it. The deity here spoken of is the God of earth, the God of its history, of the history of man. We hear at once (v. 5) that He had not yet caused the rain to fall—meaning that He is Lord also of the rain—but all this is related because of man only. The important thing here is that the earth compromises the soil (*adamah*), and that this is dependent on man (*adam*), formed out of it, and looks to him to cultivate it, to "serve" it. The earth is dependent on man not in a figurative sense but most actually. Man's rebellion brings the curse upon the earth (3, 17). When man "corrupts his way" (6, 12) the land "is corrupted" (v. 117), through their fault the deity now "corrupts" them and it together (v. 13). This is not the language of a later generation, but the genuine language of our narrator, who loves to emphasize strongly by way of such repetitions the relation between events. Again it is from this source that later generations, law-givers, prophets, preachers, and psalmists, derive the fundamental concept, even though they express it in other ways: man "brings the land into guilt," the land on which he lives (Deut. 24, 4) ; the land "degenerates under its inhabitants" (Is. 24, 5, cf. Num. 35, 33 ; Jer. 3, 1, 9 ; Ps. 106, 38). The narrator tells his people implicitly that the fate of the soil does not depend upon the pairings of deities, nor upon the rites aimed at influencing them, but upon the vital relationship of Israel to YHVH. But explicitly he says that the human lot is decided by the dialogue between God and man, the reality of which fills the whole life and the whole world, so that no ceremony can cope with it.

After the story of the sin and the curse comes the story of the two offerings (Gen. 4, 1ff). The point in the eyes of the narrator is not the tale of the fratricide only, with which the history of man after Paradise begins: he wishes to tell of right and wrong offering. The offerings described appear, both of them, to have been objectively without blemish, yet YHVH does not regard Cain and his gift. We see from the story that the non-acceptance is due to the defective intention of the offerer. When there arises the as yet indefinite passion that will grow into murder lust (v. 5), YHVH first expresses the alternative in an obscure, but yet on the whole explicable saying (v. 7): whether Cain "does well" with the intent of his offering or not, and then he compares the temper of spirit of an offerer, who does not "do well," with a closed door: a man's soul, which should be open before God, the man offering himself in his gift, shuts itself before Him, and the offering becomes worthless; and before the closed door sin lurks in the likeness of a crouching demon, waiting for a moment when it might penetrate within, its longing, like that of a woman for her husband (3, 16), being towards him that closed the door; but when the soul opens itself to God, it can control the demon, as the man can the woman.

That YHVH demands no more than the *intention* of self-oblation is quite clear—to take an extreme instance—from the second story about sacrifice, with which our "book" closes (ch. 22). The *melekh* gods of West Semitic tribes are fond of child sacrifice; [6] if they wish to gain the favor of their gods in some extraordinary situation, and especially in the hour of great danger (2 Kgs. 3, 26), they make payment to them with the offering of the firstborn. In Israel, where according to the narrative before the exodus from Egypt (Ex. 13, 2, 13) every firstling was consecrated to YHVH, and every firstborn of man was ordered to be redeemed, there was a frequent tendency to treat YHVH not as YHVH but as one of the *melekh* gods, and to acquire His aid by offering a child (Mic. 6, 7). The prophets in their fierce protests denied the belief that such was acceptable in God's sight: He demands nothing but justice and love. Not so our narrator. Even though he too knew this demand (for it is impossible not to attribute to him YHVH's speech, Gen. 18, 17ff, in which this demand is found, and which is linked by the recurring word *shaphat*, "to judge," with Abraham's intrepid pleading, v. 25): in the story YHVH actually demands the offering of the child, and in the most cruel and strange manner, for God's own promise concerning his offspring would be frustrated if Abraham fulfilled this demand.

[6] On what follows cf. Koenigtum Gottes, 68ff, 93ff, 211ff.

And He allows the demand to be fulfilled to such an extent that the intention enters entirely the realm of reality, but the intention only. YHVH does not here forgo the offering, as later the God of the prophets did, but He permits man to give a ransom, and so to hand over to God in the shape of a ransom what was demanded of himself. The deity grants him the unparalleled experience of having done what he has not done. This God demands all from man, and He grants man all, even the feeling that it is in man's power to give God something, to give Him all. But he who accumulates at his altar offering upon offering devoid of intention, without the will to offer himself, offends Him. This is what the narrator wishes to tell his people, and especially the king and the rulers.

But he even steps out of the people's domain. Indeed, he turns to the court, full as it was of foreign women, each of whom had brought with her from her father's house her gods, for whom a high place was set apart in the vicinity of Jerusalem, but at the same time he also turns to the whole world of nations, when he relates (11, 1ff) how YHVH Himself and no other was responsible for the nation's plurality. He had purposed a unity for mankind, but since the first mankind sinned and was punished for the deeds of violence, which men performed to one another, for the violence which filled the earth (6, 11), He set up a second mankind. This second mankind, unlike the first, holds together and even wishes to remain united, but it is a rebellious unity—a unity against God. They want to build a city with a tower, the top of which reaches to heaven, and there, near to the gates of heaven (28, 17),[7] they wish (so we must understand the text, if we wish to grasp the meaning of the context; the usual interpretation, that their name should be left to fame, destroys the great primeval picture) to set up the "name," which they "make" for themselves, that is to say to establish a mighty name-magic against the Lord of the lightning, in order to prevent His "scattering" them over the face of the whole earth. And now the narrator passes to the climax of his almost symmetrically arranged style of correspondences: YHVH *answers* from above to the tumult down below using the same words, words, however, which now have be-

---

[7] Jacob points with one hand at the stone but with the other at the place, where the ladder reached the heavens.

come deed. To their war cry He answers with a similar cry (11, 3, 4, 7), to the "building" (v. 4, 5, 8) and "making" (v. 4, 6a, 6b) of the town (v. 4, 8) He answers by descending, bringing about exactly that "scattering" (v. 4, 8) "over the face of all the earth" (v. 1, 4, 8, 9a, 9b : refrain) which they dreaded (v. 4) : their common "language" (v. 1, 6, 7a, 7b, 9) is divided into all the languages, and thereby the one united people of the earth is divided and becomes all peoples, and in place of the "name" (v. 4) which they wanted to make for themselves, there comes now the name (v. 9) of the city which they were prevented from completing—Babel, that is to say confusion, is its name. (It must not be supposed that the narrator did not know the derivation of Bab-ilu, gate of god; but it is over against this that he sets up his story of the name, as the *true* sense). Here is an excellent example of what has been called "the historisation of myth." [8] We know from the excavations the site of the Babylonian temple's steps-tower, which was called "the house of the foundation of heaven and earth"; we know from the cuneiform inscriptions the appearance and character of this building, which is in accordance with what we are told in Scripture; we read in the creation epic *Emuna alish* ("When above") the myth of its building by gods; and since we find in the royal annals of the Assyrian age in connection with the restorations of the tower the recurring statement that its top was to reach to heaven, we may infer that here we have the recurrence of a primitive, mythological conception which was known to our narrator. But now, apparently on the basis of an Israelite legend registered by him, he makes all this grandeur, in which the cult and culture of Babylon culminate, into a legend of revolt against YHVH, true Lord of heaven and earth, a revolt which YHVH crushes by descending from heaven, no human concentration of power being able to stand before Him. The author introduces the story of this event into the middle of his account of primitive times, where he sets out to show how the world of nations in all its manifold contrasts developed from a single human cell. This epic writer has already the daring historic view of the writing prophets and like them dares to penetrate the history of the peoples to the one divine-human secret of history. And as we find in Amos (9, 7) between the lines, that

[8] Cf. especially Weiser, Glaube und Geschichte im Alten Testament (1931), 23ff.

by whatever name this or that people call their historic liberator
god, all such gods are one, one whose true name has been entrusted to Israel, so here we are told between the lines that all
the nations, to acquire whose favor the ruler of Israel and his
men are faithless to YHVH, even they all have their origins in His
deed, and are all in His power. To express this essential concern
of his in such a form as to grasp the heart of the man for whom
the story is intended, this narrator is not afraid to use here a very
marked anthropomorphism, and his style of correspondences with
its marked repetitions impresses itself on the reader, or more
correctly on the hearer (all this work was undoubtedly meant
to be read aloud), even more strongly than ever.

These examples will be sufficient here to show the importance
of this so well and yet not fully known work in the history of
faith as the great historical document of the struggle for the
revelation in the days before the writing prophets. This severe
and free narrator is concerned, as later the prophets were, that
YHVH should indeed be recognized as Lord of the world, but
not as being removed to the far heavens—man must know that he
cannot establish in earthly life his own regime, man's regime, and
satisfy the power above by cult. The God of the universe is
the God of history. He is the deity Who walks with the creature
of His hands, man, Who walks with His elect, Israel, along the hard
way of history. He reveals Himself in history; it is not as if
He produced it but, as He accompanies man, He demands from
him that he should serve Him lovingly in all the breadth of historic life, and zealously He lets the resisting experience his fate
in history, the fate resulting from his own deeds.

The work of the great narrator, who was probably numbered
with the court prophetic circle (his attitude is that of a prophet,
not a priest) except that he has no connection with the compromising tendency of this circle, did not achieve that which the
author had in mind. In Rehoboam the last trace of the idea of
God's representative seems to have been obliterated, and in its
place there came the cold will of a tyrant; we further hear of
him that at the time when Egypt, which had been wooed by
Solomon, plundered the temple treasures, he boasts a cult with
false pomp. Immediately after the removal of the kingdom of
Ephraim, Jeroboam sets up for the official YHVH cult the baal-

istic "golden calves," and later the sons of Omri build a temple of the Tyrian Baal by the side of YHVH's temple in order to bestow sanctity upon the covenant with the Phoenicians. In the kingdom of Judah, on the whole, they keep to tradition.

Elijah's zealous acts apparently cause a great excitement of popular feeling. Jehu's revolt appears as a ruthless political inference from an essentially changed inner situation. But with Elishah and his "sons of the prophets"—who settle in common, and no longer move about the country as did the prophetic bands of the time of Samuel's crisis (Elijah had apparently thought to renew their movement as against the court prophets)—the spirit of Elijah had become the possession of a closed sect, in so far as we are able to recognize the reality through the veil of legend which is here particularly thick. Again we hear nothing of the kings except in a conventional form, and this apparently because there is nothing to tell of them; what injustice they committed secretly, and to what injustice they closed their eyes, about all this we hear only from the writing prophets. The worship of the Baal was broken down, but the prophetic protest shows us not only that the ancient sexual rites flourished in the very shadow of the temple, but also that people treated with YHVH Himself as with a mighty Baal, from whom they wished to buy at the price of many offerings the unfettered freedom of profane life. In this time of "quiet," between Elijah's revolution and Amos' call of woe (Amos, 5, 18; 6, 1), the double contradiction becomes one, on the one side, the contradiction between the true and the fictitious power of God (the power of YHVH and the power of the idols, including the human king-idol), and on the other side, the contradiction between the real and the fictitious worship of God (the living worship of YHVH as YHVH, that is to say, as He Who is present, by means of the whole presence of the worshipper, and the empty cultic worship of YHVH *as an idol,* whether Baal or "Molech"), the two unite and form an abyss. From now on the mission of those sent is to sound an alarm concerning this abyss by the word of prophecy.

7. THE TURNING TO THE FUTURE

A. FOR THE SAKE OF RIGHTEOUSNESS

If we wish to understand the first speech in the book of Amos (1, 3–2, 11), we must picture the situation in which it may have been spoken. The speeches of this prophet are without any doubt real speeches in the literal sense; unlike the later apocalyptists every prophet speaks in the actuality of a definite situation. The situation, however, serves the prophet not only as a starting point, but he throws the word of God into this actuality according to His injunction, and only if we try ourselves to delve into this actuality, can we grasp the concrete reality of the word.

The scene obviously is the space in front of the king's sanctuary at Bethel, the pilgrimage place of the Ephraimites, where formerly Jeroboam I had erected the carved image. The time clearly is almost two hundred years after Jeroboam's deed, in the days of the reign of Jeroboam II, at that great hour when the people in festal gathering gave thanks to YHVH, after the successful re-conquest of Transjordania, long controlled by the Syrians, and the re-establishment of the ancient boundaries of the Davidic kingdom. As Amos addresses Israel's neighbors one after the other, and every speech addressed to the peoples is in form and sense a definite part of the whole, we are entitled to assume that the representatives of these peoples were present at the festival.[1] And so the image rises before us: in the midst of the tumult this stranger (a sheep-breeder from the extreme border of the Judean wilderness) draws near and reproaches the delegates one by one with the sins which their peoples had committed *against one another,* and declares to them the divine punishment laid up for them. He begins each accusation with the phrase, "Thus has YHVH said," and he concludes each with the phrase, "YHVH

---

[1] Cf. Koehler, Theologie des Alten Testaments (1936), 62.

has said." He has received the prophecy, and prophesies it. It is
the prophecy of judgement. He Who thus sits in judgement upon
the peoples, on the ground that one "pursues his brother with the
sword" (1, 11), that another "remembers not the brotherly covenant" (v. 9), that another has no pity for the life, freedom, and
honor of his fellow, is none other than the Lord of the peoples.
Not only Lord of the peoples here mentioned, whom Amos is
now called upon to address, but Lord of all peoples. In another
prophecy (9, 7) it is said that YHVH is He Who has "brought
up" each one of them to their present abode: He is the tribal
god, the national god, the leader god of each one of them. And
because of this He is, according to fundamental ancient Semitic
conception,[2] the people's judge. The national gods, the leader
and judge gods of all the peoples, are here shown to be identical.
This is a different identification from that which the "fathers"
applied, when they recognized in each god they met on their
journeys in Canaan, in the power dwelling according to tradition
in this or that place, their own guardian deity, whom they had
known aforetime in the days of their wanderings. In the last
resort, however, that idea of Amos, the recognition of YHVH in
the national god of every nation with whom Israel had historic
contact, is analogous to the notion of the fathers, and flows from
this as one historical situation flows from that which precedes
it. But the essential matter, that which particularly has the character of revelation, is *for what deeds* YHVH passes the judgement
on these nations, whose God He is in truth, although they do not
know how to call Him as Israel does by His right name, the name
telling His nature; He does not judge them for their iniquity against
Him, but for their iniquity against each other. Each one of them
calls, by the name known to them, the one God as his Father: as
Israel sees itself as YHVH's son (Ex. 4, 22f; Hos. 2, 1, EV 1, 10), so
Moab sees itself as son of its tribal god that in the course of history
became its national god (Num. 21, 29, where the plural form
merely indicates the whole people as such). This epithet "son"
does not imply a notion of natural procreation—we first hear of
a female partner in connection with tribal gods, when they become blended together with the local *baal*—but expresses a relation of adoption: YHVH calls Israel His firstborn son, because

---

[2] Cf. Baudissin, Kyrios als Gottesname im Judentum III (1929), 387ff.

though young among the nations it was the first adopted by Him. And so God, the One—this is not expressly, but implicitly stated in the prophecy—wills that the peoples be truly brethren; He chastises them because they are not so. And out of the measure of punishment the leader-God peeps at times: He led the Aramaeans out of Kir (probably Ur) to their present land (9, 7), and to Kir He will again banish them (1, 5).

Of YHVH as judge between peoples we read earlier in Jephthah's proclamation to the king of "the children of Ammon" (more probably the king of Moab), an ancient proclamation fundamentally, if not stylistically. Here it is made clear, first (Ju. 11, 24) that Israel in its conquest of the land follows its leader god, as Moab its god, but afterwards (v. 27) Jephthah calls on YHVH "the Judge" to decide between the two peoples. It is only in Amos, however, that this conception is developed to include that of the Lord of history. Here we have the leader of the peoples, who sets his eyes upon the evil in every sinful kingdom (Am. 9, 8), and destroys the sinful peoples, as for instance the Amorites (2, 9), in war, but intends peace and wills a brotherly covenant to prevail between his peoples. Apart from the very deep degeneracy of the Amorite [3] and their like, there is no punishment meted out to the nations except for the fact of the despicable treachery by which they betray one another and hinder God's appointed order.

And now (the special speech against Judah, 2, 4f., dull and flabby, is certainly not from the prophet's mouth, and is only put here so that the rest of the words might be thought to be intended against the kingdom of Samaria alone) the speaker turns suddenly from the representatives of the peoples whom hitherto he had been addressing, and directs himself to the multitude of the house of Israel (v. 6ff). We must recognize the fact that all that is said here and in parallel verses to Israel is directed to all the people, and not simply to Samaria. This accusation is, however, completely distinct from the reproof of the peoples. This becomes more clear, when we take this accusation together with all the other words with which Amos reproaches Israel. Here we see the meaning of the assertion that *historically* YHVH has done no more on behalf of Israel than for any other of the

___
[3] Cf. what is said in the chapter "YHVH and the Baal" about the "iniquity of the Amorite."

peoples He has led, and that Israel has no greater historical claim than, for example, the Ethiopians who dwell on the edge of the world of civilization (9, 7), because out of the depth of history one people appears in God's eyes as another, whereas only Israel He "knew," to Israel only He had made Himself known, Israel only He had brought under the yoke of the bestowing and demanding revelation, because of this on Israel only He visits *all* their iniquities (3, 2). In revelation it was laid upon them to become a true people, that is the living unity of the many and the diverse. With regard to this, Israel was given the people's statute, the "instruction" (*torah*). The *torah* represses social wickedness and wards off the stumbling blocks liable to stand up between the members of the people through the growing social division. The *torah* combats these corruptions by means of a rhythmic social restoration, by means of a renewed levelling of the ownership of the soil and the re-establishment of common freedom. And now the revealing, lawgiving God litigates with Israel because of their iniquities against the divine will. He wished them to be a people for Him, His "firstborn son" to be "the first fruits of His harvest," the harvest called mankind: this is later clearly expressed in Jeremiah (2, 3), but the signs of this claim can be seen already in Amos (6, 1; cf. v. 6), where with bitter irony it is hinted at that those who are intended to be the first fruits of the nations, glory in this their honor and rely upon it. The people, whom God desired to become His first fruits, has not derived anything from the holy destiny laid upon them except the summons to a historical *provision*, for which they thought to pay with a well equipped cult, with abundance of offerings, and with instrumental music of rich artistry (5, 22f); whereas their whole politico-communal life they had withdrawn from the divine leading. In place of the brotherly dwelling together of a people of God, as they had been ordered, a self-seeking band, ignorant of everything except this egotism, rolled lazily and cruelly upon the people. At the hour when the poor, enslaved to them for an unpaid pair of shoes (2, 6; cf. 8, 6), already lies in the dust, they still kick his head, the head covered with dust (2, 7). The common decay of the popular body of necessity involves the decay and deterioration of the service of God. And no less than the profanation of the holy name by the shameless intercourse of a man and his father with the same harlot, is the profanation when they lay themselves down before the altar on pledged clothes or pour out a drink offering of the wine seized from a debtor and drink of it (v. 8). And this sin is committed in the sanctuary, which after being polluted by such wickedness, cannot be again designated YHVH's house, but is only "the house of their god" (*ibid*) : is it possible that the god of this desecrated sanctuary can still be He, YHVH?

At the same moment and in relation to this phrase "their god" a new thing is introduced into the divine speech by the emphatic first person "I" *anokhi* (v. 9): the act of recalling history, of reminding; and the speech passes in a neighboring verse into direct address. God reminds the congregation of Israel how He, the speaking God, destroyed at that time "from before them" a people corrupt as they are now, who had risen up against them, and gave them the land of this people at that time, when He "brought them up" from Egypt and led them in the wilderness forty years (v. 10)—those same forty years that were, as is well known, necessary to renew the people of Israel, who had become degenerate in Egypt. And for the sake of the continuous renewal in the structure of the people of God He did not send to them preachers from another region, as this present herald, but raised up for them prophets from their own sons (v. 11) near to their heart, in order to bring the living instruction near to them time and again, and to summon them to the life of righteousness. He also raised up for them Nazirites, not so as to excite the people to asceticism, for such was far from the intention of prophetic faith, but to set over and over again before their eyes the features of a pure and consecrated life. But they rejected His helping hand, they enticed the Nazirites to become drunk, and silenced the prophets (we, who know the book of Amos, are to conclude: so, here in Bethel, they will shortly rise up to silence the speaker of these words). And so—we must certainly supplement thus—they were left to themselves, and descended to that depth of depravity in which they now find themselves.

Immediately after the historical reminiscence there comes in the text the announcement of punishment. We notice here, however, a somewhat disturbing gap, which our imagination can only scantily fill up. At all events we find support in the fact that in a very similar cadence mention is made in a short fragment (5, 21–6;

v. 27 does not belong here) of those same forty years in the wilderness. There YHVH asks the people (v. 25) whether at that time they brought Him offerings in regular order and by fixed statute; whether at that time they carried as "their king" one of the idols demanding sacrifices and not the ark, over which the Unseen dwells, Who leads His people faithfully, and does not seek as His reward the peace offering of fat beasts (v. 22), nor the noise of songs (v. 23), but this alone He seeks (v. 24), "that justice should roll down as the waters, and righteousness as a mighty stream," that is to say—in contradistinction to all the streams in the land of Canaan, which in the days of rain overflow and afterwards quickly dry up—a stream flowing from of old and never running dry. And here we see what we found missing above—if not the actual form, at any rate the sense: the connection between the past and the present, albeit in an inverse order. The children of Israel want to redeem themselves through offerings and psalms; but YHVH demanded neither of these, when He led the people in the wilderness, and He does not demand them now. With both (Amos does not say this explicitly, but we must and ought to assume so from another place, in order to understand the message) He credits man, who desires to come near to Him through a sacrificial symbol (the later comprehensive term *qorban,* that is to say something brought near, is certainly derived from this basic conception), and who desires his prayer to be heard by Him. What He demands is "righteousness" and "justice." This combination of righteousness and justice, right judgement and right action, this basic concept is not ethical nor social, but religious. Amos, however, with his simile of the water, does not allude, as some think, to the divine punishment. If we compare the passages dating before the time of Ezekiel, where this twofold conception is introduced, we find consistently that we hear of it in relation to God, Who establishes righteousness and justice in the land or in Israel and not to the punishing God (Hos. 2, 21, EV 19; Is. 1, 27; 28, 17; 33, 5; Jer. 9, 23, EV 24; Ps. 99, 4), or in relation to His anointed (2 Sam. 8, 15; Jer. 22, 3, 15), and together with this we learn of YHVH as the source of this unity in relation to men (1 Kgs. 10, 9; Is. 9, 6, EV 7; Jer. 23, 5; 33, 15), or we hear of it in so far as they "keep YHVH's way" (Gen. 18, 19), that is to say, follow Him, or produce fruit of that which YHVH had planted in them (Is. 5, 7).

Accordingly we are to see this notion also in three passages in Amos (in addition to 5, 24, also 5, 7, and 6, 12).

The conception of the just tribal god, a conception apparently common to all ancient Semites, and reflected in a number of divine names and epithets,[4] grew and became in Israel an article of faith of unprecedented seriousness. The vital realism, with which the religious leaders here contemplate the relation between God and man, stands out also in the certainty that the divine righteousness desires to continue its operation in a human righteousness, and that man's fate depends on whether he submits to this will or denies it. YHVH "establishes equity" (Ps. 99, 4), He betroths Israel to Himself in righteousness and justice (Hos. 2, 21, EV 19) "for He delights in these" (Jer. 9, 23, EV 24). He appoints the king as His representative over the people, in order that he may perform justice and righteousness in His name (1 Kgs. 10, 9; Is. 9, 6, EV 7). God seeks them to follow Him, to "keep YHVH's way," the way in which He walks (Gen. 18, 19). The unity of justice and righteousness is in Israelite thought one of the basic concepts of the divine-human *relationship*. We are told here of an imitation of God for the sake of a completion of His work by human activity. Righteousness flows down from heaven, and bids fair to flood the face of the earth by means of the man-from-the-earth, the people-from-the-earth; indeed, in all the breakings and divisions brought about in righteousness at its meetings with things limited and divided by their nature, but with all this it sweeps forth continually as a mighty stream. The human people shrink, however, from the divine flood, they refuse to let it spring forth into life, and so the waters are heaped up until they tumble down and destroy, and justice is made into judgement. This is the meaning of Amos' words (6, 12, cf. 5, 7), that Israel changes justice into hemlock, and the fruit of righteousness into wormwood. And so it must be that their festal processions, with which they, lacking in righteousness, thought to serve God, will be turned into mourning, and all their songs, with which they thought to find favor in His sight, will be turned into a dirge (8, 10). "Behold I make it stop short under you, as a cart full of sheaves stops short" (2, 13)—so begins the last speech of the great Bethel discourse.

[4] Cf. Baudissin, Kyrios III, 398ff. I find no foundation for Zimmern's opinion (*ibid.*, IV, 50f) that this concept originates in Sumerian culture.

What is the meaning of these initial proclamations and also of the subsequent proclamations of destruction? We are accustomed to see in Amos simply the prophet of divine judgement, and therefore to deny him the passages which speak of the possibility of salvation and even of future days of redemption, or at best to interpret them in a negative sense. By so doing we miscontrue the special nature of Israelite prophecy. It is true, Amos denies (7, 14) his connection with the prophetic guild which, after having been consolidated under Elisha's leadership, had again degenerated to the position of a company of soothsayers, practising for money payment. But he knows that this activity, which he performs at YHVH's command, namely "prophecy" (3, 8), is the activity of the prophets (*nebiim*) from of old (2, 11), even though in his mouth, unwittingly and unwillingly, it takes on a new form, the form of solid and ordered speech, instead of that of cry and spoken chorus. In spite of this the word he has to speak remains in its inner substance the same as Elijah's call, "How long . . ." (1 Kgs. 18, 21), or Michaiah the son of Imlah's call, "YHVH has spoken evil concerning thee" (22, 23), which was delivered to the king of Israel at the moment when he obviously still had a possibility of escaping the catastrophe awaiting him. The Israelite prophet utters his words, directing them into an actual and definite situation. Hardly ever does he foretell a plainly certain future. YHVH does not deliver into his hand a completed book of fate with all future events written in it, calling upon him to open it in the presence of his hearers. It was something of this kind the "false prophets" pretended, as when they stood up against Michaiah (v. 11ff) and prophesied to the king, "Go up and prosper!" Their main "falsity" lay not in the fact that they prophesy salvation, but that what they prophesy is not dependent on question and alternative. This attitude is closer to the divination of the heathen than to true Israelite prophecy. The true prophet does not announce an immutable decree. He speaks into the power of decision lying in the moment, and in such a way that his message of disaster just touches this power. The unformulated primal theological principle of the Garden of Eden story about the divine-human relationship, namely that created man has been provided by the Creator's breath with real power of decision and so is able actually to oppose YHVH's commanding will—this mysterious article of faith rises now to awfully practical force. The divine demand for human decision is shown here at the height of its seriousness. The power and ability are given to every man at any definite moment really to take his choice, and by this he shares in deciding about the fate of the moment after this, and this sharing of his occurs in a sphere of possibility which cannot be figured either in manner or scale. It is to this personal decision of man with its part in the power of fate-deciding that the prophetic announcement of disaster calls. The alternative standing behind it is not taken up into it; only so can the prophet's speech touch the innermost soul, and also be able to evoke the extreme act: the turning to God.

In a small book, from the literary point of view late, but probably a free adaptation of an old legend, the story of Jonah, which impresses us as an epic paradigm of the prophetic nature and task, we are shown with unequivocal clarity the facts of the matter to which I am drawing attention. YHVH sends Jonah to Nineveh to announce disaster. Jonah tries to evade his charge, because he knows (4, 2), that this "gracious and merciful God" is ready "to repent of the evil"—two phrases borrowed with special intent from the dialogue between YHVH and Moses after the sin of the calf (Ex. 32, 12, 14; 34, 6)—if the people turn; and Jonah is not satisfied with being a prophet, his prophecy not seeming to him worthy of the name. Under God's powerful hand he is forced to go and make his proclamation. It is throughout a proclamation of unconditional disaster, with nothing less than a fixed time and an immutable decree. But it is just this that incites the Ninevites to turn from their evil ways (3, 8), for they say (v. 9): "Who knows, God may turn and repent, and turn from His fierce anger." Human and divine turning correspond the one to the other; not as if it were in the power of the first to bring about the second, such ethical magic being far removed from Biblical thought, but—"Who knows."

Out of this basic notion we are to understand all true preapocalyptic Israelite prophecy and especially that of Amos. It is necessary only to turn from the accepted theological conception of "the prophet of doom" to the living mediating man. He receives the most terrible task, and does not know—he, the living man, does not know, as opposed to Jonah, creature of the imagination—that his task involves a question, a summons to decision. In spite of this he refuses, apparently for a long time, to take the message as a decree. In his visions—probably the only account written by himself—he transmits to us (7, 1-6) an account of how he entreated YHVH to forgive the people, and how God both times was entreated and "repented of this." Between these and later visions, in which he does not venture to intercede again for mercy, apparently lie the speeches, in which he is authorized to call Israel directly to repentance, but he does not succeed. "Thus has YHVH spoken to the house of Israel," he calls. "Seek Me and live" (5, 4), and again, apparently after a time of vain labor, returning to the saying and clarifying it (v. 14f), "Seek good and not evil, that you may live, and so shall the God of hosts be with you, as you are accustomed to say (this is the saying familiar to the careless: God is with us!). Hate evil and love good, and set up justice in the gate, perchance YHVH, God of hosts, will be gracious to the remnant of Joseph." These words are not to be detached from Amos and ascribed to a later prophet; a line can be traced, however, from this alternative kind of speaking to the great call for decision in the book of Deuteronomy (30, 15), in which "life and good" and "death and evil" are set before Israel for choice; and, on the other hand, this quivering "perchance" is reflected later in that "Who knows" of the Ninevites in the book of Jonah. Now it is not as formerly to all the people that the prophet holds out life, because he no longer expects the people to turn; but if a "remnant" returns, perchance it will find mercy. To this the line leads from the "seven thousand" of Elijah's story (1 Kgs. 19, 18)—a symbolic number, the origin of which is not, as some think, from the time that followed the destruction of the Ephraimite kingdom, but it is very understandable in the mouth of Elijah—left as a remnant because they did not bend their knee to the Baal, and from this point it leads on to Isaiah, who calls his son by the name "A-remnant-shall-return" (Is. 7, 3; cf. 10, 21). And the development of the idea of alternative is clear: Elijah speaks about the company of men, who already proved faithful, Amos means those, unknown to him, but who, he hopes, will return in repentance before the coming of the judgement announced, and be delivered from the destruction as the remnant of Joseph.

To the time following this explanatory speech belongs seemingly the vision of the plumbline (Am. 7, 7ff) which is set on a wall to test how far this has deflected from the line of the plummet. YHVH, as builder with plumbline in His hand, tests the damage to decide whether it is possible partly or altogether to save the wall that has gone out of the straight, or whether it is necessary to pull it down completely. He does not wish to "pass by" the Israelite people any longer. And the sentence that immediately follows expresses the result of the test up to this point: the sanctuaries will be laid waste, the sinful dynasty will be overthrown—the top of the wall will be broken down.

And now—this we must conjecture to be the chronological order—there comes again a great speech entirely preserved (4, 4–13), in which the catastrophes of nature and history, the memory of which is preserved in the people, are interpreted as calls to repentance, until the last catastrophe, of which the contemporary generation was a living witness, the earthquake, which Amos, accustomed to look out from his native hill country over the Dead Sea, compares with the "overthrow" of Sodom and Gomorrah. "Yet have ye not returned unto Me"—this saying strikes the listeners' ears five times with hammerlike repetition. But linked with this is the announcement of the coming, final, undescribed and indescribable punishment, and it is to be regarded as a last call to repentance (v. 12): "Prepare to meet thy God, Israel." The meeting with YHVH approaches. Every listener knows: he, to whom YHVH shows His face without bestowing grace upon him, will die. YHVH calls the people to turn, and its turning will call upon Him for grace and mercy. But this is not, as many think, the end of the speech. This end follows (v. 13) with one of those doxologies, which the critics would deny to Amos. They misunderstand the intention of these doxologies, that are always directed towards the identification of the Lord of creation with the Lord of chastisements and destructions, the God of nature with the God of history. He Who fashions the mountains also creates the *ruah*—here *ruah* does not mean wind, but that mysterious breath, which at the beginning of creation (albeit itself a thing created) broods over the face of the waters, and afterwards storms into the midst of the historical world, and so inspires here the "man of the Spirit" that the people nickname him a madman (such a popular verdict Hosea quotes, 9, 7); by this man of the Spirit "He announces (now) to man, what His thought (literally: His musing with Himself) is." Even here there is no undialogical decree: YHVH speaks with Himself, and this can be transformed at the last moment, if it be a moment of turning to Him, into a talk with man. The disaster has already begun, it is true: He Whose name is YHVH, that is "He will be present," the God of hosts "makes now morning into darkness, and walks upon the high places of the earth."

And again after fruitless expectation there follows the last vision but one, which points to the coming of "the end unto My people Israel" (8, 2), on that day—appearing to the prophet in the image of the pestilence—on which the temple songs will be changed into this lament: "Enough! The corpse in every place! (That is to say, there is no place, where there is not a dead one!) Cast forth! (That is, cast out all the corpses into one place!)"—and this howling is put to silence by the cry of horror "Hush!" From this vision too we can understand the plague speech (6, 8–10), at the end of which also we find the same call, "Hush!" Now only Amos utters also the saying about the desolation, which does not allude any longer to an alternative (5, 2), "She is fallen, the virgin of Israel, she shall no more rise up, she is thrown down on her land, and there is none to raise her up." And now he sees the last vision (9, 1ff): YHVH Himself rises before the sanctuary, high and lifted up above the altar that stands before it, and He commands that the tops of the pillars be struck, until the roof-beams shake, and orders them to be cut off, so they fall on the head of all those assembled. The meaning here is not, as some think, an earthquake (the earthquake recalled at the beginning of the book, 1, 1, had preceded the vision, as 4, 11 shows), it is too great and simple for this: it is a symbol of comprehensive annihilation. Whoever is at first left from the guilty ones (apparently after the attack of the enemy) will be met wherever he flees by God's wrath, and even in the midst of those marching into captivity in front of their enemies YHVH's sword will rage (9, 4). From this vision, which compels us, as we read it, to recall the destruction of Samaria, which followed a three-year siege by the Assyrians some decades after this, and the carrying off of the greater part of its inhabitants into exile in Mesopotamia, from this vision apparently there springs a great speech of the prophet, scattered fragments of which are in my opinion preserved in 6, 1–7, 11–14, and 5, 27. Here (6, 11) the image of the pulling down of the house returns (here it is the pulling down of a "great" house and a "small" house, apparently the temple and the king's palace are meant), more realistically than symbolically, so much so that we are inclined to think of a destruction by the conqueror; and in the same speech again and again (5, 27; 6, 7, 14) banishment to a far country is announced. This is clearly the speech, after which the priest of Bethel informs the king (7, 10ff) about the rebellious prophecy, and then bids the prophet hasten and remove himself from the twofold authority of the king's sanctuary and the royal house (we recall the great house and the small house), and return to his native land of Judah, where he will be able to find his sustenance with ease by such rhetorical art. In his answer Amos says that true prophecy is not a human calling, but a mission of God, Who takes a man from his work, "from following the sheep," and sends him to the people with his message. Man's will, which tries to hinder the word, is destined to meet God's punishment. The answer ends with the same words, which the prophet transmitted to the king: yes, Israel will verily go into exile from their land.

We do not know whether Amos' public activity in Samaria ended here. It is possible, however, that to this time after the prophecy of the exile belongs the verse (9, 9) about the sifting of the people in the sieve of the world of the nations (considered by most, though without sufficient evidence, unoriginal): the "remnant" will be preserved even in the midst of the dispersion. And so the saying (8, 11f), which is perhaps to be understood as a bequest to Amos' intimates in Samaria, about the coming days—days of the loss of counsel and direction—when there will arise in the land a hunger and a thirst for YHVH's word, now driven out with His prophet, a hunger and thirst, which they will not then be able to satisfy. And finally, this is the place, it seems to me, of the original nucleus of the saying about salvation which ends the book (9, 11, 13, the first five words of 14, and the last three of 15), which it is customary to date, without foundation, at the end of the Babylonian exile or soon afterwards. This speech is directed to one listener, as the last words "YHVH thy God has spoken" prove. Perhaps it is the farewell to a disciple, whom the prophet had won during his wanderings in Samaria, and who is now left there. What is here promised for the future is the restoration of "the fallen hut of David," that is to say, unlike the seceded particular Samaritan power, doomed to destruction, the whole Israelite community will arise in its former shape, as in the days of David. In order to understand the real meaning of the figure, we must not forget that here we have a shepherd speaking about a shepherd: such huts of shrub and branch work Jacob made for his flocks (Gen. 33, 17); David built his kingdom as a hut for his herds, and only such a people-hut was worth rebuilding "as in the days of old." Its renewal is promised according to a primitive oriental conception [5] as a time of blessing for all nature. And God's speech ends with the saying: "And I will restore restoration to my people Israel."

Here in a passage, not directed to the public, the saying about the "remnant" is being developed. Earlier Amos had sharply denounced (5, 18ff) the people's false trust in salvation, and had attacked the widespread popular notion, apparently of many generations' standing, that the coming "day of YHVH" would be altogether a day of light and splendor for Israel: the day of YHVH will indeed come, that is to say a day in which He will rule without restraint, but it will be for this sinful kingdom a day of darkness, in which the sun shall sink at noon (8, 9). Now, however, Amos announces to his faithful ones another "day," on which YHVH brings the restoration. It cannot be otherwise—so may the man from the desert border think—with a God, Who walks forty years with His people in the desolate wilderness: He will still walk with them in the midst of the desolation which is the work of His own judgement.

"Amos," so I read in a recent commentary,[6] "approached near to monotheism, but did not actually reach it, for in his eyes there are, apart from YHVH, other gods, standing, it is true, on an inferior level to Him (5, 26)." And so, because Amos denounces the people's idols before them, and asks them whether they carried with them in the wilderness the images of their star gods,

---

[5] Cf. Duerr, Ursprung und Ausbau der israelitisch-juedischen Heilandserwartung (1925), 102f.

[6] By T. H. Robinson (in the Handbuch zum Alten Testament I Reihe, 14 Bd., 1938).

"which they made for themselves" (and not YHVH's ark of the
covenant and the testimony), or because he declares to them—
according to the commentator's interpretation—that these images,
which they made for themselves, they will carry into exile, therefore he was not a "monotheist"! Remarks like these appear to
me calculated to reduce in value the question of the presence or
the absence of this "monotheism" of which so much is said. Amos
did not introduce a new element into Israel's relation to the deity,
a relation founded and constituted in another age, but he did set
up the exclusiveness of a people in its relation to its God, as to
the liberator, leader and judge of the peoples, lord of righteousness and justice, he set it up under the divine demand and chastisement in a manner such as nobody before in man's history, so
far as we know, had achieved. It may be uncertain whether he
reached some "ism" or other; all the pretension of such distinc-
tions comes to nothing when it tries to assert itself in the face
of what is to be found here: a man, given up to the oneness of
his God.

B. FOR THE SAKE OF LOVINGKINDNESS

Not many years after Amos was driven out of the land of Samaria, possibly in the latter days of the same king to whom the
priest had sent his report, something happened, the like of which
had not been heard of from of old, to a young as yet unmarried
farmer, who lived not far from Bethel, apparently on the southern
border of the kingdom of Ephraim. He certainly listened in his
youth to the hard sayings of the prophet of Judah (cf. for example
Hos. 4, 15, with Amos 5, 5) ; he had come to know that the prophets
were the iron chisel with which YHVH chiselled Israel in order
that His justice "might go forth as the light," [1] although Israel
is a living substance and being "slain" by the terrible sayings (Hos.
6, 5) ; and he set himself up to serve his Lord as a speaker. But
the expected event, when it began (1, 2), was quite different from
what he had expected. Indeed, he was required to become that
very thing of which the simile was given only to Jeremiah, his
posthumous disciple; namely, to become "as a mouth" of YHVH

[1] Read מָשְׁפָּטִי כָאוֹר וְיֵצֵא "And my judgment shall go forth as light."

(Jer. 15, 19). Not only his mouth, however, was required for this, but his whole personality, his whole personal life. With everything that he had and that was in him, even including the most private things of his life, he was to become a speaker; his most personal lot was to be presented before the people and to express God's concern. His marriage with a "woman of whorishness," that is to say a woman whose heart inclines to whoredom, represents the marriage between YHVH and this land, his love which his wife has betrayed represents YHVH's love which Israel has betrayed, his separation from the faithless one the divine separation, his mercy on her God's mercy. In the book of Hosea (which, it seems, includes only a few remnants of the original corpus, saved from the destruction of Samaria and bound up together) we have preserved only an incomplete testimony to what happened, namely a fragment in the third person (1, 2–9) and a scantily patched up one in the first person (3, 1–5), to which when the patching up was done a sentence was attached (v. 2) upsetting the sense, a sentence from a lost account also written in the first person, and fitting, if we change it into the third person, a definite place in the opening story (in the middle of chapter 1, v. 3).[2] Added to this is an utterance (2, 4–25, EV 2–23), in which there is apparently a hint of what is missing. From all this the unprejudiced reader can see that there is here not simply an allegory or inner ecstatic experience. But also he who regards God's cruel words, "Take to thee a woman of whorishness" (to which may be added by way of completion "whom I shall show thee," or something like this) as a belated interpretation, with which Hosea seeks to see his private experiences as God's decree, fails to recognise the "mortally factual" character of the word, that resists all psychological attenuation. And finally it is not permissible to regard chapters 1 and 3 as parallel representations of the same event, because then both God's word to the prophet and the utterance of the second chapter, would lose almost all their biographical background. Indeed, we cannot reconstruct this background out of the remnants in our hands; but we have enough

---

[2] In its present context the verse has apparently been understood by the redactor to mean that the woman, driven away, became a temple prostitute, and had to be redeemed from the sanctuary (cf. Budde, Der Abschnitt Hosea 1–3, Theologische Studien und Kritiken, 1925, 68, and also Hans Schmidt, Die Ehe des Hosea, Zeitschrift fuer alttestamentliche Wissenschaft XLII, 267ff).

before us to show how a *nabi* in the sight of the multitude, which defames him now and afterwards as a fool and a madman, experienced his lot as a sign of what is experienced by God. God loves, and He endures suffering for the sake of His love which is betrayed. "Go on, love a woman, beloved of a paramour, and an adulteress," He says to Hosea (3, 1), "as YHVH loves (He puts Himself in the third person before His prophet, as a model for his drawing) the children of Israel" —that is to say, with a suffering love, like His. And Hosea does as he is bidden. But this does not at all mean that he "feels with" God, as some think ; [3] the sensation assailing him is the sensation of his own love and suffering, but in feeling it he feels that he is following in the divine footsteps. In his own feeling the divine feeling is figured so strongly that in every stage he can read from his own lot the course of relations between YHVH and Israel, as when a stigmatized person, contemplating the marks of the wounds on the palms of his hands, comes to know the wounds of the crucified. But the comparison does not go very far : the stigmata are only like the copy of the original, whereas in the prophet's marriage we see the man himself with the secrets of his blood and soul and, just because of this, bound up with the secrets of God and, just because of this, able to embody them in the form of signs. This is to be understood only from the world of Israelite faith, where the blood and soul of theomorphous man know about his likeness character, which alone makes possible for him the imitation of God.

But there is another problem that arises before us from the divine saying with which the fragment preserved from the first person report begins. This is written in what I call the hammering style. Four times in one verse the verb "to love" recurs, each time signifying a different type of love : straightforward love of a man for his wife, adulterous love that breaks the bond, divine love of YHVH for Israel, and the so-called "love" of the Baalim for the raisin cakes brought to them. The first time, however, the verb occurs in the imperative, "Love!" A rare and strange form : is it possible to order love—not a general kind of order, as is found in the Torah repeatedly in relation to God and man, but a particular order like this? When Amos says, "Hate evil and love good," we take the saying without hesitation, because it is spoken

---

[3] Cf. especially Heschel, Die Prophetie (1936), 76ff.

in so general a way (cf. also Zech. 8, 19) ; but that a particular person should be bound to love another particular person in utter concreteness, is there such a thing as this? The word can only be spoken to one who already loves. He loves, he still loves the faithless one, he cannot suppress this love, but he does not want it, for he feels himself degraded by it. The personal side is stronger at this hour than the imitation of God, and the personal side is an inner conflict and shame. Into this state of soul God's word descends, "Continue loving, thou art allowed to love her, thou must love her; even so do I love Israel." From the sphere of God, the eternally loving, man's feeling gets back its right.

Hosea does not use the precious word "love" lavishly. At any rate in the book preserved for us he says all the essential things about God's love once only. They are three things. First, it is a demanding love. YHVH confesses that He called Israel as His son out of Egypt (11, 1), and drew him "with cords of love" (v. 4), when Israel was young and He grew fond of them ; and they went away from Him (v. 2). Second, it is a wrathful love. YHVH says (9, 15), that a hatred of Israel was stirred up in His heart, and He would drive them out of His house, and not love them any more. And third, it is a merciful love. YHVH promises (14, 5, EV 4), "I will heal their turnings away, I will love them freely." These are sayings of that "zealous God" of Sinai, the same demand (Ex. 20, 3–5a), the same wrath (v. 5b), and the same mercy (v. 6), all translated into the language of a great love story, a story of guilt and purification. All this is indeed very anthropomorphic, but I think that if Hosea had to explain the matter to us in terms of our conceptions, he would say that the theomorphism of man, that is to say, the fact of God's image in him, has been preserved only by God's own becoming anthropomorphous over and over again in such a manner.

In the use of the word "to love" in the book of Hosea there is something noteworthy: the prophet does not use it, even as a demand, of Israel's relation to YHVH. The symbolic passage (chapter 2) many times describes the Baalim by the name "lovers" of Israel (2, 7, 9, 12, 14, 15, EV 5, 7, 10, 12, 13), but nowhere is it said that Israel "loves" them. What we find in earlier and later passages of the subject of those that love God—in the Decalogue (Ex. 20, 6), in Moses' speeches in Deuteronomy (*passim*), in

literary speeches of Joshua (Josh. 22, 5; 23, 11), in the Song of
Deborah (Ju. 5, 31) etc.—is here, in the book of the "prophet
of love," completely lacking. Reciprocal love between YHVH and
Israel is expressed intensively in the passages in Deuteronomy
apparently influenced by Hosea's words (especially 10, 12, 15),
whereas in his own book such expression is lacking. It is true
YHVH charges Israel again and again that they commit whoredom in forsaking Him; but He does not say that He demands
or expects from them that they love Him. Love is not, in the
book of Hosea, a concept of reciprocity between God and man.

What this means can be elucidated more exactly by comparison with another concept, a concept taken apparently by Hosea
from the Decalogue, and readily used by him, in contradistinction
to Amos, in whose book the concept is lacking: the almost un-
translatable concept of *hesed,* which originally may have sig-
nified the right relationship between a lord and his men, his
hasidim, a relationship of goodwill and loyalty. So YHVH leads
with His *hesed* the people redeemed by Him out of Egypt (Ex.
15, 13), and the faithful man that pleads His cause is called by
the name "His *hasid,*" His devoted liege (Deut. 33, 8). But real
hesed cannot of course be done by the subject to the decidedly
superior one. Like Amos' double conception "righteousness and
justice," which is varied somewhat by Hosea and linked with "lovingkindness and mercy" (2, 21, EV 19), so also this lovingkindness
is in fact no reciprocal concept. To be sure, YHVH, Who prac-
tises "lovingkindness and faithfulness" (Gen. 24, 27; Ex. 34, 6), demands these very qualities from Israel (Hos. 4, 1) and in particular
hesed (6, 6; 10, 12), in connection too with justice (12, 7, EV 6).
But *hesed* is not demanded as something to be done to God, but as a
general goodwill manifested to all; and that not only appearing
temporarily and transitorily like a morning cloud and like the
early departing dew (6, 4)—for such passing and unreliable feelings deserve to suffer themselves the fate of a morning cloud and
the early departing dew (13, 3). Here too the text speaks of a following in God's footsteps and so serving His work in the world:
His lovingkindness to Israel must continue and operate in Israel's
lovingkindness to all. And so here too there is no concept of *reciprocity* between God and the people, but rather one of *conjunction*
between God and the people: a divine and human, divine-human,

virtue. All these concepts of conjunction by means of the good that flows from God and will spread itself by man's agency are gathered together in a solemn figure in the pardoning words of the symbolic saying (2, 21f., EV 19f): "I will betroth thee unto Me for ever, I will betroth thee unto Me in righteousness and justice, and in lovingkindness and mercy, and I will betroth thee unto Me in faithfulness, and thou shalt know YHVH."

This last word, "knowing," is in the book of Hosea the proper concept of reciprocity in the relationship between God and the people. "To know" here does not signify the perception of an object by a subject, but the intimate contact of the two partners of a two-sided occurrence; that the meaning of the verb "to know" is associated with the coupling of man and wife is doubtless included in the concept of Hosea, whose outlook is steeped in matrimonial imagery. In the passage about the election in Amos (3, 2), YHVH says that He has known Israel only of all the families of the earth. This "knowing" is the contact made through revelation and the establishment of the covenant. In Amos there is here no idea of reciprocity. It is otherwise in Hosea. He returns to the saying of Amos: "I knew thee in the wilderness," YHVH says to Israel (Hos. 13, 5); but the expression of reciprocity precedes it, "thou knowest no god beside Me" (v. 4); the circle is completed. In order, however, that this last sentence should not be understood in a relative way, in the sense that every people has its own god whom it can know, there follows a saying, in which Amos' teaching about YHVH's "bringing up" of the peoples (Am. 9, 7) is condensed: "there is no saviour but Me"; Amos' saying "you only" is here completed by the saying "I only" contained in these words of Hosea. YHVH only is the god to be known; to Israel only has He made Himself known. His contact with people through the revelation is balanced by the people's contact with Him in receiving the revelation. But the people no more wish to know Him; the reception of the revelation, which must be renewed in every generation, is interrupted. "There is no knowledge of God in the land" (4, 1), "they do not know YHVH" (5, 4). They think that by means of offerings they can dispense themselves from the devotion of themselves to receiving God's covenant; YHVH, however, delights not in sacrifice, but in the knowledge of God (6, 6). Therefore His people must "perish for lack of knowledge"

(4, 6). He slips away from them, He returns "to His place," to heaven, until they recognize their guilt and "long for His face" (5, 15), and say to one another: "We will know, we will follow after knowing YHVH" (6, 3). In the phrase "long for YHVH's face" (cf. also 3, 5), as in the kindred phrase "seek YHVH" (Am. 5, 4, 6; Hos. 10, 12), an important cleavage of meaning has taken place as against the earlier connotation, search for an oracle: they do not here seek the god in order to hear future things at his mouth, but in order to come into contact with him, in order to know him. This has already been emphasized in Amos' antithesis (5, 5f) "Seek not Bethel . . . seek YHVH and live!" In Hosea it is developed still further out of his conception of the "knowing."

About the election of the fathers Hosea says as little as Amos: neither of them have any interest in the prehistorical era of the people, but merely in their historical beginning, in order to confront the present with it. Over against this, Hosea differs decisively from Amos in his view of the redemption from Egypt. He does not see in this redemption, as his predecessor did, one of the acts of the living leadership of the peoples, which stands out from the rest of history through revelation alone, but an act of love, a summons to the people adopted to sonship (11, 1). Like the rest of the early writing prophets he too does not know the term "election." But the two key words of the Bush dialogue with which YHVH's dealings with the people Israel begin—the word *ammi*, "My people," (Ex. 3, 7, 10), and the word *ehyeh*, "I will be," that is to say, I will be with thee (3, 12, 14; 4, 12, 15)—the two words with which God binds Himself to the people, before making the covenant, and even before the meeting of YHVH and Israel, the two of them burn in the heart of the man who had plunged deep into the history of the Exodus from Egypt. The last child of the marriage ordered him Hosea calls by the name *Lo ammi*, "Not-my-people," for so God says in ordering the name (1, 9): "You are not my people, and I am not *Ehyeh* to you." It does not say, "I will not exist for you," but the meaning is: I, YHVH, said that I would be with you when I told Moses to say to you: "*Ehyeh* sent me to you" (in that unravelling of the name, the central importance of which Hosea knows; compare the idea of "the memorial" of the Tetragrammaton in 12, 6, EV 5, with Ex.

3, 15); but from now on you are no more entitled to rely on this, that I am with you as one that assists, protects, leads; indeed I will be where you will be, but no more to you as *ehyeh*, for you are no more my people.[4] From the word *ehyeh* the accompanying word *immach* is detached, the word by which the divine tie is expressed, and now the saying *Ehyeh asher ehyeh*, "I will be present as ever I will be present," reveals itself as the awful proclamation of the divine freedom to be what He wills: His being present becomes now the presence of the "consuming fire" (Ex. 24, 17). The might of the election is balanced by that of the rejection— but this is again balanced by the might of the new promise, directed at the perfect turning of the people (3, 5), the promise of the return (apparently originating from a later stratum of Hosea's prophecy): "And I will say to *Lo-ammi*, thou art my people, and he will say, my God" (2, 25, EV 23).

In the next step Hosea is distinguished from Amos in a noteworthy manner. Amos recognizes the redemption and revelation in the Exodus from Egypt only as YHVH's work upon Israel, only from above downwards, so to speak; he has nothing to say of a movement from below upwards, until there follows ingratitude, treachery, and the perversion of God's gifts. Hosea sees the moment at which in the Sinai desert Israel, which had grown to be "His people," stands before God, as a true meeting. YHVH "finds" Israel in the desert (9, 10), and this discovery is as if a wanderer finds grapes in the desert, that is to say, finds something precious where he did not in the least expect it. More than this: He sees the hosts encamped at the foot of the mountain, "your fathers," and they appear to Him like the first fruit of a fig-tree "in its beginning," that is to say, a fig-tree that produces fruit for the first time. This addition (not to be deleted, as some think) points beyond the comparison given in the first simile: God's great fig-tree, that is mankind, produces fruit for the first time, and its first fruits are those hosts of Israel. Here we have the origin of that theologically farther-reaching saying of Jeremiah (2, 3) about Israel as the "first fruits of God's increase." What Hosea shows us here is the happy meeting of the planter with the blessing of the first fruit of the tree he had planted. But this harmony between YHVH and Israel lasts only a moment:

[4] Cf. the commentary of Van Hoonacker.

when Israel enters the realm of the Baal, it falls into his bondage, and immediately all the freshness and deliciousness is lost, they "become abominations like the subjects of their love" (Hos. 9, 10). And the God Who has met this treachery suffers, as His prophet suffers, betrayed by his wife.

Israel's sin in the eyes of Amos is unrighteousness, that is to say, instead of serving humanly God's work of setting up righteousness and justice in the world, they stop and pervert it. Hosea not only transfers the chief emphasis from the faithful, God-serving justice and righteousness in relation to the fellow man, and lays it on faithful, God-serving lovingkindness in relation to him, but also adds the principle of reciprocity, which is absent from Amos. Israel has been sent on its historic way (10, 12), in order to sow for itself "in righteousness," to reap for itself "at the command of lovingkindness," and to break up for itself fallow ground: it is time to seek YHVH "until He come and instruct you in righteousness"; for without His *torah*, "His instruction," that which is established and that which is about "to come," there is no consummation of righteousness. It is not accidental that, in contradistinction to Amos, Hosea accepts emphatically the tradition of the covenant made between YHVH and Israel and inscribed in the Torah (6, 7; 8, 1; cf. 8, 12), the breaking of which he sees in the image of the breaking of the marriage tie. Here the meaning is not simply that man follows God as a pupil his master, that he imitates God and pursues as far as he is able the line of God's actions, but that by "knowing" Him he enters into reciprocal relationship with Him, and returns in a human way God's knowledge of him. This is the reason why Baalism is the chief subject of Hosea's indictment, here again in contradistinction to Amos. But here it is not the cult of local fertility spirits established before Elijah that is meant, nor the cult of the Tyrian storm god, defeated by Elijah and destroyed by Jehu, but the syncretism which followed them and set out to baalise YHVH Himself and to conduct His worship with rites belonging to the worship of the Baal. This syncretism implies first that they now imagined YHVH, the leader-God, Who goes out before them, the God of hosts and battles, in the likeness of a *baal* adhering to a holy place and again that they begin to introduce into the sanctuary of God, Who controls sexuality, ruling and hallowing it, the ancient sexual rites, and even began to regard Him as a husband, the Baal of the land. Both things together prevent the "knowledge" of God, setting up between the people and His face images essentially foreign to Him. From this we can understand Hosea's fight against the holy places, and especially those of the Samaritan "calf" (8, 5f; 10, 5; 13, 2), and against all "sacred" whoredom, a fight which is exemplified in the cry "With the temple harlots they sacrifice!" (4, 14). It is for the prophet to plead unremittingly against the degenerate sacrificial cult, in which the offering is changed from being a sign of the extreme self-devotion and becomes a ransom from all true self-devotion, from all lovingkindness and all God-knowing. "If Ephraim multiplied altars, they have become for him a sinning—altars a sinning!" (8, 11). For all that his land becomes more fruitful, for all that he has to give thanks to YHVH, the more Israel builds altars upon hills, beneath trees (4, 13), instead of returning thanks to God by living for Him; therefore He "will break the neck of their altars" (10, 2). For although they call God's name on the altars, they are, according to the quality of the cult, devoid of all true intention, altars of the Baal. A faithless people and faithless priests, these are rejected as one (4, 9). After this, at the beginning of the collapse, it will happen that just as formerly they went (Ex. 10, 9; 3, 18) into the wilderness "with their flocks and with their herds" to sacrifice to YHVH their God, so they will again go (Hos. 5, 6) "with their flocks and with their herds" to seek Him in a pure place and to appease Him, but "they will not find Him, for He has passed away from them." Only if they return truly to YHVH, and take with them, on their way to seek God, not animals for sacrifice but "words," that is to say, words of knowledge and profession, to make payment through oxen with their lips (14, 3, EV 2), then they, the destitute, will find mercy (v. 4, EV 3). And as Hosea fights against the soulless and degenerate cult, so he fights against the baalisation of YHVH Himself. This he does by dealing in a particular way with its fundamental concept. It is true that he readily uses the verb *raham*, "to have mercy," in connection with God (unlike Amos, who does not use this verb at all), a word that is related to the noun *rehem*, "womb," and so originally a term of maternity. But the image of YHVH as husband of the land he takes up and reshapes with the force of his personal experience to become such a sublime picture of a divine-human soul, passionate and suffering, he sets so powerfully *the people* as acting in the place of the land (although at the beginning, 1, 2, he has to call the land by the name of the wife), he raises so clearly and equably all the events of the reciprocal relationship, marriage, childbearing, adultery, divorce, reconciliation, into the sphere of *symbol* (and nevertheless they remain perceptive and alive just by the participation of his own experience), that it is scarcely possible for a true hearer or reader of Hosea to return afterwards to the nature image. The baalisation of YHVH appears to be overcome where Israel is thought of as His wife, and so His husbandship pictured as something not of nature but of history.

Although it is "the land" which is designated by YHVH in His first speech (1, 2) as the faithless wife, this marriage bond was not made in Canaan, nor can Canaan be the place of its renewal. To be sure, the farmer Hosea—he is so expert in field and village life, that there is no doubt about his being a farmer—is no kindred spirit to the sons of Rechab. When his God reproves the faithless and says (2, 10, EV 8) that it was not the *baalim* but He Himself Who gave her the corn, and wine, and oil, these appear as the great acquisitions of life, and what is required is only the recognition that the lord of the soil, bearing them, is none other than the God of the people, that came with them from the wilderness, and now controls the settlement and the waste land as well. But in the eyes of the man near to nature in Syria and Asia Minor, vegetative fertility is, as in bodily necessity, intertwined with the mystery of animal procreation and birth, a mystery perceived by men in their own life and magnified to god-pairings, superhuman pairings, which nevertheless need human imitation and strengthening by man. Into this seductive net of plant life Israel fell, as Hosea emphasizes strongly (9, 10), even at the first contact with agriculture, and from that time has been unable to stand up against it. The iniquity of Baal-peor continues in all that riotous Baalism, and therefore YHVH's curse fastens upon it. He wishes to chastise the people itself with barrenness (v. 11): "Ephraim (here the derivation of the word from the root *parah*, 'to be fruitful,' is suggested, cf. 13, 15; 14, 9, EV 8), like a bird their *kabhod* shall fly away (that is to say, their weight, their irradiating substance), from birth, from womb, and from conception (that is, all these things shall be no more)." It is easier to relate to one god the multiplicity of history than the multiplicity of nature. Although Hosea has no "nomadic ideal," he is forced to admit that the people has to be brought into a more simple nature surrounding, in the wilderness, in order that they might be purified and then make a new and eternal covenant with their God. In the wilderness, "in the burnt out land," their God knew them formerly (13, 5); in the future, after the accomplishment of the fierce chastisement, He will raise them up from their exile and settle them in tents "as in the days of the meeting" (12, 10, EV 9, that is to say, as in the days of the first meeting between YHVH and Israel, their meeting in the wilderness, and naturally here too we have echoed the memory of the "tent of meeting," the holy tent of the migration), and there, in the wilderness, He will "speak unto the heart" of Israel (2, 16, EV 14), until Israel calls Him as a wife calls her husband—but not by the epithet *baali*, "my husband," for He is no *baal*, but *ishi*, "my man" (v. 18, EV 16).

Here we are able to look right into the depths of the baalization of YHVH. The whole "whoredom" in question means ultimately that Israel forsook the true YHVH for the baalized YHVH. The small *baalim*, venerated in domestic cults as fetishes (13, 2), were never rivals of YHVH, and even the great Tyrian Baal, which for political motives was brought to Samaria, was attacked by Elijah only as an accessory god. A chief danger came rather from the mother-goddesses, just because they, approaching YHVH, contributed towards His baalization. No god was in a position to displace YHVH, saving only His own distorted image. It was for this that the people exchanged Him in the hour of their apostasy for YHVH-Baal and YHVH-Molekh. The super-sexual god the people exchanged for the husband of the mother-goddess. The righteous God-king, demanding righteousness from His kingdom, they exchanged for the cruel Molekh-idol seeking human sacrifice. The people are unfaithful, because they make YHVH into an idol instead of knowing Him, and fill His service with sacred whoredom instead of serving the God of *hesed* with *hesed*. This is what speaks to us out of the depths of His wrath: His name is profaned. This Amos had declared already (Am. 2, 7); Hosea makes it the fundamental subject of his prophecy, although he does not use this actual phrase.

The whole history of Israel, beginning with the entry upon the settlement up to the time of the prophet's words, appears here as a succession of acts of desecration. Hosea is imbued with the feeling of history, the history of Israel, as no other prophet is. And everything that the recollection of the times brings before him appears to him as a betrayal of YHVH's love; everything, both past and present, is bundled up together before the accusing God: "I remember all their evil, now their own deeds surround them, they are present to my face." (Hos. 7, 2) The lewdness of Baal-peor and the lewdness of the Baal of this hour are one. In Gibeah, where once the horrible deed was done (Ju. 19), Israel "has stood" (Hos. 10, 9), it has not moved from this place until this day. All history lays bare its shamefulness. Jehu's bloody deed, after the site of which, Jezreel, Hosea is bidden to name his first born, cannot be justified on the ground that it was performed out of zeal for YHVH; here already appear signs of Isaiah's simile of the rod of God's wrath, which does more than it is commanded and therefore is broken; the dynasty must be "terminated." But the king's murder, by which this announcement is fulfilled, and the murder which followed soon afterwards, are represented as an image of horror (7, 3ff), in which the murderers, the "consumers of their judge," and the kings, which even in the hour of their fall do not call upon YHVH, constitute but different sides of one vast situation of sin. Hosea sees the disorders, which occurred after the death of Jeroboam II, not only as a continuation of all the corruption in the history of the kings of Israel, but also as leading up to and expressed in present events.

The lawsuit between YHVH and the unfaithful royal house is here brought to a close by Hosea in Samaria before its fall, as in a later age by Jeremiah in Jerusalem before its fall. Recently [5] an attempt has been made to explain the many verses in Hosea about kingship as referring not to a king of flesh and blood, but to the god Melekh or Molekh, the so-called "Moloch," worshipped in the likeness of a bull. But it is difficult to apply this explanation fairly to more than two verses (10, 7, 15). Clearly, however, Hosea means to combine the man sitting upon the king's throne in Samaria with his master, the bull-Molekh in the sanctuary at Bethel, the distorted image of YHVH. Such a saying as "they have made kings but not from me" (8, 4) is best understood—if the connection between it and the end of the verse is to be seen as original—as referring to both together, the pretender in the sanctuary and the pretender on the royal throne, ruling in his name (he himself means: in YHVH's name!) And if the test that Hosea puts upon his wife, whom he takes back to his house, that is to say, that for "many days" she shall not be to others nor to him (3, 3)—if this test is substantiated by the point (v. 4) that the children of Israel are to be "many days" without king and without prince, it is difficult to relate this to the kings of flesh and blood only, but it is best interpreted as meaning that in this lengthy between-time Israel will have as king neither YHVH nor His adversary, and will not have a true representative of God nor one of the authority-usurping princes (and so, as appears from the end of the verse, there will be no cult, neither true nor false); and then the last verse of the story, the authenticity of which has been wrongly doubted, becomes clear (v. 5): "afterwards the children of Israel will return and seek YHVH their God and David their king": the true God and His legitimate representative shall return.

Hosea sees himself as the prophet of the turning. Moses was a prophet, by whom YHVH brought up the children of Israel out of Egypt, and by whom they were preserved (12, 14, EV 13). Now it is no longer the prophet's task to lead and to protect. Solitary, called mad because he is the man of the Spirit (9, 7), he finds "a fowler's snare in all his ways" (v. 8), but he is walking as "a watchman" "with his God"; [6] he was appointed to this task of watching and looking out not only for the approaching disaster, but also for the men whom his word may induce to turn to God. Here, too, Hosea starts from the prophecy of Amos who reproves the people (Am. 4) because they have not turned to God after any of the chastisements that had come upon them; but here too he deviates from him. Hosea stands in another historical situation from that of Amos; he does not prophesy in an hour of triumph about coming adversity, but he sees it descending and coming at first in inner troubles, afterwards in the vain giving of tribute to Assyria, in the revolt, in the covenant war with Syria against Judah and her neighbors, in the Assyrian invasion, in the break

---

[6] The word "Ephraim," that interrupts the connection, is an apostrophe, which was indeed plain in speech, and was misunderstood when it came to writing.

up of the Galilee region, in the transportation of a large section of the people to Assyria. And at every stage of the unfolding history as he time and again announces the judgement, at the same time he calls out of the ever more weighty actuality of the moment to turn to God; and all the time that it is still possible to come to political decisions, he calls to a turning that includes the political domain: to the abandonment of all alliance illusions. So he demands from those turning at the time of the giving of tribute that they should recognize that "Assur will not save us," and that they should decide that "we will not ride upon horseback" (14, 4, EV 3). When the evil advances, he sees that "for all this" they do not turn to YHVH (7, 10), that they refuse to turn (11, 5), yet he calls still more loudly (14, 2, EV 1): "Turn, O Israel, to YHVH thy God." But he does not only call to turn, he also prophesies that the turning will take place (3, 5). The motive of this prophecy, which appears nowhere in Amos, is that Hosea has and pronounces a divine promise, the like of which we never hear in Amos, "I will heal their turnings away" (14, 5, EV 4). This saying Jeremiah (3, 14, 22) is to develop to a perfect dialogue: "Return, O children that turn away, I will heal your turnings away," so YHVH expresses the reciprocal movement, and the people reply: "Behold us, we have come to Thee." It is not only the wounds which God inflicted on them in chastisement that He Himself is to heal (Hos. 6, 1), but even the turning away which caused this chastisement, for it is a disease. To be sure, it is laid upon the sick to make a beginning, before the healer can intervene: it is for the sick to *turn himself* to the healer. To return does not mean going back to conditions before the sin was committed, for this is impossible, but turning ourselves with all our being to God, in order to know Him. We do not return to ourselves but to Him Whom we have forsaken. Of course we do not yet stand again in the covenant, which God, and not we ourselves, renews, but we stand before His face. Him we do not yet have again, but neither do we have the Baal any longer, we stand in the test of the "many days."

"The virgin of Israel is fallen, she will no more rise up, she is forsaken upon her soil, there is none to raise her up," says Amos (5, 2). Hosea's returning ones (6, 2) do not think that the people will escape the fall, the death; in spite of this, however, they believe, "after two days He will revive us, on the third day He will raise us up, and we shall live before Him." It is not known, nor is it important, whether the image of the three days is connected with the myths of the resurrection of Adonis and other "dying and rising" gods;[7] the days are days of God, and it is not known how long such are, the three days of testing death correspond to the "many days."

The contemplation of the future that begins with Amos in a hidden form in an oracle to the elect, one of whom (it may have been Hosea) he addresses with his saying "YHVH thy God has said" (9, 15), here becomes stronger and is expressed publicly. YHVH promises Israel, rising to life again, a twofold covenant (2, 20ff, EV 18ff). First there is the covenant of peace that He makes for Israel with all living creatures and all the world of nations; and second there is the new marriage covenant, by which He betroths Israel to Himself forever in the great principles that make up the two-sided relationship between deity and humanity. This promise is fitted into a *dialogic* connection. In the wilderness where the inner change takes place and whence the change of all things proceeds, the woman "gratifies" her husband "as in the days of her youth" (v. 17, EV 15), and He "gratifies" (v. 23f, EV 21f) not her alone, but the whole world, while a stream of gratification pours from Him to heaven, and thence to the earth, and thence with all its productive blessing to Jezreel. Everything is changed: as *Lo-ruhamah* becomes *ruhamah,* and *Lo-ammi* becomes *ammi,* so Jezreel, formerly called by this cursed name after the place of a bloody deed, now becomes revealed according to the significance of this name, that is to say "he whom God sows." He stands here for a new generation. YHVH sows the land with a new seed. And at the end of the book the dialogic concept of "gratification" returns. YHVH heals the turning away of Israel, for His anger "is turned from them" (14, 5, EV 4). He wishes to be as dew to Israel, and they "will return" to dwell in the shade of Lebanon (v. 8, EV 7), and to blossom "as the vine." For "I am He Who has gratified" (v. 9, EV 8).

The moment, however, in which the wrath turns and mercy awakes, YHVH makes known as a present one (11, 8): "How shall I give thee up, O Ephraim, and deliver thee, O Israel! . . . My

---

[7] Cf. Baudissin, Adonis und Esmun (1911), 403ff.

heart turns within me, my compassions boil up together." That "soliloquy" of Amos (4, 13), which is "imparted" to man, is here developed by the prophet of *hesed*: it is the moment of a divine turning.

C. THE THEOPOLITICAL HOUR

Isaiah's story of his call, that took place at the same time as Hosea was prophesying in Samaria, comes in the book of Isaiah after two small collections of non-political material, that is, sayings which do not include extra-political demands or criticism of this kind (ch. 2 and ch. 3–5 basically, collections which for the most part belong to the early days of the prophet. Whereas after the chapter about the call, there follows immediately the account of his most important political act (ch. 7), probably copied from the prophet's own record, and after it the rest of his political memoir (8–9, 6)—to the beginning of which he apparently joined the story of the vision, which he wrote later—to which again were added mostly political sayings. Thus we understand why the story of the call was put not at the beginning of the book—where it should be—but in this place; because it was indispensable to a right understanding of the account of the political act and of the memoir, and whoever reads them must have these things continually before his eyes. The redactor, certainly one of the prophet's disciples, wishes apparently to assist to the best of his ability in the clarification of this intrinsically obscure position of his master.

"In the year of the death of king Uzziah . . . my eyes saw the king YHVH of hosts" (6, 1, 5)—only here does Isaiah himself designate his God by the attribute "the king," name and style together being used here for the first time, and he calls Him not king of the world or the like, but "*the* king," which clearly means: the true king, our true king. A hint is given us: it is not he that sits upon the royal throne, who is the true king, but He Whom mine eyes now see. But we must examine this account more closely. Evidently it has not been written by the youthful Isaiah shortly after the vision, but at a more mature stage of the prophet's development; it is a skilfully constructed account, every word of which has its fixed essential place. The phrase "in the year of king

Uzziah's death" is to be understood as meaning *before* his death, for there is no reason to doubt the opening words of the book, according to which Isaiah had visions in the days of Uzziah. And indeed we know that Uzziah no longer reigned then, but lived as a leper in a separate house (2 Kgs. 15, 5). A chapter of the Chronicles, which is apparently otherwise historically trustworthy and valuable, and also on this subject seems to follow a special tradition, even if this has been worked over from a definite point of view, relates (2 Chr. 26, 16ff) that Uzziah caught leprosy because he took upon himself the right of offering sacrifice in the temple, that is to say because he opened afresh the struggle over the question of authority in sacred matters, a struggle that had continued from the beginning of the kingdom and after the early successes of the kings had begun more and more to pass to the advantage of the priesthood. Leprosy, according to the Biblical view, is the uncleanness of a person or thing breaking out and affecting that person or thing; and uncleanness in Scripture means the upsetting of the relationship between God and the world in a certain place. At the beginning of his account of the vision he saw in YHVH's sanctuary, which Uzziah had wished to penetrate, Isaiah recalls the unclean man who had been taken down from his throne; he mentions him before he hears the seraphim praising God, enthroned upon His royal seat, as the thrice holy one: and so here they stand over against each other, in a terrible though veiled contrast, the true king and his unfaithful vicegerent now no longer entitled to the style of "the king."

At the time of the vision Isaiah is apparently in the hall of the temple, looking into the depths of the sanctuary right into the darkness of the Holy of Holies, where the ark, YHVH's throne, stands. At this moment the darkness becomes light, the confined space extends without limit, the roof is lifted, in place of the ark a throne is raised up to heaven, so great that the skirts of the clothing of Him that sits upon it fill the temple. Isaiah says: "I saw the Lord," but this seeing is probably like that related of the elders on Sinai who "saw the God of Israel" (Ex. 24, 10): what is said of what was actually seen is on that occasion what is "under His feet," and here "His skirts." The antiphonal cry of the seraphim in its second half helps us towards an understanding: as the skirts of God's clothing fill the temple, so His *kabhod,* that is to

say, His radiating "weight," fills the earth. Tradition tells (Ex.
40, 35, a verse which, whatever its date from the literary point of
view, is at all events from the religious point of view earlier than
Isaiah) that His *kabhod* once, when it descended in a cloud upon
the wandering tent in the wilderness, filled the "dwelling place"
while the covering cloud "dwelled" upon it; whereas now Isaiah
hears that it is not only the earthly-heavenly sanctuary which he
sees, but the whole earth that YHVH's *kabhod* fills. Whenever
we see "Him," we really see His radiation, which the earth can
scarcely contain. The earth contains the *kabhod* which fills it,
because this *kabhod* is merely God's radiation, the nature and purpose of which is to fill the earth. The point about this cry of the
seraphim is the present tense used. It is not in the future that the
kabhod is to fill the earth, as later "eschatological" passages, already apparently influenced by Iranian religion, have it (Num. 14,
21b,[1] Ps. 72, 19), now and ever it fills it, as the skirts fill the
temple; but no one sees it except he to whom it is given to see it.
This means here the prophet; it is only later passages (Is. 35, 2; 40,
5) that represent all creation as seeing it. Isaiah sees it as he sees
the "skirts." More than this even the seraphim, who cover their
faces, do not see.

This same thing from the other side is expressed in the first
half of the antiphonal cry: "Holy, holy, holy is YHVH of hosts."
The word "holy" is a concept which cannot be understood unless
its definition is followed by a limitation. Up to the Babylonian
exile "holy" means distinct but not severed, distinct and yet in the
midst of the people ("a holy one in thy midst" Hos. 11, 9); distinct and radiating. Here in this double character of being detached and joined at once we find the origin of the peculiar power
expressed in this conception: YHVH is absolute master of the
world because although He is definitely distinct from the world,
He is not in any way withdrawn from it. And for this very reason
this conception makes possible a new and the highest expression
of the demand to imitate God: that Israel should be holy, as their
God is holy (Lev. 11, 44f; 19, 2; 20, 7, 26); this had already been
expressed in that earlier verse about the "holy nation" (Ex. 19,
6), and the verses based on this (Deut. 7, 6; 14, 2, 21; 26, 19;
28, 9), in these last more in the form of a promise than in the

---

[1] A later addition, evidently occasioned by the mention of *kabhod* in v. 22.

form of a demand. Indeed Israel must—this is the meaning—be distinct (cf. the ancient Balaam speech, Num. 23, 9), but not in order to withdraw itself from the world of nations, but in order to influence them by the radiance of its way of life. In Isaiah we do not find the attribute "holy" applied to the people; but in a passage, the date of which is much disputed (Is. 4, 2–5), an undoubted Isaianic fragment is found (v. 3): "And it shall be that whoso is left in Zion and remains in Jerusalem shall be called holy." By the "turning remnant" (7, 3; 10, 21f), preserved from the catastrophe, it will be proved true that the people can follow even God's holiness. This, that YHVH is present to Israel even with His most sublime and essential characteristic, His holiness, and that Israel is thereby able to receive His influence to follow His footsteps, and to place human activity at the disposal of His activity, in other words, the hallowing of Israel by the holy YHVH (cf. Ex. 31, 13), this is the root idea of the divine attribute so dear to Isaiah; for this he is mocked (Is. 5, 19; 30, 11), his response being an even more emphatic "the holy one of Israel." As with the "righteousness" of Amos and the "lovingkindness" of Hosea, so also this third basic concept, the greatest of them, is a concept of the divine-human relationship, its chief meaning being that YHVH wishes to work through the independence of man created as independent and to continue His work on earth by this means. In one generation Israel's faith developed these three basic conceptions of the relationship to God, and only all together could express what is meant by the being present of the One Who is present to Israel, Who is "with it." The name YHVH was unravelled at the revelation to Moses in the thorn bush; in the revelation to the three prophets it has been unfolded.

At the moment when the door posts move at the cry of the seraphim and their burning breath mingles with the smoke rising from the altar of incense, Isaiah cries (v. 5), "Woe is me, for I am undone, for I am a man of unclean lips, and I dwell in the midst of a people of unclean lips, for mine eyes have seen the king, YHVH of hosts." It is customary to explain this by saying that Isaiah, as YHVH's emissary, needs clean lips—but he is not yet appointed an emissary, nor does he know that he is about to be such; others explain that he wishes to join in the songs of praise, but cannot do so unless his lips be clean—but such an explanation disregards the awfulness of the song and the terror of the "un-done" man; and there are even those who prefer to strike out the word "lips" and to leave simply the general uncleanness, but in this way the event is robbed of an essential element. We can understand the matter if we realize the contrast between the leprous, unclean king and the thrice holy God. In the Law (Lev. 13, 45) a statute, the antiquity of which most scholars have not recognized, orders: "The leper, who has the plague, his clothes shall be rent and his head bared, and his moustache he shall cover and shall cry 'Unclean, unclean.'" The lips must be covered as far as the moustache so that with the vapor which rises from the sick body and defiles the lips with every breath, the uncleanness shall not pass to that which is round about, defiling it. The reverse is to be seen in the mourning customs (Ezek. 24, 17, 22), where the unclean substance of the dead is not to be breathed in; and there is the symbolic behavior of him who is isolated from the world (Mic. 3, 7). Isaiah identifies himself and his rebellious, faithless people with the rebellious, faithless king: as the king is unclean, so is Israel, and so too is Israel's son Isaiah; his lips and the lips of the people he feels to be specially unclean in consideration of the contact with God and the world, because through them the unclean breath is spread abroad, and at this moment is even mingled with the temple air saturated with holy smoke. Only the act of the seraph, who, himself apparently of a fiery species, cleanses with a live coal Isaiah's lips and thereby atones for his iniquity, makes the lips a possible vehicle for the divine mission. For it is in order to decide, in the moment of question, whether he is willing to accept the hitherto unknown mission, that the young man is brought from the circles of the royal residence into the sphere of this vision.

The question is not directed to him, all the initiative is left in his hands. The situation here is different from that of the rest of the prophets: Moses and Jeremiah even wished to resist the vocation and it was forced on them from above; whereas here it is God's will that man should do something excessively heavy, and therefore man has to ask that God should load the burden upon him. The question which Michaiah ben Imlah heard (1 Kgs. 22, 20) was directed to the host of heaven; from their midst came the one who was ready for this service. Not so here. The seraphim are no emissaries; their Lord does not speak to them, He speaks to Himself; but it is His wish, that the man called to His presence should hear; He "declares to man what is his soliloquy" (Am. 4, 13). Without being asked, Isaiah submits himself as an emissary and he is sent. The mission which he now accepts is the most terrible thing in the whole vision. The duty which is laid upon him is this: to say "to this people" that they may listen but will understand nothing, and that they may see but will know nothing. And in order that it may be really so, in order that the people shall not understand nor know what they see and hear, in order that they may not perceive the signs of the times so as to interpret them rightly, in order that they may not return and be healed, it is further laid upon Isaiah to "make fat" the heart of "this people," to "make heavy" their ears and to "becloud" their eyes. This is a very strange command. Not because YHVH wishes to harden the people's heart, though this perplexes us; but because evidently the prophet has to achieve this aim through the words God will put in his mouth. He is not to deceive his hearers with lying promises, as did that wind-spirit of Michaiah ben Imlah, but he is to hand on the true sayings of God. And so if we here consider every word with such seriousness as is right and proper, we cannot avoid the question as to what prophecy is fitted to act so—in other words, what prophecy of this kind we find in the extant sayings of Isaiah. It cannot be a proclamation of punishment and disaster; for if such a proclamation does not succeed in shaking the heart of the people and bringing them to repentance, and if they do not return "to Him that smites them" (Is. 9, 12, EV 13) in spite of all the warnings about historical afflictions, certainly it does not aim at such a failure, and certainly we cannot see in it the execution of the command to make the hearts fat. What then is it that is made to serve as a true prophetical announcement and at the same time to make the ears of the multitude heavy and to becloud their eyes? It can be nothing else than a great message of salvation, a sound so new, so strong and clear, that it silences all prophecy of disaster in the ears of the many, who only long for the securing of the people's existence, for the quieting of their soul's unrest, and for the confirmation of their illusions.

We stand here on the threshold of Isaiah's testimony—and on the threshold of the tragic contradiction in his prophetic way.

Will he hold out the message of salvation to the people as poison?
Will he refuse to obey his God? His way cannot be either of these,
and it can only be a tragic way and one full of contradiction. Of
the first stage of this way we hear in the story of the meeting with
king Ahaz, of the second in the remaining part of the memoir,
and of the third afterwards. It was an exposition and justification before the generations to come, when he wrote down at the
prime of his life the story of his first vision, putting it at the
beginning of his memoir written many years before.

The moment he accepts the task of making fat the people's
heart Isaiah asks (v. 11): "Lord, until when?" The meaning of
this "until when?" can only be, to what time, until what term
does this awful task hold? He hears the reply: until the people be
reduced to a tenth, and the land be wasted. The same thing was
known to Isaiah from the prophecy of Amos, in which, as we can
see from many passages, he was well versed; there (Am. 5, 3) it
had been said that a tenth should remain. It is only possible
to understand the nature of this remnant if we refrain from cutting
out (as is often done without adequate reason) the last verse of
the account of the vision, or its last words, which from the point
of view of content and character are the most important. But
neither should it be explained that the tenth too is appointed for
extermination. As if to facilitate the correct understanding of this
saying the same very rare expression: "it will be for grazing" [2]
occurs in a connection that cannot be mistaken, in the small collection of Isaiah's sayings which the editor of the book placed
before the account of the vision. In the parable of the vineyard
(Is. 5, 1–7), in which God appears as a careful vinedresser and
Israel as an ungrateful vineyard that brings to its lord, who has
done everything in his power for it, wild grapes instead of good
grapes, it is said in the declaration of punishment (v. 5) that
YHVH would "remove its hedge and it should be for grazing,
break down its wall and it should be for trampling on" (that is
to say, by small cattle cf. 7, 25). Destruction cannot be meant
here; and as if to guard altogether against a misunderstanding,
another fragment is put before this in which the elders and princes

---

[2] Outside the book of Isaiah we find this phrase only once, in the prophecy of
Balaam, Num. 24, 22, a difficult verse and one which does not prescribe an interpretation.

are addressed in these words (3, 14): "Ye have grazed the vineyard, the spoil of the poor is in your houses." What Isaiah declares at the end of his vision as God's will means: then, when the people is decimated and the land again given over to pasturage,[3] will take place what sometimes happens when a tree is felled; a stump is left in the ground, and after a while a branch comes out of the stump, and from it springs a new tree. This new branch Isaiah calls here—as the "remnant" is designated holy in 4, 3— by the name "seed of hallowing." This is no more the natural propagation and maintenance of the people, it is selection by removing, revival by selection, hallowing by revival. When we find this metaphor again centuries afterwards, eighty years after the return from the Babylonian exile (Ezra 9, 2), it has become an accepted term of self-reliance; but in Isaiah it appears as something that is seen for the first time. Hallowing for him is the acting movement of God's holiness towards the world, towards man; if he says "mount of hallowing" (Is. 11, 9), he means the place where truly takes place the hallowing of Israel by YHVH, "to see Whose face" they come—until the people's depravity rends the bond, and the pilgrimage, emptied of its content, becomes repulsive to God (1, 12). And so the meaning of the "seed of hallowing" here is a particular kind of propagation of the people, set apart in the personal, removing and preserving interference of God, a kind of propagation that conducts the people through death to life, and now the regenerated people is hallowed. This is what Isaiah now wants to present to the people in living signs by calling his son *Shear-yashub* ("A-remnant-will-return"), though apparently not yet as later acting at God's command (8, 3). He has realized directly that this remnant, which will return "to the valiant God" (10, 21), will come forth from the "determined consumption" as the divine-human "righteousness" carried on the crest of its flood (v. 22). The dialectic of the event to take place is awake in his heart. Who will be swallowed up by the waves? and who will seize the plank of faith? The boy walks the streets of Jerusalem as a call to decision, a call in bodily dress. If the passers-by, who look at the boy with the strange name, the boy known to all, see and do not know what they see, their blindness is not because his father has been "beclouding" their eyes. Salvation and desola-

[3] For the right interpretation cf. especially Budde, Jesaias Erleben (1928), 22ff.

tion are so intermingled in this sign that it is able to point the way to deliverance, but can certainly deceive no one into a cheap assurance. It is true that Isaiah's words at this period, his first sayings—so far as we can distinguish them as such—point much more to the judgement than to the possibility of escape. But their influence upon open hearts cannot possibly be "fattening"; behind every prediction of disaster there stands a concealed alternative.

*   *   *

A few years only elapsed after the call before that hour arrived for which the prophet had then been equipped, as he tells us by placing the vision account in front of the narration. Damascus and Samaria, who had made a covenant after a protracted war, united their armies and set out to fight against Judah. In the king's house and among the people hearts trembled "as the trees of a wood move before a wind" (7, 2). The young king Ahaz decided to summon the help of a power interested in interfering on such occasions, that is, Assyria. But at the sight of increasing danger he also did (2 Kgs. 16, 3 can hardly refer to another occasion) what West Semitic kings used to do in such circumstances (cf. 3, 27), he "makes his son to pass through fire"—a deed which may be understood as a real offering of the first born, or as a substitution for it by a symbolic act, the consecrating passing through or over the fire in the valley of Hinnom; [4] at all events there is here a transformation of YHVH the *melekh* into "Moloch," an extreme profanation of the name of the true god-king by the abominable worship of the perverted king called by his name. After this, but before the departure of the messengers to Assyria, YHVH sends Isaiah to Ahaz and orders him to take with him his first born *Shear-yashub*. The boy taken and brought by his father represents in bodily form the divine protest against the sacrifice of the first born, and at the same time the divine warning: now the decision begins, who is of the remnant, who will return to Me, and whom I shall preserve. Perhaps this will be only a handful of faithful ones, perhaps the whole of Judah—now the decision begins. The boy, in a language at once silent and great, expresses the decision power of the hour. The time to return has not yet passed, all that return are the remnant. Isaiah has to take the boy with him *as a visible word* expressing the demanding mercy of his God.

[4] Cf. Koenigtum Gottes, 69f, 211, 222.

The decision to which Ahaz has to be called is to give up the plan of a covenant with Assyria. With this mission Isaiah's struggle against covenant politics begins—first the covenant with Assyria, afterwards with Egypt—the war against the desire that persists in spite of changing objectives (Is. 30, 1) "to take counsel but not of Me, to weave a web without My spirit." Many have regarded this attitude as important indeed from a religious angle, but from the historical angle of reality as imprudent, "utopian." But the world of prophetic faith is in fact historic reality, seen in the bold and penetrating glance of the man who dares to believe. What here prevails is indeed a special kind of politics, theopolitics, which is concerned to establish a certain people in a certain historical situation under the divine sovereignty, so that this people is brought nearer the fulfilment of its task, to become the beginning of the kingdom of God. Men trust the Lord of this kingdom, that He will protect the congregation attached to Him; but at the same time they also trust in the inner strength and the influence of the congregation that ventures to realize righteousness in itself and towards its surroundings. Covenant policy is not suitable for such a people from a religious point of view, because it puts the people under obligations and in a position of dependence, contrary to that one such relationship which is true; but at the same time it is unsuitable from a political point of view also, because it involves the people in other nations' wars of expansion, in wars liable to rob the people of its independence and finally to destroy it, especially when, as with little Israel, it has to live between two great powers. Isaiah begins his speech to Ahaz, standing in front of him at "the end of the conduit of the upper pool," with the words (7, 4): "Take heed and *keep still*." More than two decades afterwards, when in an advanced early stage of the complications announced by him it fell to Isaiah to fight, no longer the covenant with Assyria, but that with Egypt against Assyria, the prophet further clarified the content of that same instruction (30, 15): "Thus hath YHVH, the Holy One of Israel, spoken: In turning away and in rest you will be saved, in *keeping still* and in confidence will be your strength, but you would not." This is a reliable political program for the people living at the time in Canaan. And it is not merely a negative program, if we take it in connection with all the prophetic teaching about the right ordering of community life; if this order is established, *keeping still* lends the people a downright magnetic power. But this attitude, too, as theopolitical, as the acting of the divine will through a chosen company of men, means the imitation of divine attributes. In a somewhat later fragment, of a still more critical time, where it is revealed to the prophet that Jerusalem will survive the great danger awaiting at the hands of the Assyrian host, YHVH announces to him how He regards the war of the peoples threatening to strangle the little Judah (18, 4): "*I keep still* and look on my foundation place (that is from heaven I look upon Mount Zion, cf. 4, 5) like a clear heat above light, like a cloud of dew in the heat of harvest." Israel must keep still, as YHVH keeps still. Then will there be poured out from on high, as is said in a messianic prophecy not to be denied Isaiah (32, 15ff), a spirit upon the people and righteousness shall dwell there and its working shall be "*keeping still* and confidence for ever." Only in these four verses from Isaiah do we find this verb "to keep still." Together they form the core of his theopolitical teaching. To understand them aright it is necessary to consider afresh what he means by "holiness": *distinction and radiation together.* "Keeping still" is holiness in regard to the political attitude of God and His people.

From the days of Samuel on, the faithless vicegerent of God and the unofficial advocate of God's sovereignty stood over against each other; but only here is there direct word of the crux of the matter, of *the kingdom.* But at first Isaiah does not, like the others, come reproving and demanding. He does not hold the king's guilt before his eyes, he does not address him as a private person, but as the king of Israel, whom he urges not to miss the political decision that conforms to God's regime. For this reason he tells him that if he takes heed and keeps still, that is to say, if he does not call on the help of a great power, thereby making himself a bone of contention and a light ball in a game between the kingdoms of the world, there is no need to fear "these two smoking torch stumps," that have no longer the power to burn up Jerusalem. Against their intention to "break up" Judah YHVH sets His word (7, 7): "It will not stand, it will not be." And with this word is the authority. The head of Damascus is named Rezin, and the head of Samaria Pekah, whereas—this is intimated to Ahaz—you know who is the head of Jerusalem, if you believe, if you confide. And now suddenly there is cast into the midst of the decision power of the hour the decisive saying about the choice given by God, and this comes in its negative, that is to say, in its prophetic form (v. 9) : "If you will not confide, you will not abide." We feel the force of this central saying of Israelite prophecy still more, if we compare the adaptation of it given by the Chronicler (2 Chr. 20, 20) in the positive form, which wrongly refers to the prophets: "Confide in YHVH your God, and you will abide." Not only is the absolute "confide" greater than this "confide in YHVH," which by adding obvious words weakens the force of the verb, but in the adaptation the awe-inspiring actuality is lost, meaning that people and prince lose the stability accorded to them from the Lord of history, as soon as they no longer confide, as soon as they break the covenant. He who has dealings with the powers renounces the power of powers, that which bestows and withholds power, and loses its help; whereas he who confides and keeps still thereby gains the very political understanding and strength to hold his ground. The unbeliever demands acceleration of God's actions and mocks His slowness, as Isaiah related earlier (5, 19), for he, the politician, cannot wait: "Let Him make speed and hasten His work, that we may see, let the counsel of the Holy One of Israel draw near and come, that we may know." Against them the prophet takes his stand in a later prophecy (28, 14ff), in which the destruction of the "torrent-scourge" and the salvation of the "precious battlement," which abides because it is tested and tried, are declared together in a saying, meant for finality (v. 16) : "He that confides will not hasten." The true believer does not wish to hasten God's work, the work of salvation, even if he could. Small politics is a monologue of man; great politics is a discourse with the God Who "keeps still." For Damascus and Samaria there was laid up an hour of danger from Assyria, God's "rod of anger" (10, 5), more than was laid up for Judah from them; but if the kingdom of Judah, instead of confiding and keeping still, called this rod of His anger, she brings her own head under the stroke.

Ahaz does not answer; he apparently does not wish to see himself as one questioned. And now (the idea [5] that king and prophet silently went asunder for the time being does not fit the stress of

[5] So Procksch, Jesaia I (1930), 118.

the situation: already in the next hour the embassy can go forth!)
YHVH demands through Isaiah, but in accordance with the
importance of this step he is designated here—and only here—as
speaking not to the prophet but to a third person, He demands
of Ahaz that he asks for himself a "sign" and he is permitted to
choose this sign from the whole domain between the uppermost
and the lowest spheres of existence. And intentionally it is said
that he should ask the sign "from YHVH his God" (this phrase
"thy God" is only found this once in the actual words of Isaiah):
in spite of all, YHVH is his God, and wills to be so.

In no original non-legendary prophetic saying, related not to
past events but directed to present or future occurrences, does
the word *oth* ("sign") mean a miracle. What the special significance of this concept in Isaiah is, we know from the fact that the
symbolic act of his going naked (ch. 20) is called a sign (v. 3);
so too he sees his sons or his pupils or both together set in the
world as a sign (8, 18). Of course a sign can be also a *pele,* a "wonder," that is, something beyond our comprehension; but if anyone
is given or promised a sign of what God tells him, there is no other
meaning than that he receives or shall receive a visible, material
token, a pledge so to speak. The content of the divine saying is
linked to something actual, which has to present, to recall, and
again and again to ascertain it. The passage before us, and only it,
goes beyond this: the choice is given to the hearer to determine
the sphere from which the sign is to be taken. Hence they are
mistaken [6] who think that the passage is simply concerned with
a miracle, and all the further conclusions bound up with this notion
are futile. Ahaz shall not content himself with the word, he shall
seek the embodiment of the word, in the likeness of which there
will abide in the material world of man the binding, obligating
force of the promise.

But the king knows that if he does so, he will take upon himself
an obligation, that is to say he will be compelled to forgo his plan
for deliverance. He declines: he will not "tempt YHVH." He is
pious: he was pious when he passed his son through fire for
YHVH—for Him and no other god!—and he will be pious when he
sends from Damascus the pattern of the Assyrian altar (2 Kgs.
16, 10ff), so that a copy could be made in YHVH's temple—His

[6] Cf. Procksch, *op. cit.,* 120.

and no other's!—and when afterwards he offers on it all the sacrifices in their order. He wishes to give to religion that which appertains to it; but it must be far removed from the sphere of politics, that is from the sphere of real decisions. If this—so he thinks—is expressed in religious language, this unofficial emissary of religion must see the drift of it. Indeed, this man has brought him an important oracle, which, as sometimes the priestly oracle does (cf. Lam. 3, 57),[7] began with the exhortation "Fear not," and afterwards he went far beyond this function—the expression of the divine "yea" or "nay," the acceptance or rejection of a request—and even came to promise him the destruction of his enemies. But of course such a comforting view is not sufficient to abolish a *political* resolution, adopted through political considerations only. To the messenger—one moreover from an honorable family, and who can therefore be expected to adapt himself to the benefit of the state!—the pious reply is then given, fitted to close the conversation.

But this same man now unexpectedly gives Ahaz the "sign." It can hardly be called a miracle. In the same form of speech as is used otherwise in Scripture only in direct apostrophe to announce the birth of a son to a pregnant woman or one about to become pregnant, here it is announced in the third person that "the young woman" (*almah*) has conceived or will quickly become pregnant, and bring forth a male child. As it is difficult to conjecture that a woman was present,[8] the reference must be to a young woman just married or about to be married, well known to the king and so understood by him to be meant by the indefinite words. From this we find the explanation of this most controversial verse: if Ahaz, as he hears the word *almah,* knows to whom it refers (and only then does the sign truly concern him), it can only be a woman near him, and moreover hardly another than the young queen; we may even suppose that it was customary in court circles to call her the *almah.* That Isaiah refers in the name "Immanuel" of his declara-

---

[7] Cf. also Begrich, Das priesterliche Orakel, Zeitschrift fuer alttestamentliche Wissenschaft, Neue Folge XI (1934), 81ff.

[8] The idea put forward by some, that Isaiah speaks to Ahaz in these words about a figure who appears before him at that moment in his vision (Hans Schmidt, Die grossen Propheten, 74) is unconvincing; neither does it suit the language of the dialogic situation to explain the matter as referring to any woman or number of women, as other commentators think.

tion to Ahaz to the anti-king, opposing to the faithless vicegerent of God the faithful one—this is unmistakably clear from the words "thy land, O Immanuel" (Is. 8, 8). And that the true anointed can only come from the house of David is clearly expressed in the central part of this Messianic memoir, in the song about the boy that "is born to us" (9, 5, EV 6) and especially in its conclusion (v. 6, EV 7). "Immanuel" is the anti-king but not "a spiritual anti-king," as some explain it, for the fulfilling, the Messianic kingship too is a real, political kingship, or rather a theopolitical one, that is to say, it is a kingship endowed with political power to the scope of the political realization of God's will for people and peoples— no other view is held by Isaiah or by any other prophet of the period of the monarchy. Immanuel is the king of the *remnant*, from which the people will renew itself. As the man called to the fulfilment, as the man who, while yet a youth, in the days of the great darkness (8, 22; 9, 1) knew "to refuse the evil and choose the good," he will live with the remnant in the land made into pasturage, he will eat again together with them the twin food of the pre-agricultural age, the primitive and holy food, cream and the honey of wild bees (7, 15, 22), until the yoke of Assyrian servitude be broken (9, 3, EV 4), which the political covenant of Ahaz had brought upon Israel. Only then will his hidden destiny become manifest. His first name, God-is-with-us, designated him as the man in whom is represented YHVH's being present, His remaining with the remnant that has become His people; but now his secret name, his wonder name (the word "wonder" belongs to "his name," as in Judges 13, 18, the similiar word "wonderful"), is revealed. In accordance with the three stages of the process of salvation, namely war, victory, and peace, this secret name is composed of three parts [9] (not, as it is usually stated, of four): "counsellor of the valiant God" (that is, of the God as leading the battle), "father of the spoil" (this spoil is the world of peoples delivered from the "rod" of the Assyrian tyrant, v. 3, EV 4), and "prince of peace" (that is, of the "peace that has no end," v. 6, EV 7, which in a later prophecy of Isaiah is pictured in the image of the peace of the animals, 11, 6–9). These are not names—as the customary translation suggests—speaking of divine rather than

[9] Cf. the commentary of S. D. Luzzatto, who is, however, interpreting the passage in another way.

human attributes; they are exalted titles, befitting the executor vicegerent of YHVH, who shares in His work, first in the counsels of God, then in God's war, and finally in God's re-ordering of His world, as the human leader of the human helpers.

In the word to Ahaz mention is made only of the first, hard period of the invasion and the desolation. It may be conjectured that the prophet did not yet fully recognize the decisive, "Messianic" importance of the child that was born. But probably something else was added to this.

Until his meeting with Ahaz Isaiah prophesied mainly judgement. Now he had to make known an unambiguous message of salvation, which ended, it is true, in a great alternative, but itself had not the alternative form: he had to announce the downfall of hostile devices and the overthrow of those allied against Judah, which would take place without any action from within. He did so, and saw that the declaration only hardened the heart of the hearer: Ahaz thrust away the sign of obligation. YHVH's terrible announcement in the vision of the call is fulfilled: the prophecy of disaster does not stir the people to repentance, and the message of salvation hardens them still more. In this hour—so we must take it—Isaiah chooses his way. He says no more to Ahaz than he must hear. What he revealed to the king about the fate of the enemies, he will now tell also to the people and will attest it by the strongest symbolic embodiment, in order to put before them directly the doubtful character of the king's politics (8, 1–8, cf. also ch. 17). But what is revealed or will be revealed to him about salvation without any order to transmit the good news to the people or to any definite recipient, he will conceal within the circle of the faithful, which has begun to gather around him as the original community of the holy remnant. Obviously it is not yet clear to the prophet what the nature of this revelation will be, and at the time he may experience only a little of the promise of "a great light" which he will receive, and so we should not suppose that at this time the decision had yet matured in his heart to "seal" it (8, 16); but here is the first hour of its appearance, and also the hour of the beginning of the tragic conflict in the prophetic way of the man, whose prophecy was itself the starting point of the special "Messianic" hope of the people of Israel.

*   *   *

What is the nature of this hope? We shall not understand its nature and origin if we start from "eschatology," that is to say from a doctrine or conception of the "last things," no matter if we mean by this an element of Israelite faith or an element of ancient oriental myth. By so doing we just miss its special, concrete, historical core. It is true a primitive and popular figurative essence, a dream plasma of a Garden of Eden world and its return, becomes crystallized around this core: but the core itself does not belong to the margin of history where it vanishes into the realms of the timeless, but it belongs to the center, the ever-changing center, that is to say, it belongs to the experienced hour and its possibility. This can be quite clearly recognized in Isaiah.

The fragment preserved for us in Hosea's autobiographical account of his marriage prophesies for the time after the testing and trial of the "many days" in a verse (3, 5), the authenticity of which need not be doubted, if we understand the character of Hosea's rejection of the kingdom, which is historico-critical and not fundamental: "Afterwards the children of Israel shall return and seek YHVH their God and David their king." In Amos (9, 11) YHVH promised to raise up the hut of David that was fallen. In Isaiah's prophecy about the shining of the light in the darkness the everlasting peace (9, 6, EV 7) comes "upon the throne of David and upon his kingdom." It is clear that, even in the first writing prophets, the hope for the fulfilment of God's will regarding the right ordering of the people—and radiating from it the right ordering of the world—was already linked to one of the house of David. But this was not to be any son of David, it was to be the man of the house of David who fulfils YHVH's words, the "righteous" to whom already (2 Sam. 23, 3) those "last words of David" had referred, i.e., the last will of the "anointed of the God of Jacob" (v. 1), which most probably is a contemporaneous text and may even have come from David's own mouth,[10] having been attached to the book about the beginning of the Israelite kingdom as a testimony of fundamental importance. Because he is the righteous, he rules "over man," shines

[10] Cf. Procksch, Die letzten Worte Davids, Kittel-Festschrift (1913), 112ff. Also Lagarde in a course of lectures on the Psalms (Goettingen 1878/9), notes of which are in my possession, expresses such a supposition ("if anything is Davidic this is").

upon the sons of men as the morning light, as the sun of a morning, when "for brightness no mist remains," and as after a shower of rain grass springs up from the earth to meet the new sun, so now after the clouds have dispersed, he the righteous makes all the salvation and the delight of God to spring forth. Whereas the wicked, the worthless element, which arose in the evil days as thornbushes and became an unsurmountable wall,[11] is now subdued and destroyed by him who is invested [12] "with the iron and the wood of a spear" for the battle of liberation. This monumental little song is already filled with that same vision of darkness and shining light, struggle and triumph, as Isaiah's prophecy about the child. And in order to know how the activity of the righteous one as ruler is to be imagined in detail, we must have recourse to two royal psalms referring to one another, which in my opinion come from the period of Isaiah: the second of them, in which there are recognizable traces of the influence of the prophecy of Amos on an upright though very eulogistic courtier, from the time of Uzziah, and the first, which suggests the influence of Isaiah himself, from the time of Hezekiah (cf. Is. 11, 4). The first is the thanksgiving of Hannah which stands at the opening of that same historical book (1 Sam. 2, 1–9), and sets YHVH the "holy" (v. 2) as a type and pattern of "His anointed" (v. 10), as He Who raises the poor out of the dust and seats him with nobles upon the throne of glory, Who guards the feet of His *hasidim,* that is to say His faithful tenants, and the wicked He condemns to be silent in darkness. The second psalm is that instruction to princes (Ps. 72, 1–17), in which God is besought to give the king His judgements and His righteousness to the king's son, that is, to assist the king in imitating the divine righteousness and thereby continuing God's work by vindicating the afflicted of the people, saving the children of the needy, and crushing the oppressor (v. 4, cf. v. 13). The human king appears before us here as the faithful vicegerent of the divine king. Gunkel [13] has argued against taking this psalm as a Messianic psalm that the Messiah is prophesied as coming in the future, whereas here prayer is made for the present. This

---

[11] *Munad* means: become a wall (denominative from *ned,* "wall").

[12] "Invested," lit. his hand is "filled," as the priests' hand in their consecration, i.e., he is fitted with special power.

[13] Die Psalmen (1926), 307.

argument brings us to the very source of the Messianic problem. The original Messianic faith has no reference to "the Messiah" in the sense of a special category: the man, whose absence is felt, the expected, the promised, he is the anointed king, who fulfils the function assigned to him at his anointing. There is no need for more than this. The son of David, who will prove righteous, is the announced. YHVH, Who in primitive days awaited the answer of mankind, and in the age of His rule by the men of His choice the answer of the people, now since He had granted Israel the hereditary kingdom on condition that "the ordinance of the kingship" be observed, that the task be fulfilled—now He awaits the answer of one of the anointed ones. The *nebiim,* who over and over again summoned the insubordinate vicegerents to judgement, were the mouthpiece of this expectation of God, they expressed it *critically.* Now Isaiah gives it the *prophetic* expression. The waiting God promises the coming of the one awaited. He, Who says in "the last Words of David," that He "has" a just ruler and that He will give him to the world, even so awaits the human fulfilment. There is something essential that must come from man. Again we stand—on a higher plane—in the paradox of man's independence, which God has willed and created; we stand in the dramatic mystery of the One facing the other. The "Messianic" prophecy too conceals an alternative. This too is no prediction, but an offer. The righteous one, whom God "has," must rise out of this historic loam of man.

Hence we can understand the problematics of the Immanuel prophecy. Who is "Immanuel"? Perhaps Hezekiah, Ahaz' son, who may have been born the year after the meeting at the "conduit of the upper well." [14] It is easy to understand that in place of the son sacrificed the prophet announces to the king at that time a new son who would be born to him but would not be like him. If so is Hezekiah meant by the promised son of David? He would have been if he had fulfilled the possibility placed in him. But is Immanuel not identical with the child, given to "the people that walk in darkness" as a "great light"? He is, according to the intention of this prophecy; but its intention also depends on the human vital decision and is made to be frustrated thereby, is indeed frus-

[14] We cannot depend upon the Biblical chronology; as is well known there is a contradiction between 2 Kgs. 16, 2, and 18, 2.

trated. The prophecy remains in substance, but the reference to a particular man is suspended. To the burden of the experience of hardening is added for Isaiah the burden of disappointment on account of the non-fulfilment of the message of salvation.

*　　*　　*

For the moment we must speak of the first. Some time after the meeting with Ahaz, after having been told by God to call his second son by the name which linked desolation and salvation together, "Speedy-booty-prey-soon," a symbol of the conquest of Judah's enemies by the might of Assyria, and at the same time also of the future threat to Judah from the same source, Isaiah receives a singular divine communication (8, 5–8). This is to be explained, if we take the verses as they are, without striking out or changing anything as many are accustomed to do. He is told: "Because this people have refused the waters of Shiloah (they are apparently the same 'conduit of the upper pool' at the eastern end of the tower hill, by which the meeting took place and by which three decades later the Assyrian envoy was to demand the surrender of Jerusalem, cf. 36, 2; 2 Kgs. 18, 17), which go slowly, and delight in Rezin and Remaliah's son," therefore YHVH will bring "the waters of the river, the mighty and many," the power of Assyria, first upon the two northern states and afterwards upon Judah, "thy land, Immanuel." If we accept the entire passage as it is, the words "this people" can only refer to the whole people of Israel (so it is used in all the early passages of Isaiah, although with varying degrees of emphasis). It, the people, despises the sovereignty of YHVH "Who dwells on Mount Zion" (Is. 8, 18), the sovereignty that works slowly but without hindrance, and it relies upon kings of flesh and blood and delights in them: the Samaritans rely upon their son of a Nobody, king slayer and throne stealer, and upon his exalted ally, and the Judaeans— this addition every Judaean who heard had to make in his heart —rely upon their king, Ahaz, who is faithless to his Lord Who commands him, and from whose attitude Isaiah appeals to the coming one, "Immanuel." Therefore the host of the king of Assyria will first overflow those lands, then this land. Here ends the announcement. In a much later time, in the first days of Hezekiah's reign, before he had by his Egyptian politics disappointed the prophet's hope, Isaiah whose outlook now embraced the world of nations far more comprehensively and clearly than that of Amos, apparently attached to the memoir a new saying (v. 9f), in which— if this is its right place—these counterplans appear to be included in the great counterplans of the nations, which threaten Mount Zion this way and that, but—the word of Ahaz (7, 7) is repeated—the thing "will not stand"; and the reason follows immediately: "for *immanuel* ('God is with us')," that is to say God is with the remnant, whose leader's name is Immanuel—and perhaps in the secret of his heart Isaiah still at that time called Hezekiah by the name Immanuel.

The pronouncement of YHVH concerning the people's rejoicing in the kings, the prophet seems to have opposed most ardently; the faithful of the house of David set himself up against the Word of God, that confuses the son of David with those kings: so was his heart one with the people of Judah, it wished to be one with them. That this was the hour of a storming of this soul against God's hard judgement, we learn from Isaiah's account (v. 11ff). "With the force of the hand," which is heavy upon him, YHVH "warns" him and the circle of his disciples "against going in the way of this people," who decry it as rebellion, when men see the king in his real nature. Those who know YHVH dare dread no earthly power. He who so gives himself to YHVH's will and "sanctifies Him," to him "He will be for a sanctuary," in which he will find a refuge. Whereas to all the rest, "to the two houses of Israel," when He arises to act terribly in History He will be for a stumbling-block, upon which they will stumble and fall. For— so it is said afterwards in a prophecy of Isaiah, long after Samaria had been laid waste and when Judah was in great danger (28, 21)—"foreign," barbarian, as if it came from one to whom Zion and Jerusalem are strange, is "His work"; only he who has given himself to His will can credit Him, the Lord of Mount Zion, with such a work, and lay hold of the utmost edge of his plan of desolation and salvation.

It was at the same hour of the "force of the hand," it seems to me, that Isaiah was given the promise of "the great light." He receives it, and with it all that flows from it, as *teudah* ("testimony")—apparently a new word and designed to indicate something new—and as *torah* ("instruction") (8, 16, 20). In this two things are involved for him: the revelation of God's coming mercy, and the revelation of man's way to meet it.

In the depth of the prophet's reflection the decision, which had originated and grown out of his meeting with Ahaz, now comes to maturity. Isaiah had through bitter experience realized that YHVH "hides His face from the house of Jacob" (v. 17), but he also realized how great was His longing to show it again. Now the point is that those who know this "wait for YHVH" and "hope for Him" (this verb originally means to be stretched out to meet something, like a line). But the bright prospect shall not be revealed to the people, lest it contribute to "the beclouding of the eyes." It is necessary [15]—so the prophet tells himself (v. 16)—to bind up and to seal like a valid document the testimony received in the spirit "in my *limmudim*"—this word, found here for the first time, is only found here in this sense and in verses dependent on this and referring to this—to whose hearts it is entrusted. Them the prophet joins with his own sons, who present in their symbolic names the two sides of the coming process, into a single company which he designates by the name "the children which YHVH has given me." These with the symbolic power of their names, and the others with the bright rays of the promise hidden in their hearts, are united with the prophet as those appointed by YHVH, in this time of expectancy, "for signs and tokens in Israel" (v. 18). You must wait—so Isaiah addresses them—until, in the hour of "distress and darkness" (v. 22), people thrust out in the darkness, hard pressed, hungry, enraged, will come cursing "their king and their God" (v. 21, presumably we are to read "Molech their god"), will come running to you who are patiently waiting, to you recognized now as the knowing ones, and will entreat you (v. 19), as men make entreaty who "have no dawn" (that is, who are utterly sunk in the darkness without hope of again seeing the sun), will entreat you to seek the necromancers and their spirits—the same people of which it was said in an early prophecy of doom (9, 12, EV 13) that they did not seek YHVH of hosts. Then you shall answer, "What? these sons of nought, that chirp and murmur from under the earth?" And they will say, "Shall not a people seek its gods?" And you will

[15] The two following verbs are to be read as Infinite Absolute.

again reply, "What? on behalf of the living the dead?" (that is, the departed spirits, which they call by the name of god, although really they are not god at all but the dead). Then has the hour arrived: "To the instruction! to the testimony!" Then break open the seal and remove the binding of the document in your hearts, then reply, "The people that walk in darkness see a great light" . . . then will those, who still can see, see it.

*   *   *

The memoir of Isaiah closes with the song of the child, with the saying about the "zeal of YHVH of hosts," the zealous God, Who zealously demands decision and brings decision. It was much later—not at the same time, as most people think—only under the influence of his disappointment over Hezekiah that Isaiah could compose his second Messianic song (11, 1–9). Only in its subject, the person of the coming prince is this second song akin to the first; the view expressed is fundamentally changed. Isaiah no longer acknowledges the ruling dynasty. The idea of the kingly authority has disappeared, he even refrains from mentioning the name of David, although the descent of the expected one from him remains certain; the image, which appeared in the inaugural vision, of the cutting down of the tree that renews itself and now grows from its stump, he applies to the kingly stem of the kingdom: from the *rootstock* of Jesse a new branch will be brought forth. Apparently the expected destruction of the people is now meant to include the destruction of the dynasty, and after it something new will arise, also a "remnant" that will be made into the new substance.[16] But more important is the fact that God's part in the future operation receives very special emphasis. It is YHVH too Who in the song of the child breaks the yoke and establishes the kingdom; but now it is emphasized with incomparable force, that it is the Spirit of God alone, which alights upon the expected one and "inspires"[17] him to fulfil his office. This spirit not only rushes upon him, as it rushed upon the judges and also upon the first king (1 Sam. 10, 6), whom it left to make room for "an evil spirit from YHVH" (16, 14) at the very hour

---

[16] Mowinckel (Psalmenstudien II, 308) thinks that because mention is made here of a stump the passage must be exilic or later. This view can only be upheld if one denies the prophet any sight into the coming catastrophe.

[17] So, as denominative of *ruah,* the verb should be understood.

when it rushed upon the anointed David, in order to rush again upon him "from that day forward"—this spirit rests upon the coming one. The ruler in the song of the child was God's "counsellor," and the operative force was that of the "valiant God" alone; whereas here both—counsel and "valiant strength"—are only the gift of the Spirit to the bearer of the Spirit. And not only wisdom and understanding, which according to the Biblical view come from above, but also everything which otherwise comes from man or is liable to come from him, as part of man's God-willed independence, even the "knowledge of YHVH" and the "fear of YHVH," are given him by the Spirit. He that "rules in the fear of God," as the "righteous" one of the Last Words of David, is only fitted for this in so far as the Spirit inspires him with this fear. Man can only "go forth," as this branch goes forth and sprouts from the stump; in order that it should grow into the tree of fulfilment, God must empower it to do so. Therefore is it brought about that he "vindicates with righteousness the poor," and "settles with equity for the humble of the earth" (cf. Ps. 72, 4), and that "with the breath (*ruah*) of his lips he slays the wicked." In this certainly there is no new "theology" when it is compared with the first Messianic song, but the emphasis is clearly different.

*   *   *

There are those who, not without justification, find the origin of the description of blissful peace among the animals (Is. 11, 6–8) in the pictures of the return of primeval blessedness which are common in ancient cultures; but it seems to me that this idyll of the beasts of prey "staying" with the domestic animals is intended merely as a symbol of the peace of the peoples, perhaps even a symbol in which under the name of wild beasts certain nations were to be recognized. This passage stands between the picture of the just reign of the coming ruler and the prophecy (v. 9) that there shall no more be done any evil in all the holy mountain, for "the earth shall be full of the knowledge of YHVH"—no longer is the earth only to be full of God's radiation as in the song of the seraphim, but it will also be full of human perception, of human acceptance and reception of God's activity. The peace of peoples suits this connection much better than the peace of animals —and especially if we notice that this is the holy mount to which, according to another Messianic prophecy (2, 1–5) all nations "flow" that God may teach them His ways, and that they may receive His arbitration to settle their disputes, so they can beat the swords into ploughshares and nation no more lift up sword against nation. What in the song of the child was proclaimed for the liberated Israel in the image of the burning of the soldiers' boots they had noisily tramped in and of the battle garments rolled in pools of blood, a burning as a fiery ban for YHVH—all this is completed in a greater picture prepared for the whole world of man: the battle of one against another turns into common work upon the earth.

This prophecy, which there is no foundation for detaching from Isaiah (it has been incorporated in the book of Micah 4, 1–5, because he omitted the important last verse and added in its place a nationalistic conclusion, weakening substantially the universalistic element in it), we are certainly right in regarding as the prophet's last Messianic prophecy. And it is remarkable as well for its great historical prospect, in which Mount Zion is the center of the *torah* of the nations, because it makes pronouncement not for an indefinite future, possibly already very near, but for a far-off time, for "the lateness of the days." Only here has Messianic prophecy, which hitherto stood in the full reality of the present hour and all its potentialities, become "eschatology"—even though here too not in the sense of a real ending of history, as in apocalyptic. The conclusion also is important. Announcing that the peoples will then say one to another, "Let us go to the mountain of YHVH," the prophet adds a call to his own people: "Let us go (now) in the light of YHVH." Here the prophet again stresses the part of man: if Israel will go now, as the peoples in after time, in the ways of YHVH, He will not "hide His face" any longer from them, but will make His light to shine for them. It is for Israel to begin this "going," that the nations may be able to follow and that there may arise among all, between Israel and the nations too, the great peace of God in which, as is said in a short passage (Is. 19, 23–25)—which I regard, contrary to the accepted view, as inimitably Isaianic, and ascribe it to the last period of the prophet's life—Israel will stand as "a blessing in the midst of the earth," the center of a peaceful commerce between the two world powers, Egypt and Assyria, which formerly over and over again made use of Israel in their struggles against one another.

And there is something else to note: in the prophecy about the peace of the peoples the figure of the Messiah is missing. This too shows no theological change. Where the matter in question is the ordering of the people and the state according to God's will— as in the two songs—there the personality of the representative, whose task it is to watch over its realization and maintenance, is indispensable. Whereas the prophecy about world peace belongs to a *later* stage of the age of salvation; the Messianic order upon Mount Zion is assumed here to be already accomplished. But the great arbitration and the great instruction upon the mount are YHVH's concern and not His agent's. In neither place is, as some think, the sovereignty of Israel in the world discussed; the peoples persist in their independent existences as before, but they receive the common teaching about God's ways and the common law of peace, and both of these they receive directly from YHVH and not from His representative in Israel. There is here no declaration about a world state under the rule of a world king, but about the reception of a universal revelation, after which—so we may assume without being contradicted by a single word of the prophet—the peoples will continue to live their life, but they will be united in the ways of God, Whom they have come to know. This view of the Messianic continuation of history, that is to say, a history out of which its poison had been taken, Micah afterwards overemphasized and upset its sense by saying that after receiving the revelation every people would again go "in the name of its god" (Mic. 4, 5). Over against this is the consistent view of Isaiah that, together with the "ways," the "name" of God too is become the possession of all (for the strong connection between these two, as also with *kabhod*, cf. Exod. 33, 13, 18; 34, 5ff), this God Who has revealed Himself now to the world of nations, so they bring Him tribute to Mount Zion as the dwelling place of His name, as was said in an earlier prophecy to the Ethiopians (Is. 18, 7), those Ethiopians for whom Amos said that YHVH cares, as He cares for the Israelites.

* * *

Here the question arises: what special function is assigned to the "Messiah" in the early picture of the age of salvation? There are those who think [18] that he is "in fact a superfluous attendant on YHVH's king, and so a kind of double of YHVH." Such views

[18] Mowinckel, *op. cit.*, 298 (cf. also Sellin, Der alttestamentliche Prophetismus, 1912, 173).

are based upon a misunderstanding of the origin of the Messianic belief. The origin of this belief is the treating of God's rule seriously. In the pre-monarchic period YHVH leads the people according to His purpose through those seized by His Spirit, and in the period of the kingdom He rules according to His purpose through His vicegerents anointed in His name, the "kings." Both types of mediation are in accordance with the *realism* of Israelite belief. In order that the divine regime may be truly real, it is necessary that all the actual life of the community be subject to it. This regime cannot be compressed in the "religious domain," that is to say, in the "upper spheres" of being, it is not to be reduced to special holy times and special holy places only. At the center is the holy *God*, Who demands all and gives all. His regime cannot but be political in the highest and most comprehensive sense. The human representation of God, which is indispensable in order to realize the absolutely obligatory character of the divine ordering of the people, cannot by its very nature be the concern of the priests, but only of a "judge" or "king." The institution of the judges passes over to that of the kingdom as soon as it becomes clear that the people now cannot actually acknowledge the divine representation except in the form of the continuity, that is to say, that from now on the people's order is only to be realized as a state order. The dynastic continuity implies a continuity of responsibility to fulfil the divine commission. Connected with the anointing, the sacramental expression of the continuity—this natural substance, oil, which is found in all Israelite rites of anointing, is designed to preserve things from corruption, and so here means, as mentioned, the *preservation* of that which has been given—is the bond of the "ordinance of the kingship." The fundamental and practical opposition of the kings to this constitutional obligation resulted in the mission of the prophets. Unlike the "judges," who come and go, the kings appointed to permanence must be called to account. Against the tendency of the kings (frequently supported it seems by the priests with their sole concern for the autonomy of the sacred domain) to sublimate the commission into a divine right without any obligation, a divine right granting the kings to stand, in accordance with ancient oriental custom, as sons of the deity invested with full power (cf. Ps. 2, 7)—against this tendency the prophets set up the theopolitical realism which does not admit any "religious" subtlety. Over against YHVH's vicegerent on the royal throne, acting unrighteously and therefore unlawful, but powerful, there stands the bearer of YHVH's word, without any power, but certain of his mission, reproving and claiming, reproving and claiming in vain. Sometimes (for instance at the time of the division of the kingdom, and afterwards in the northern kingdom, which unlike Judah had no great tradition of primal legitimacy) this situation turned into a revolt: in place of the unfaithful dynasty a new one arises—which soon brings about the old disappointments once more. In Judah it is different; experience becomes crystallized more and more, but only in enthusiastic prophetic words, the explosive matter increases more and more, but when the outbreak comes, it is not a revolutionary but a Messianic outbreak. The Messiah—whether he is regarded more as the man whom God has found, or as the man whom God has sent—is the fulfiller, he who at last fulfils the function of the vicegerent, through whose agency the ordering of the people under YHVH's leadership will be realized. He is anointed to set up with human forces and human responsibility the divine order of human community. In order to be able to do this, he receives the Spirit. This figure is not drawn from myth, but grows out of history; it is not its form but its garb that is given it by myth, just as was done for YHVH. But—however mythical the garb of the Messiah, as he is shown us in the prophecy of Isaiah, he is in no way, as some scholars imagine, "more than man," [19] nor "of a divine rather than a human sort." [20] As there is no foundation for ascribing to Israel "an idea of the king as the incarnation of the national deity," [21] so there is no foundation for reckoning the Messiah, the fulfiller king, "in the class of the *elim*." [22] Such ideas never made their way into Jerusalem from the great conceptions of the ancient East, but only in late forms showing Persian influence or a "Hellenistic" origin. The Messiah of Isaiah is godlike, as is the man in whom the likeness has unfolded, no more and no less. He is not nearer to God than what is appointed to man as man; nor does he pass over to the divine side; he too stands before God in indestructible dialogue. He is God's "counsellor," because God

[19] Mowinckel, *op. cit.*, 302.
[20] Staerk, Soter I (1933), 4.
[21] Mowinckel, *op. cit.*, 301.
[22] Staerk, *ibid.*

allows this expression too to the human independence which He created in mystery; he accepts the task and accomplishes it, because God wills to operate in human affairs through man. The prophets are afraid of designating him with the name Messiah, Anointed, because the sacrament of anointing is desecrated by its recipients. They are afraid to designate him with the name king, not because the political domain is far from him [23]—he is and remains a "political" figure—but because they set up against the errors of the "kings" who still boast themselves in history the truth of the only true *melekh*, whom the most exalted man can only approach if he serves him. Just because Isaiah was the first to be bold enough to declare that he had seen "the king YHVH of hosts," he can no longer concede the royal dignity even to the rightful anointed one who is to come.

[23] Eichrodt, Theologie des Alten Testaments I, 271. Cf. also Kittel, Theologisches Woerterbuch zum Neuen Testament I, 566.

8. THE GOD OF THE SUFFERERS

A. AGAINST THE SANCTUARY

However forcefully Isaiah fought against the cult emptied of intention, however fiercely his God reproved those who honored Him with their lips, while their hearts were far from Him (Is. 29. 13), and besought them not to trample His courts (1, 12), all this was directed only against the *desecration* of the sanctuary; but the desecration cannot—this is the undoubted conviction of the prophet—remove from the sanctuary its basic sanctity, and it is this sanctity that establishes its inviolability. Even if the land is punished for the guilt of the people, the "flame" which YHVH has kindled in Zion (31, 9) will not be extinguished, the place of His "dwelling" (8, 18), of His "name" (18, 7), will not be broken down, all the nations that fight against this mountain will be scattered like chaff (29, 5, 8) before YHVH, when He descends Himself to fight for Zion (31, 4), and, as they shake their hands against her (10, 32), defends her (31, 5; cf. also the sayings against Sennacherib, which in the midst of the context of the later story are to be regarded as original, 37, 22–29, 33–35). For this mountain is appointed to be the center of God's future kingdom (2, 2; 18, 7). The catastrophe, prophesied by Isaiah, which only the "remnant" shall outlast, does not touch the sanctuary. The sanctuary is that which continues: here already divine reality dwells on the earth, no more to leave it.

But we possess the prophecy of a contemporary of Isaiah, and possibly also a pupil of his, which, unlike the prophecy of his master, announces the destruction of the sanctuary. Micah, a villager from the southwest coastal plain, comes to Jerusalem after prophesying, while still in his native place, the destruction of Samaria and the danger awaiting Judah, and apparently takes to himself the teaching of Isaiah, of which we find many traces in his sayings, once even a verbal repetition (4, 1–5) completed in his own style. But obviously this teaching was not sufficient for him. More radical and inexorable in manner, "full of power by YHVH's spirit and of justice and of might" (Mic. 3, 8) he preaches God's word. There are three things in which he goes further than his master. The first is the criticism of social order: not as one who joins himself with the oppressed, but as one of them he demands an account from the overlords. At the beginning he merely calls (2, 1–5) woe upon those who rob the peasants of field and house, following Isaiah's example (Is. 5, 8–10), although more ardently; but afterwards, apparently when he has been brought to trial (we have only fragments of his account, 3, 1ff), he defies the "heads of Jacob" to their face for "eating the flesh of his people" (v. 3). The second matter is the crystallization of the divine demand. In a dialogue (6, 6ff), which nowadays some would deny to Micah on account of its peculiar style—although such unusual language at moments of high concentration is found in the religious literature of all times—he puts into the mouth of a man from the people the question directed to himself: With what can I obtain the favor of my God? The man goes on adding to his offer until he reaches the offering of his son. The prophet in his reply puts in place of the ethos tied to sacrifice a free religious ethos, but a *religious* ethos indeed. In this the two elements of the imitation of God, the "righteousness" of Amos and the "kindness" of Hosea, which latter here rises to be a "kindly love," are blended with the essence of the relation of faith; to go with God, but humbly: faith, which boasts itself and glories in the relation of faith, faith without shame is no longer faith. And the third thing: the completeness of the punishment for doing that wrong, for refraining from doing this "good." The city "built with blood" (3, 10) cannot stand. All those "who abhor justice and twist all equity" (v. 9), the chiefs who are no chiefs, the priests who are no priests, the prophets who are no prophets, misunderstand Isaiah's message and misuse it, perverting the sense of a sublime verse from a psalm akin to Isaiah (Ps. 46, 6), which speaks of the city of God that will not stagger because "God is in the midst of her," so relying upon the belief that "YHVH is in our midst" and so "no evil will come upon us" (Mic. 3, 11). "Therefore, on your account," Micah calls to them (v. 12), therefore because you feel safe

in all this wickedness, the stronghold of your safety will fall;
"Zion shall be ploughed as a field, and Jerusalem shall be
a heap of ruins, and the mountain of the house as the grove
high places." The verse refers to those places, natural and
artificial, taken over by Israel from the Canaanites. Such a high
place in the wilderness overgrown with a grove will be the mountain of the temple; of the sanctuary itself there will apparently
be left only a few stones, and they will bear witness out of the oaks,
as they resemble the ancient pillars.

In the book under consideration, preserving, as it presumably
does, only a small part of Micah's prophecies and these mingled
with later matter, there follows—clearly in order to temper the
declaration of punishment with the consoling promise of salvation
that would be hereafter—the Isaianic saying about "the lateness
of days," in which "the mountain of YHVH's house will be set
in the top of the mountains." There is no reason to deny Micah
the complete text as found here; that it was taken into the book
is probably due, as I have said, to the conclusion limiting the
spirit of universalism in the passage. Micah believes that the sanctuary will again be established and that YHVH will reign in
Mount Zion over the "remnant" of Israel (4, 7). But the declaration of the rebuilding does not take away from the tremendous fact
that here a Semitic deity wishes to punish his rebellious people by
decreeing destruction upon his sanctuary which they have desecrated.

We know from the Ras Shamra texts what it meant for a Canaanite deity to be without a "house"; "I bring you good tidings,
Baal," cries the goddess Anath, "a house is appointed you, as your
brothers have them." The nomad deity YHVH, however, has not
come with His men to Canaan in order to tie Himself to any house.
The problematics of the Jerusalem temple building can be seen
clearly in the words of Nathan (2 Sam. 7, 4ff); certainly that of
the Shiloh sanctuary in former days was no less considerable. One
may conjecture even in these early days a true religious dilemma.
The ark, which in the Davidic wars still served as a movable
center of the divine might, could no longer now, in the era of
final repose, gather around itself the sacred acts; the high places
are liable to shatter the unity and uniqueness of God and to turn
Him into a multiplicity of local deities; the prophet does approve

the construction of the sanctuary, but he fears lest it trouble his God to be bound "to dwell for ever" (1 Kgs. 8, 13) in the dusky house. This fundamental feeling grows and deepens later in Israelite prophecy. If the sacred order of God's kingdom, as it was appointed in former days, is preserved, it may be hoped that the grace of God's presence will endure for the people; if the order is broken down, YHVH will depart from "His loft" (ibid), "His stronghold" (ibid, cf. Isaiah 18, 4), and will return to heaven, and the sanctuary, which has ceased to be a house, is forsaken. This prophecy, which Isaiah could not prophesy concerning the sanctuary that in his vision had grown to heavenly proportions and in which he had seen "the King," this prophecy now proceeds from the mouth of Micah.

The influence of Micah's words on his hearers and especially on Hezekiah (Jer. 26, 19) can be seen as a historical fact. We may attribute to it Hezekiah's reform of the cult (2 Kgs. 18, 4): the cult is cleansed so that YHVH should not take away His favor from the sanctuary. But in this reform alone—and even as such it was defective—there was no appropriate answer to the denunciation of the social sin by Micah, and by Isaiah before him. We hear nothing of a change of thought and life; but it seems to me that the reform of the cult alone would not have been sufficient to warrant the elders in Jeremiah's day saying (Jer. 26, 19) that Hezekiah was stirred up by Micah's words "to soothe the face of YHVH." Here we must suppose a somewhat deeper change. As Amos had done at Bethel, so Micah in Jerusalem linked his denunciation of the social sin with the prophecy of the destruction of the sanctuary. In the former case the prophecy is quickly fulfilled, after YHVH, Who again and again had "repented" of His decision, said that He would do so no more. Whereas in the latter case we are told a hundred years after Micah's words (ibid), that then YHVH "repented." From Isaiah's connection with the royal court too we may probably conclude that Hezekiah tried to restrain the social unrighteousness. But the attempt was apparently stopped at the outset. At all events nothing of this or of the cult reform survived in the days of his son Manasseh.

*   *   *

The situation was fundamentally different when, a hundred years afterwards, Jeremiah again took up Micah's prophecy. His word, spoken three months after the death of Josiah, presupposes the late king's act, the radical reform of the cult—purification and centralization—with which was linked a great social initiative (cf. Jer. 22, 15f). Jeremiah's speech at the temple gate (7, 1–15; 26, 1–6) was delivered in the hour of the *crisis* of this work. Josiah, who dreamed of a new Davidic kingdom freed from all foreign cultic elements, fell at the first encounter with the Pharaoh. The Pharaoh removed Josiah's son after a reign of a few months, and in his place enthroned another son; the short time, it is true, was not sufficient to put a stop to the cult reform (verses 7, 6b and 9b are not to be understood in this sense), but it was certainly enough to give the social exploitation free course under royal leadership and thus to deprive the reform of its true character, that is the fulfilment of God's will for the order of the people and the sanctuary *as one,* in a unity of "holy" common life. In order to grasp the intention of Jeremiah's speech, it is necessary to set before us the basis of the reform in this its character.

This basis is to be seen in the discovery of a book (2 Kgs. 22, 8ff), which can be identified with the central kernel of Deuteronomy. This book contains, together with homiletic elaboration of a special oral tradition of Moses' Logia or Moses' Hadith,[1] statutes and other traditional writings of many ages adapted and arranged not in Josiah's time certainly but in the days of Hezekiah, when a lot of such collecting seems to have been done. Those responsible for this adaptation and arrangement probably came from a circle of young priests and cult-prophets, who had taken to themselves the spirit of the fragments of Hosea's prophecies referring to Jerusalem, but were also related to the school of Isaiah. Their intention was presumably to form, out of the mass of tradition in their hands, a program for Hezekiah's reform which had come to a halt after the first stage. In the days of Manasseh, who adopted from his environment every remnant of star-worship and magic in Israel, the book was apparently hidden, to preserve it from destruction, and it was brought out of this hiding place in the days of Josiah. In this way the nature and influence of the book become plain to us, for in it are fused into one a legal tradition, which had grown into an organic whole, the spirit of the first writ-

---

[1] Cf. Albright, The Archeology of Palestine, 156f; From the Stone Age to Christianity, 197.

ing prophets, a priestly organizational tendency and a preaching style, schooled on great examples.

It may be said of this book that it is designed to bring the torrent of prophecy into a regular channel: on the one hand the realization of the social demands had to be set within the realm of the "politically possible," and on the other hand the sacred domain, which seemed menaced by the prophetic fight against the degenerate cult, had to be at once purified and supported. The spiritual principle at the basis of this great attempt at a practical synthesis becomes apparent when we consider the Deuteronomic statutes not, as usually, in isolation but in connection with the core of the preaching, without which it is impossible to grasp the character of the book discovered in the days of Josiah. It is the purpose of this principle to fix the authentic interpretation of the ancient formula "YHVH God of Israel." This principle is made up of two chief sources: the one is Hosea's conception of the election of Israel by the love of YHVH and YHVH's expectation to be loved by Israel, and the other is the saying about the eagles' wings (Ex. 19, 4–6a), from which there come two fundamental ideas of the goal of election, namely Israel as a "peculiar treasure" of God in the midst of His world, and Israel as a "holy nation" (in our book of Deuteronomy we find them, 7, 6; 14, 2; and 26, 18f). A third concept, Israel as a "kingdom of priests," could not be adopted, because in the Exodus passage *kohanim* simply means "direct servants," while in Deuteronomy its meaning is naturally the sacred position of sanctuary officers. The idea of love comes first. Of love YHVH has chosen Israel (Deut. 4, 37; 7, 7f; 10, 15); and what He looks for from Israel is that they shall love Him "with all their heart and with all their soul" (6, 5; 11, 13; 13, 4). The early saying about those who love YHVH, which we hear in the Decalogue and as far as the Song of Deborah, is here changed under the influence of Hosea's message into the comprehensive expression of a divine desire. The love of God, which He bestows, and the love of man, which He expects, appear here to correspond to each other with significant emphasis: now it begins from above (7, 8f), and now from below (10, 12, 15). All else that YHVH seeks from Israel comes from this one thing: because they love Him, they cleave to Him (10, 20; 11, 22, 13, 5), follow Him in His ways (10, 12; 11, 22; 13, 5; 19, 9), hearken to His voice (13,

5, EV 4), keep His commandments (10, 13; 11, 1; 13, 5, EV 4),
serve Him (10, 12, 20; 13, 5, EV 4); and one has also to fear Him
because one loves Him (10, 12, 20; 13, 5, EV 4)—the fearing Him
is not to be understood to mean that He is fearful, it is fear and
love in one. Because they love Him with all their heart and with
all their soul, they do what they do for Him with all their heart
and with all their soul (26, 16). Moreover the love between a man
and his neighbor flows from the love of God. In the ancient legal
text the prohibition about oppressing the *ger* ("sojourner") is
joined to the admonition, which brings it home to the hearers,
"for you were sojourners in the land of Egypt" (Ex. 22, 20, EV 21),
and more clearly still: "And you know the soul of the sojourner,
for you were sojourners in the land of Egypt" (23, 9), that is,
you know from experience what is in the heart of the sojourner;
do not bring upon him suffering and affliction, because now you have
the upper hand, do you not know the taste of this suffering! We
find the same argument in a later legal passage (Lev. 19, 33f), also
in connection with the command about loving the sojourner.
In the Deuteronomic passage, however, it is said (10, 18f), that
YHVH Himself loves the sojourner, and therefore Israel should
love him, "for you were sojourners in the land of Egypt." The saying has a new sound and a new sense: in Egypt you felt as sojourners the nature of the longing for the liberating love of God,
but you also know how great is the privilege of partaking of it
(v. 21f); when you were sojourners God bestowed His love upon
you; so then because you love Him, love the sojourner beloved
of Him, Who gives him "bread and raiment" (v. 18, cf. what the
sojourner Jacob says, Gen. 28, 20).

This is the basis set up by the adapters of the traditional material for the cult statutes and the commandments about purification
and unification, codified by them and strongly connected with the
ordinance of social righteousness. It may well be that not all
the sayings recorded were written in the book discovered in
Josiah's day and either all or in part read to him (2 Kgs. 22, 11;
2 Chr. 34, 18). But, at all events, it was not only a collection of
statutes with the addition of blessings and curses which the king
felt so strongly when he listened that he rent his clothes and wept
before YHVH (2 Kgs. 22, 11, 19), but closely attached to this
there was certainly this great preaching, telling Israel that their

God loves them and that all His words—law, blessing, and curse—
flow from His love, and again that YHVH demands nothing from
them but love, and expression of this love in the ways of life. It
is true the prophetess, when questioned, only mentions cultic sins
(v. 17), true the writer tells only of the reform ˙of the cult (23,
4–24)—both apparently were influenced by the priests—but the
covenant, Josiah's renewal of which for "all the people" "before
YHVH" is here related, embraces all "the words of this covenant
written in this book," and the writer emphasizes in Deuteronomic
language that this renewal of the covenant, this return to YHVH,
is made "with all the heart and with all the soul" and in accordance
with "all the instruction of Moses" (v. 25). It is not a fear of
dread that stirs the spirit of the young king, but a love-fear, and
what he sets out to do is not only a reform of the cult, but a
restoration of the holy order of the people. Rightly has the book
been designated "the closing of a social revolutionary movement,"[2] striving "for the reform of the state and state cult in
general," but this reform really means the restoration of the old.

Evidence of this is to be seen more clearly than elsewhere in
Jeremiah's obituary notice (22, 15f), where in the midst of strong
reproof of the deeds of Josiah's lawless and oppressor son, of whom
the prophet prophesies that he would be buried like an ass, he mentions the deeds of his father, who "did justice and righteousness"
and "vindicated the cause of the poor and needy."

Here too there occurs a saying which, in my opinion, has always
been misunderstood. "Your father," says Jeremiah, "has he not
eaten and drunk, and done justice and righteousness?" This is vari-
ously explained to mean, "your father has done well for himself,
enjoying in measure the pleasures of the table,[3] and yet . . ." or
"he has lived well frugally and . . ." or "justice to your father was
as natural as eating and drinking." None of this can be drawn out
of the text, nor does it fit the underlying tone. Josiah's "eating and
drinking" here belong, it seems to me, to the *covenant making* as
much as the "eating and drinking" of the elders on Sinai (Ex. 24,
11) ; he takes part in the holy covenant meal, enters the covenant
with YHVH, and henceforth fulfils it by himself practising justice
and righteousness, and as regards men by vindicating the cause of

[2] Galling, Die Erwaehlungstraditionen Israels (1928), 82.
[3] Skinner, Prophecy and Religion (1922), 248.

the poor and needy. "This is to know Me," YHVH says by Jeremiah—that is that knowledge which Hosea declared to be the innermost essence of the relationship of faith: whosoever helps the suffering creature, comes into close contact with the Creator, and this is here called "knowing YHVH." The most sublime conception in the teaching of his master Jeremiah sees realized in the life of the king.

In Josiah, as distinct from the lukewarm Hezekiah, we see true emotion and change. Already in his youth together with his plans for restoring the kingdom to its old position he had set out to free cult and culture from Assyrian influences,[4] now he removes all Canaanite traces too, and presses on towards primitive purity, which means for him apparently not only the purification of the sanctuary but also of the order of the community, the borders of which he strives to enlarge so as to embrace the original pan-Israelite kingdom. In all his successful works and struggles for the new kingdom he ventures to take part in world power politics, in order to defend the newly won freedom against Egypt on her way to help the tottering Assyria; he goes forth to meet the Pharaoh and falls. Together with him falls the whole reform, operation and plan. The kingdom of Judah survived him by less than a couple of decades.

* * *

Jeremiah was the son of a priestly family of the country, connected, it is reasonable to suppose, with Abiathar of the house of Eli, whom Solomon drove out of Jerusalem; from this we may infer that it was traditionally linked with the recollection of the first catastrophe, the capture of the holy ark, and the destruction of the sanctuary at Shiloh by the Philistines. If this supposition is right, then Jeremiah is completely independent of this tradition: like Samuel, whom he places next to Moses (15, 1), so he too sees (7, 12) in that catastrophe the action of YHVH Himself: having "made His name (that is to say, the earthly presence expressed by the Tetragrammaton) dwell" in Shiloh, the name has been desecrated by the iniquities of the priests, and therefore He has removed it from the house and renounced the ownership of the place.

Moses and Samuel appear to Jeremiah as representatives of the

[4] Cf. Procksch, Koenig Josia (Festgabe fuer Th. v. Zahn, 1928), 25ff.

faith of the people's early days: true prophets, great intercessors, but at the same time having in their hands the conduct of the cult. He, the priest, who at his call was uprooted from this as from all his inherited associations, adjudges to the free prophet the unqualified leadership of the religious life of the people. Not the priest but the prophet he regards as the mediator between heaven and earth, messenger of God and intercessor in one. The contact between godhead and manhood in his view is not bound up with the rite but with the *word*. The rite is a work of man and it is accepted or rejected by God, according to the feelings of the men performing it; whereas the word comes again and again from heaven as something new, and makes its abode within man. It is true, the priests too (and together with them the professional prophets attached to the sanctuary of king's court) have the duty of administering the word; but this is partly the treasury of traditional sayings and songs which they watch to see that it is not changed, partly the oracular sentence they impart to the inquiring persons, and partly psalmody and preaching—the latter, as we know from Deuteronomy and the kindred books of the Bible, being especially a concern of the temple prophets. But the word of God, the bearer of which Jeremiah knows himself and every true unofficial prophet to be, is of another sort altogether; again and again it breaks into the whole order of the word world and breaks through. The aforementioned is an addition to rite, and is even nothing but rite in the form of language; whereas the other, the divine word, which suddenly descends into the human situation, unexpected and unwilled by man, is free and fresh like the lightning. And the man who has to make it heard is over and over again subdued by the word before He lets it be put in his mouth (1, 9; 20, 7). This is not the expression of a familiar deity, with whom man comes into regular contact in fixed places and at fixed times. He, Who speaks, is incomprehensible, irregular, surprising, overwhelming, sovereign. Therefore it is the virtue of this word, and of this alone, to lead, that is to say, to show the way.

He, to whom and by whom the word is spoken, is in the full sense of the word a *person*. Before the word is spoken by him in human language it is spoken to him in another language, from which he has to translate it into human language, to him this word is spoken as between person and person. In order to speak to man,

God must become a person; but in order to speak to him, He must make him too a person. This human person not only adopts the word, it also answers, lamenting, complaining to God Himself (15, 18), disputing with Him about justice (12, 1), humbling himself before Him, praying. Only Jeremiah of all the Israelite prophets has dared to note this bold and devout life conversation of the utterly inferior with the utterly superior—in such a measure is man here become a person. All Israelite relationship of faith is dialogic; here the dialogue has reached its pure form. Man can speak, he is permitted to speak; if only he truly speaks to God, there is nothing he may not say to Him.

Because man, who is addressed, is person in the full sense of the word, the occurrence here is not one of the divine "formation" alone, the formation of the individual person "from the womb" (1, 5), which recalls the divine "formation" of the first man from the dust of the ground, but before this formation there is a "knowledge," a first contact of the Creator with the single creature, and after the formation, still in the womb, there comes a "sanctification" for the special vocation. In the account of the call the "boy" (v. 6) is told what it is for the sake of which he is sent: he is appointed to be "a prophet to the nations."

It is again beginning to be acknowledged now [5] that the oracles against the nations, collected in chapters 46–51 of the book of Jeremiah, are for the most part original and come from the period of the prophet's youth. But the phrase "I have appointed thee a prophet to the nations" is not to be paraphrased in the words "I order thee to speak in My name to the single nations"; it means rather: I authorize thee to declare my will for *this hour* in the history of the nations. It can only mean this, however, if and because this is a *special* hour in the history of the nations. And such is in fact the hour in which the end of the Assyrians and of the supremacy of Egypt occurs. Amos, living in the period of the greatness and the greatest rivalry of the two empires, had only to call certain peoples to justice and to declare that YHVH's eyes are upon the sinful kingdom to destroy it; Isaiah prophesies the decline of the insolent Assyria and Egypt; after an eventful century Jeremiah, in his position in face of the shaking of the ancient

---

[5] Cf. Bardtke, Jeremias der Fremdvoelkerprophet, Zeitschrift fuer alttestamentliche Wissenschaft, Neue Folge XII (1935), XIII (1936).

oriental powers, receives the task of seeing all individual things in one and of interpreting the world hour as God's action in history, judgement and renewal. He is appointed (1, 10) "this day over the nations and the kingdoms, to root out and to pull down, to build and to plant." It is not laid upon him to express the different verdicts of God upon the death and resurrection of the nations, but to show God's sway, the pulling down and building up of the world's architect, the rooting out and the planting of the world's gardener. God lets the prophet note His action, as such, in the chronicles of the Spirit. That he is "appointed" "to root out," means that he has to say of the rooting out that it is such. He has to *say* what God *does*.

This core of his prophecy Jeremiah expresses in various forms, but not in his speeches to the nations, only in those to his own people; for in the shaking of the great powers, preparation is made for the fall of Judah, and to announce this is the essential mission of Jerusalem's last pre-exilic prophet. In the potter's house he sees how clay is made on the wheel into vessels, and imperfect vessels made into clay again so that new vessels can be made out of it, and he hears YHVH saying (18, 6) that Israel in His hand is as clay in the hand of the potter: the human clay which is not perfect suffers the fate of the imperfect clay. To uproot and pull down is God's planning for the rebellious nation and the sinful kingdom, but if they return to Him, He will repent of the evil; so too, if nation or kingdom turn to evil, He will repent of the building and planting, which He intended to do for them (v. 7–10). Here once more the prophetic alternative is clearly shown. Israel indeed pays no heed to God's "plans," and follows its own plans (v. 11f)—to its own ruin. But many years later, after the punishment had taken place with the deportation by Nebuchadrezzar of important sections of the people, Jeremiah in the parable of the figs announces to the deported God's word (24, 6), that He will bring them back and build and no more pull down, plant and no more root out. And again later, when those left in Palestine wish to go to Egypt, God's word comes and promises the same thing (42, 10) in the same image, if they remain in their place. This the people refuse to do; so the other thing is far from them. There is no other divine activity in Israel at this world hour but pulling down and rooting out, as it is too at this time in the

world of nations. This is expressed in the last of these announce-
ments supplementing one another on the meaning of the hour (ch.
45), in the form of a last and final word. This is God's word to
Baruch, Jeremiah's trusted disciple and scribe. It belongs to an
earlier time, but Baruch is certainly right in putting it at the end
of his book. He had complained of the course of events, YHVH
adding day by day grief to his sorrow, and giving him no rest;
now God sends him the answer: "Lo, what I have built I pull
down, and that which I have planted I root out, even all the earth
—and thou, dost thou seek great things for thyself? !" The "great
things," which the suffering man seeks for himself, the "rest" without grief, is not even found with God Himself at the hour when He,
acting in history, comes near to destroying the work of His own
hands: He suffers by His doing. No longer as formerly in His
words to Isaiah (Is. 18, 4) does He look down in silence and patience "as a cloud of dew in the heat of harvest"; He stands over
the wheel, and presses the misshapen vessels into a lump of clay
—but He shares in the trouble of this rebellious human clay which,
on the potter's wheel of world history, takes shape and loses it
again through its own fault.

It is in Hosea's words that we first hear of the God Who is
zealous and suffering at once, suffering for His betrayed love and
zealous for it. Here, in the words of a later disciple of Hosea, the
same deity speaks to us. Now indeed He no more "repents" (Jer.
15, 6), after having done it again and again in vain, because He
sees that the people no more change their impure manner than
the leopard his spots (13, 23); but in the midst of punishment,
when he "hears" that the Ephraimites, long before carried into
exile, repent in a foreign land and return in penitence, there occurs
in his soul again what is described in Hosea's words (Hos. 11, 8):
His inward parts are moved for "His firstborn" (Jer. 31, 19, 8, EV
20, 9). And for Jerusalem itself too he makes complaint in the
midst of the punishment (12, 7): "I have forsaken my house, I
have abandoned my inheritance, I have given the friendship of
my soul into the hand of her enemies." The temple is not yet
destroyed, but after He had in Jeremiah's temple speech announced its destruction, and even then the people had not returned
in penitence, YHVH "forsook" His house: His protecting *kabhod*
is therein no more.

It is on this basis, on the basis of these acts and sufferings of God, that the temple speech is to be understood.

*   *   *

Josiah's reformation meant not only the purification of the cult, externally (by removing foreign objects and rites) and internally (by a practical instruction concerning the necessity of the intention: there is no true worship of God where there is no righteousness), but also its centralization at the temple in Jerusalem. Probably the most rigorous version of this demand (Deut. 12, 4–12) does not belong to the Hezekianic arrangement and adaptation of the book, but was introduced later. In this case this is one of the passages against which Jeremiah's protest concerning "the lying style of the scribes" (Jer. 8, 8) is directed. Supposedly in the priests' house at Anathoth there was preserved in an oral tradition the contents of a collection of Moses' words, which could not have been published in writing in Manasseh's days. If this is so, it is very possible that the prophet's strong emphasis upon "the words of this covenant" (11, 2) refers to the book of Deuteronomy, that is to an extract known to the community chiefly through public reading, whereas the sections later disseminated among the people and apparently influenced by the special views and needs of the Jerusalem priesthood, stirred up his opposition. In these matters we can do little more than conjecture, but the silence of Jeremiah, which extended so many years between the reform and the death of Josiah, is best understood as meaning that he did not wish, on the one hand, to oppose the action of the king, while, on the other hand, he was no longer able to approve of it. It may be supposed that the strict centralization of the cult, which affected not only the syncretistic sanctuaries but also those which had remained pure, was not easy for his sense of faith. Some argue for the religious merit and value of the centralization, that the many local places of worship opposed the concept of YHVH's unity, as this is most powerfully expressed in the Deuteronomic confession of unity (6, 4); in their opinion the idea of an omnipresent God was "above the grasp and imagination of antiquity." [6] But it is not necessary—as they maintain—to see in this picture the fruit of a later development: this deity had never been linked to any particular place—in the beginning He had travelled before

[6] Westphal, Jahwes Wohnstaetten (1908), 114.

His nomadic believers, afterwards He had come in the storm to the aid of the settlers, and wherefore should He not be sought out of every man seeking his God in a holy place? Against this the absolute centralization takes from the religious life of the people much of its simple continuity and thereby of its naturalness: hitherto meal and offering were bound up together, now they are to be separated, hitherto there was everywhere holy soil, now it is in Jerusalem only. Villagers, such as Micah and Jeremiah, felt the danger of the predominance given to the one sanctuary, a danger which was hidden from the Jerusalem aristocrat, Isaiah. Isaiah knows only the holy awe which fills his own soul for the place chosen by YHVH, whereas they—Micah and Jeremiah—feel also the false pride and confidence attaching to the idea of the center of the world. It is true Jeremiah also loves the popular pilgrimage to the holy mount, and prophesies (31, 6, EV 7) that the day will come, when the watchers in the re-inhabited Ephraim shall cry from the mountains, "Arise, let us go up to Zion unto YHVH our God!" But the beginning and the renewal must be preceded by the breakdown and the great age of affliction, in which faith so renews itself that even the strictest centralization can no more injure it, but only serve as its most worthy symbol.

The fact that the vain confidence is the enemy of faith appeared to Jeremiah as the problematics of the reform, the vain confidence of those who say they have the sanctuary and the vain confidence of those who say they have the book. "How," he addresses the false leaders of the people (8, 8), "do you say, 'We are wise, and YHVH's instruction is with us!'?" They have the book, but YHVH's *word,* this living, ever new, unforeseen, unforeseeable, the prophetic word, they reject, and without the rousing and renovating life of the word even the book does not live—"What wisdom have they?!" (v. 9). But the prophet also recognizes this, that they find in the midst of Deuteronomy itself the food for such confidence, reading its attempt at a synthesis as a compromise. The book claims to stand good forever, to continue its existence without addition or subtraction (Deut. 4, 2; 13, 1, EV 12, 32), that which is revealed is forever deposited in it, handed over and belonging to Israel, whereas the other side, the secret things, are left in the hand of YHVH alone (29, 28, EV 29). Against such an exact division there stands the fact of God's word itself, the word spoken afresh, the word *happening*, the "fire," the "hammer" that "smashes the rock" (Jer. 23, 29, cf. 5, 14); over against it stands the experience of the actual divine speech to man, the speech that time and again reveals the secret things.

Centralization and codification, undertaken in the interests of religion, are a danger to the core of religion, unless there is the strongest life of faith, embodied in the whole existence of the community, and not relaxing in its renewing activity.

Jeremiah knows that he is appointed to be a tester in the great people's foundry (6, 27); [7] not only does he receive a function and message like all true prophets, he also has to scrutinize the present disposition of the people. And so he sees how the bellows of the reform work "pant" (v. 29), but also that the strongest fire can only succeed in melting the lead but not in removing the dross; the tester shows YHVH the result, and the deity rejects the useless silver—"rejected silver" it is called henceforth (v. 30). The tragic king and his helpers cannot refine the people. From three points of view the reform apparently failed fundamentally. Socially, the powerful ones did not let it touch them, and Josiah's son and heir became the worst among them. The second aim, the purification of the cult, lasts only during the lifetime of Josiah, after his death the vile confusion of gods returns again. Only the third, the centralization of the sanctuary, survives—in the hearts the action of the priests has not begotten anything but confidence in the temple. It is to the temple that the judgement sentence is directed, and it is to proclaim this that YHVH now sends His tester to the temple gate.

*   *   *

Only a few months had passed since the battle at Megiddo. These months mark a most important incision in Israelite religious history. The question "Why?" presses upon all hearts. Why has the king, who unlike his predecessors did YHVH's will in everything, been snatched away in the prime of his life and in the midst of his plans for the realization of God's word, at the hour when he went forth undismayed, trusting in God's word (Deut. 20, 1), to fight the superior force? Why is the land that had become

---

[7] The verse is based on a play on words: first the prophet is appointed as *bachun*, a watch-tower (against the people), cf. 1, 18, whereas now he is to act as *bachon*, a tester (of metals).

strong and independent in the days of the idolater Manasseh, now once more fallen under a foreign yoke? The question penetrates the innermost depths of faith. YHVH has been proclaimed by the prophets as the God of justice. The question comes to include the justice of the leadership of the world. Jeremiah himself apparently is seized by it although from a personal motive; for at this time probably the question addressed to God arises, later to be deposited by the prophet in his strangest of all diaries (Jer. 12, 1) in conjunction with his personal experiences (biography and history are mixed together in this prophet, as will be seen): "Wherefore does the way of the wicked prosper?" The ready teaching about reward and punishment in the life of individual and community is shaken. This deity is no more to be formulated. What Isaiah and Micah regarded as the characteristic of the coming age (Is. 8, 17, Mic. 3, 4), what the book of Deuteronomy announced most emphatically for the day of wrath, has happened now: YHVH "hides His face," He has become an enigma. And it is the same thing that God's answer expresses, which Jeremiah may have felt already at that time and later noted in his diary (Jer. 12, 5) in connection with personal matters: "If thou hast run with footmen and they have wearied thee, how wilt thou contend with the horses?" As life, so history will lead to even deeper suffering and mystery. The prophet sees a barrier stretched across his prophetic outlook.

One thing indeed now becomes clearer to him than ever: the reform that did not reform the life of the people is nothing in God's eyes. But the people have no knowledge of this, the people calm the anguish of their hearts for the coming fate with the possession of the indestructible temple; they run to the house and cry (7, 10), "We are delivered!" As the fugitive, seeking asylum, "seizes the horns of the altar" (1 Kgs. 1, 50f; 2, 28), so they cling to the delusive idea of the inviolability of God's house and city: "YHVH's temple, YHVH's temple, YHVH's temple, are these!" (Jer. 7, 4). Jeremiah sees himself as sent to the temple gate to combat this illusion.

His words here simply mean this, that God does not attach decisive importance to "religion." Other gods are dependent on a house, an altar, sacrificial worship, because without these things they have no existence, their whole nature consisting only of what the creatures give them; whereas "the living God and eternal king" (10, 10; a post-Jeremianic saying, but in his spirit) is not dependent upon any of these things, since He is. He desires no religion, He desires a human people, men living together, the makers of decision vindicating their right to those thirsting for justice, the strong having pity on the weak (7, 5f), men associating with men. He rejects this people here, which "enter these gates to throw themselves down before YHVH" (v. 2), He rejects them, because by the iniquity they commit one with another they frustrate the divine order of the people and profane God's name, as the name of Israel's Lord, and therefore He also rejects the desecrated sanctuary (v. 11): "Is this house, upon which My name is called, become a den of robbers in your eyes? ! Behold, I too have seen (that this is truly so)." A sanctuary, in which robber men oppress and plunder, enjoying the refuge it gives them against the enemy without, *is* a den of robbers and nothing else.

"Stealing, murder, adultery, and false swearing . . . and following after other gods" (v. 9)—it is the decalogue, the tablets of the nomad tribes, which Jeremiah holds out before the religion-confiding people as the law they daily transgress; but here, in contradistinction to the Pentateuchal text and order, the sins against religion come at the end (as in v. 6), because the prophet has to proclaim just this, that God seeks something other than religion. Out of a human community He wills to make His kingdom; community there must be in order that His kingdom shall come; therefore here, where He blames a people for not having become a community, man's claim upon man takes precedence of God's claim.

Over against the "lying words" of false confidence (v. 4 and 8)— and here we are forced to recall that "lying style of scribes"—the prophet sets the decalogue. It is as if he, standing at the gate of the temple, put forth his hand into the innermost room and took from the ark the tablets in order to show them in a changed order to the people. Opposite the self-reliant, spirit-forsaken civilization religion there stands here for all to see God's ancient instruction of the nomad tribes.

Later, immediately after the fulfilment of the prophecy and the destruction of temple and city, a saying is handed down to us (3, 16f), which comes probably from the mouth of Jeremiah and, if not, then at all events from his school; it says about the ark, that in the days of the return it will no more be remembered nor missed, nor shall they think any more of making a new one. The ark had a double function—and again it is not important why and how the two functions became blended: it contained within itself the tablets of the covenant, and it carried YHVH's throne. In those days, the saying adds (v. 17), there will be no need of a special throne any longer, for the whole of a sanctified Jerusalem, in which according to this prophecy, as according to Isaiah's prophecy, the nations will meet, will be God's throne. And again there will be no need of the ark of the tablets, for the people will no longer be dependent on tablets. In the little book of comfort (ch. 30 and 31), which apparently Jeremiah wrote after the catastrophe, a new covenant is promised the assembled people. This will not be written on tablets as the covenant YHVH made with the fathers when He "seized them by the hand to bring them out of the land of Egypt" (31, 31, EV 32), and concerning the fulfilment of which the prophet had been struggling with the people (11, 3), but it will be written upon the hearts of all (31, 32, EV 33); only by this means can the word of the first covenant-making reach perfect realization: YHVH Israel's God, Israel YHVH's people. The Deuteronomists thought (Deut. 30, 14) that already it was so, that God's word was found in the heart of the people and needed nothing save "to do it"; whereas Jeremiah, who, in spite of the importance of the personality as such in his eyes, ascribes less power of decision to man than did the prophets before him, thinks it necessary that first the revelation should touch the souls, and he believes and promises that it will indeed come: YHVH Himself will write His word upon Israel's heart, without tablets, without any intermediary. No tablets and no ark—as Samuel did not restore the ark after the catastrophe of Shiloh to which Jeremiah refers in his speech at the temple gate, so apparently he too would not return it if he could. When God puts His word in the heart of the people, there is no longer need of any external support. Indeed, the prophet in his little book of comfort blesses the redeemed Jerusalem and the Zion of the future, which shall see the realization of God's will (Jer. 31, 22, EV 23): "YHVH bless thee, O pasture of righteousness, O mountain of hallowing!" Zion is to be the place of pilgrimage for the nations. But of the future temple which Ezekiel, the man on the borderline of prophecy and apocalypse, knows how to describe in all its details, Jeremiah is silent, not even allowing place in the meantime for Micah's "grove high places." In Baruch's story of the conquest of the city (39, 1–10) too, there is no mention of the temple; its overthrow and the capture of its vessels is not recorded at all. It appears that Jeremiah himself only once trod the temple area after his speech at the gate; this was presumably at the festival following, in order to declare to the people assembled that the fate of the city would be that of the pitcher he had broken at the potter's gate (19, 15); afterwards the officer not only has him flogged and put in the stocks, but also forbids him further entry (36, 5).

The protest of the prophetic generations against the spirit-bereft cult reached its extreme expression in the passage about the robbers' den. In the trial, when the elders recalled in Jeremiah's defence Micah's forgotten prophecy and its effect (26, 17ff), there appears once more in the prophet's mouth the alternative (v. 13, cf. v. 3). After this the prophetic "if" ceases. What is still heard is different: the tester's accusation of the mighty ones and their attendants, and the complaint of the witness about the approaching evil—with no more hope except of the future "return."

*   *   *

With the accession of Jehoiakim, that is with the temple speech, Jeremiah's fight against the kings begins, and we have evidence of this in the prophecy about the royal house (22, 1–23, 4), words unparalleled in the literature of the ancient Orient for their liberty of spirit. But this fight against the kings, as with all the former prophets including Hosea, is not fundamental: with the same expression as is used in the "last words of David" (2 Sam. 23, 3), in the same language as is used in the prophecy of Micah (5, 1, EV 2), so here promise is made of a "righteous sprout," which performs "justice and righteousness on earth" (Jer. 23, 5), of the "ruler" whom YHVH will let come near to Him so he may approach Him (30, 21), as distinct from those who reigned after Josiah. It is not meant to suggest that the priestly office was to be laid upon him. The traditional picture from Samuel (1 Sam. 10, 6, 10; 16, 13) to Isaiah (Is. 11, 2) of the approach of the chosen one to God: that the Spirit descends upon him, originates in prophetic experience; Jeremiah the priest prefers the cultic image (Num. 16, 5, 9, 10; Ex. 28, 43, and 30, 20) : the priestly experience is not that of a sudden inspiration from on high, but of man's regular approach to the altar, of permission to draw near. Just as Jeremiah has nothing to say about the future of the temple, so he says nothing about the future of the priesthood (the prophecy about its future establishment, 33, 18, 21, 22, is not to be regarded as genuine) ; but just as we may not infer from the silence in the first case, so it is wrong to infer from the silence in the second case, that he denied such a future; it is simply that according to his view it was no longer possible to make a pronouncement concerning the temple domain. From the beginning of his prophesying he had been fighting against the priests who "handle" the Torah but do not ask after God's presence and do not know Him (2, 8), against the degeneration of the priestly station, not against the station itself, just as his fight against the cult was directed against its deterioration. He was indeed, more than all his predecessors, inclined to feel that, for the sake of hallowing the whole life, the partition between sacred and profane should be removed; but it was certainly clear to him that this was not the appropriate hour to obtain a picture of the future order of the relationship between God and man. With the expectation of a new covenant which would come after the end of the distress, and in which God's living word would be written on the heart of the people, there was no place to foretell the forms in which the changed heart would express itself. The difference between Jeremiah and his contemporary, Ezekiel, is the difference between pure prophecy, bound up altogether with the historical hour and God's direct speaking in it, and a prophecy becoming problematic, which peeps into a future which, so to speak, is already at hand and so describes it. The pure prophet is not imaginative or, more precisely, he has no other imagination than the full grasping of the present, actual and potential. His God is the God of a truth which, as far as it is open to mortal man, enters really into time, interwoven with human deeds and misdeeds, that is, it can never be depicted beforehand. "For there is no divination in Jacob, nor soothsaying in Israel," so it is put basically in Balaam's speech (Num. 23, 23). "It will be said in time to Jacob and Israel, what God is working." The true prophet, this quivering magnet needle, pointing the way to

God, is altogether bound by this "time." He is bound by the situation of the hour in which God is preparing the work He has in mind, and therefore the decision is not yet made, but is being made. Men cannot hear from his mouth, the mouth of the true prophet, what they wish to hear; they can only· hear what they shall hear, that is what is designed in this hour and set before them, that they may let drop into it their "Yes" and "No," their decisions and their refusals to decide, the molten metal of their hour, and supply God with the material for His work.

It is in the light of these Biblical theologoumena that we are to see Jeremiah's chief battle, that against the "false prophets." These are court and public servants, professional speakers who, in the hour of decision, when all depends on recognising YHVH's historic warnings and attending to His behests, set up themselves against the warning with promises of salvation, and think that with such empty talk they will easily heal the rupture of their people (Jer. 6, 14) by encouraging them to meet the historical danger with the usual historical action. In them Jeremiah necessarily sees the worst enemies of his mission, for over against the reproving and challenging word of God, over against God's word that burns within him they set a soothing sham word, which the people naturally prefer to the word of the prophet. The priests lead astray by teaching the empty cult as the way to YHVH; whereas the false prophets misuse and pervert the manifestation of God itself, by declaring the wishful vision of their heart as proceeding from YHVH's mouth (23, 16). So long as the fraud works outside the actual domain of truth, it can but seduce; and the seduced ones can be rescued by those who succeed in showing them that there is a domain of truth. Whereas when the fraud enters with its activity the very domain of truth, if it sets up over against the hard divine word of demand and judgement the easy word of a pseudo-deity, a compromising deity, who is ready to help unconditionally, then it introduces confusion into the heart of the hearer, who is addressed on two sides, and with the greatest of ease confounds the severe grace, which only the entirely devoted person can experience, with the promised favor of the people's patron. Over against such confusion the true word is almost powerless, in no respect here appearing as endowed by the heavenly Lord with supernatural might. God does not corroborate it; He leaves to man the choice of opening his heart to the hard truth or of accepting the easy fraud as truth; He does not in any way lighten this choice for man; He does not endow His declaration with energy; He does not throw onto the scales of man's soul even a particle of His limitless power. His prophet, this man without office, without influence, weak and shy, pronounces His word undismayed even to martyrdom, he is "as His mouth"; whereas the mouth itself, God's mouth, is silent towards the people. God will speak to it only in the language of history, and in such a way that it will be able to explain sufficiently what happened to it by the coincidence of adverse circumstances. This God makes it burdensome for the believer and light for the unbeliever; and His revelation is nothing but a different form of hiding His face. The tradition of Sinai had another story, and certainly Jeremiah kept to it, not only to the making of the covenant on the mount, but also to the preceding speech from the midst of the fire. But his own solitary powerlessness, in which nevertheless the word lived, stood as reality beside that tradition. And from time to time it seems as if this powerlessness was changed into might. The *nabi* Hananiah who, seven years before the destruction, after the temple vessels had been carried off, took from Jeremiah's neck and broke the heavy yoke, the sign of the ordered subjection (28, 10), and prophesied three times as YHVH's word that so He would within two years break the yoke of Nebuchadrezzar (v. 11), died two months afterwards according to Jeremiah's word—according to the word spoken (this is significant) not in immediate response but some time later, after Jeremiah had waited in silence for the word and after he had heard it. Sign had stood over against sign, now the true sign was proved to be deadly real; certainly the people received the news with feelings of terror; but we are not told that the people's way of life was influenced by this news.

As distinguishing marks between "true" and "false" prophets, Jeremiah declares in his first reply to Hananiah (v. 8f) that the false prophets prophesy salvation and that their prophecy is not fulfilled. The first mark which Jeremiah repeatedly stresses (6, 14; 14, 13; 23, 17) we find already suggested in the words of Micah, in whose eyes the false prophet is the intoxicator (Mic. 2, 11), and the second mark we find in the statute of the prophets in Deuteronomy (Deut. 18, 21f). Both hints are an expression of the starting point of problematics. Surely there is no need to make it clear that the fulfilment or non-fulfilment of any prophecy is not a sufficient mark—apart from the fact that anyhow the hearer cannot in this way distinguish at the time of hearing; unfulfilled prophecies of true prophets are numerous enough.[8] But the very nature of true prophecy, its character of manifest or concealed alternative, forbids the use of such a criterion; the prophetic theologoumenon about the future, in the determining of which human decisions share, the principle which we also find as the basis of Jeremiah's attitude, is in opposition to all assertion of prediction in the apodictic sense. Likewise the distinction between a prophecy of salvation and a prophecy of disaster, widespread until our day, is unsuitable and can only be understood of a time in which the promise of salvation silenced the call to return. Isaiah before this time prophesied clearly that the city would not be captured, although he knew in the depths of his heart the contradiction into which the promise of salvation ventured, and bore this contradiction within; and Deutero-Isaiah after this time has simply and solely a message of good things. It is not whether salvation or disaster is prophesied, but whether the prophecy, whatever it is, agrees with the divine demand meant by a certain historical situation, that is important. In days of false security a shaking and stirring word of disaster is befitting, the outstretched finger pointing to the historically approaching catastrophe, the hand beating upon hardened hearts; whereas in times of great adversity, out of which liberation is liable now or again to occur, in times of regret and repentance, a strengthening and unifying word of salvation is appropriate. Jeremiah opposes the dogmatics of a guardian deity, Deutero-Isaiah the dogmatics of a punishing deity; both of them venerate the living God Who is exalted above all dogmatic wont, and His historically expressed will, which they interpret. Jeremiah, who announces the disaster, and Deutero-Isaiah, who announces the salvation, both prophesy so for the sake of the covenant between godhead and manhood, for the sake

[8] Kuenen has collected them clearly and on the whole correctly in his book "The Prophets and Prophecy in Israel" (English edition 1877), even if he is not right in every point.

of the kingdom of God; the "false prophets" announce what they announce for its own sake, that is to say for the fulfilment of man's wishes. They "dream dreams" and recount them (Jer. 23, 25, 27), or even declare the "phantom of their heart" (v. 26); this does not mean that they are to be denied integrity—certainly many of them are honest patriots—but that they brew out of the wishes and impulses, common to them and the people, the stupefying illusions, "causing forgetfulness," which they give the people to drink, as their predecessors, the prophets of the Baal, "their fathers," "forgot" YHVH's name (v. 27; cf. the saying about the change of generations in the people itself, 16, 11f) for a world of Baalic myth and ritual which had grown out of wishes and impulses. In times of danger and common doubt men come to them—whether they are attached to cult or court or are unattached—they come to them to obtain through them information on fate; and they tell them, not only by "Yes" and "No" as was done apparently by the priestly oracles, but in short sayings they tell their questioners what they want to hear, and this is also what their own ear wants to hear from their own mouth. They do not speak only in order to please the men who inquire of them, but also to please their own "dream" and "phantom"; they do not simply deceive on purpose, but they themselves are entangled in the delusion of the world of wish. In the language of psychology: the false prophets make their subconscious a god, whereas for the true prophets their subconscious is subdued by the God of truth, Who absolutely transcends everything discoverable in the psychic domain, and Who is recognized in this very transcendence as the vanquisher. This process we see in a notable example from the life and prophecy of Jeremiah. In both he stands opposed to the new idolaters, who submit no longer to the Baal but to the wish-deity himself, calling him by the name of YHVH. Deuteronomy is right in saying (13, 3; 18, 20) that the false prophet calls to follow "other gods"—but it must be added he does not know that they are other. And so in the life and prophecy of Jeremiah, Moses' word in Deuteronomy (18, 15) comes exactly true that YHVH will raise up for Israel—that is from generation to generation—a prophet like himself. In both—and in no other prophet—in the man Moses of the tradition and in the man Jeremiah of his own confession, we find this conquest by God, this intensive dialogue with Him, this ardor of intercession, and this suffering for the rebellious people and their lot.

*   *   *

Jeremiah is the one among the martyrs of the ancient world, whose afflictions are not only told us, but who himself opens for us the door to share in them by occasionally committing to writing an expression of his sufferings with that same directness as he whispers or cries about them to his God. Why does he act so, why does he make known to us complaints and pleadings, and even resentments and shouts of vengeance? Obviously because he thinks all these supra-personally important. Jeremiah is no "religious individualist"; he is not interested in his own person, as Augustine is, for example, he is only interested in it as in a vessel of the divine word, and also as in the creature in whose personal existence the great discussion between YHVH and Israel and the fate resulting from it are consummated in personal condensation. In his youth he resisted with all his might the designation to become the central man of the catastrophe, but God "befooled" him (20, 7). He longed to live in the midst of his people, but was compelled to sit lonely under God's hand (15, 17). He refused again and again to pass sentence in YHVH's name upon his beloved people, but the word remained in his heart "like a burning fire," "shut up in the bones," and he was weary of the vain effort to contain it (20, 9). The divine wrath heaps itself up in him and forces him to pour it out in cursing his people, without discrimination, upon children playing in the street, upon the company of merry youths (6, 11), and moreover he feels as if he did not announce a coming disaster, but as if fire actually proceeded from his mouth and consumed the logs of his people (5, 14). He knows that the avenging God is just, even though sometimes he no longer understands His actions. He sees around him the "assembly of traitors" (9, 1, EV 2); in vain he searches first among the lowly of the people, afterwards among the great ones, for one man doing justice (5, 1ff); he longs to go out from this people to the desert and to find a refuge in the humble night's lodging of wayfarers, but he has to remain and fulfil his service (9, 1, EV 2). He suffers both from the stubbornness of Israel and from the punishment already beginning before his eyes. It is not that he only sees from time to time what is happening; through the present he gazes into the coming destruction in immense proportions; the earth is returning to chaos (4, 23). Then he breaks down on the people's breakdown in his vision, and his soul weeps in secret (8, 21; 13, 17). He longs to pray for Israel, but YHVH forbids even this, He "will not hear" him (7, 16). And now when, after being driven out from the people in mockery and torment, even his Lord withdraws from him the communication of prayer, he curses the day of his birth (20, 14); he complains against the God Who first called him and afterwards renounced him, untrustworthy "as failing waters" (15, 18). But for an answer he hears just what time and again he carried to the people as God's message: he is told to return to God, putting out of his soul that which is vile, so God "will let him return" (v. 19). And from the manner in which Jeremiah notes this answer as something indisputable and final, we learn that he has accepted it fully. The great man of prayer is not pious and patient; but even his revolt turns out to be prayer, and that which is assigned to him afterwards turns out to be that for which he had prayed without knowing it.

In all these things something of the personal is always mixed, too personal it may be said: complaint about all the enmity, all the abuse, petition for protection and even for retaliation. But no word of Jeremiah is simply personal; his sufferings, though he does not know it, are transparent into the sufferings of Israel—not the sufferings of one generation, still less of this corrupt generation, but the sufferings of the eternal people. His intention is to express things; but the fact is that they are not in any sense private. His "I" is so deeply set in the "I" of the people that his life cannot be regarded as that of an individual. In general those who tend to distinguish precisely in Scripture between the collective and the individual "I" are mistaken. The "I" of the individual remains transparent into the "I" of the community. It is no metaphor when Jeremiah speaks of the people of Israel not only as "we" but also as "I," just as it is no more figurative language to speak of Rachel weeping for her children (31, 15): primeval mothers do not pass away, and Israel could not have been chosen if it were no person. But it is necessary to listen even more exactly. The approaching military disaster appears so corporeally to the prophet, that the sound of the trumpet strikes the walls of his heart, de-

struction upon destruction is called, and in the midst of this call
he hears the words of Israel itself: "Ah! all the land is ravaged,
suddenly ravaged my tents!" (4, 19ff). Here the "I" of Jeremiah
passes over directly into the "I" of the people; but in another
passage (10, 19f) Israel in the same language laments alone for its
ravaged tent—and afterwards, when the prophet has instructed
it about the foremost cause, the "stupidity" of the "pastors" (v.
21), it recognizes God's leadership and requests to be corrected
"but with just measure" (v. 23f; v. 22 does not belong here, and
v. 25 is not Jeremianic). In such an association of the individual
and the collective "I" the fact emerges that, in the last resort, the
sufferings we are told about are one and the same. This, however, is
not only because Jeremiah identifies himself in moments of inspiration with the people, but because he really bears the people within
himself. The contradiction that destroys the people resides in his
very self. The prophet fulfils in himself instead of the rebellious
people purification and repentance. The sufferings which he bears
because of Israel he bears for Israel.

And so he bears them for YHVH. For this is the hour in the
history of Israel and Israel's faith when, in the accomplishment
of the disaster, the divine appearance again undergoes a change
in the eyes of the believer, even though the conception of the divine nature itself is unaffected by this change. Formerly the God
of the nomad tribes had become the God of the land of Canaan,
and it was the great achievement of the prophets that all the attributes of the local and national Semitic deities were kept away
from Him. The prophets were enabled to do this by their fighting
for the covenant. But now, YHVH having abolished the covenant
violated by Israel, a new situation between Him and the people
had arisen. He "leaves His house," He withdraws to heaven, now
only He becomes wholly God of heaven, God of the world, God of
all; He wants to be recognized as "God from afar," filling heaven
and earth (23, 23f), perceiving all and yet remaining above all.
But at the same time He remains near the outcast, near those who
suffer. He does not wish, according to the words of a post-exilic
prophet (Is. 66, 1f; 57, 15), that man should build Him a house
again, for heaven is His throne and earth His footstool, but it is
not only in holiness and in the height that He delights to dwell,
but "with the contrite and lowly of spirit, to revive the spirit of

the lowly and to revive the spirit of the contrite." He Who is infinitely above the domains of the mighty and secure descends to those who lie in the dust of the earth and shares their afflictions. His growing incomprehensibility is mitigated and even compensated by His becoming the God of the sufferers and by suffering becoming a door of approach to Him, as is already clear from the life of Jeremiah where the way of martyrdom leads to an ever purer and deeper fellowship with YHVH. Between God and suffering a mysterious connection is opened. In every generation God's emissaries not only worked and fought by His order, they also bore suffering in the course of their work and fighting. But hitherto these sufferings were only something incidental, having no intrinsic import of their own. Henceforward the sufferings themselves began to rise into prominence.

B. THE QUESTION

From the moment when a national disaster appears inevitable, and especially after it has become a reality, it can, like every great torment, become a productive force from the religious point of view: it begins to suggest new questions and to stress old ones. Dogmatized conceptions are pondered afresh in the light of the events, and the faith relationship that has to stand the test of an utterly changed situation is renewed in a modified form. But the new acting force is nothing less than the force of extreme despair, a despair so elemental that it can have but one of two results: the sapping of the last will of life, or the renewal of the soul.

From the primitive organic unity of the family, and later of the tribe, there arose in Israel, as in other peoples, a sense of the solidarity of the community, which manifested itself especially at times of general suffering. Even in the early days the Israelites saw in such occurrences an act of heavenly retribution coming upon the people, united by covenant relationship to their God, for their guilt, corporate and individual. Indeed, it was sometimes actually thought possible to find the guilty, as for example by the casting of lots (Josh. 7, 13ff; cf. 1 Sam. 14, 38ff) and to redeem the community from the sin by the punishment of the individual; but generally such a breaking up of the unity was not feasible and, for this reason, probably already in early times ordinances came into being to accomplish the individualization immediately after the discovery of a crime, the perpetrator of which was not known (Deut. 21). Questions concerning the righteousness of the collective punishment were apparently first raised in connection with natural disasters. The story of Abraham's intercession for Sodom (Gen. 18, 22ff) speaks in clear language: under the impression of destruction descending without discrimination upon whole countries, men discuss the divine justice and endeavor to grasp its nature. In a cult legend of the temple, written down apparently in the days of Solomon and purposely put at the end of the book of Samuel after the first redaction had been completed (2 Sam. 24), David rises up in defiance against the afflictions of the people, "these sheep," afflictions due to the guilt of the pastor; the verse is certainly an interpolation, but to judge from its language not a late one. In order to make the plague which does not distinguish between righteous and wicked consistent with the justice of God, the numbering of the people has been taken to be only the direct cause of the disaster, whereas the true reason for it has been seen in a previous sin of the *people,* for whose sake YHVH enticed David to sin; to a late theological outlook this idea proved intolerable, and Satan—here already used as a proper name, not as hitherto as an epithet of the "hindering" or "adversary" spirit—comes perforce to take the place of God (1 Chr. 21, 1).

Of course utterances, such as these related of Abraham and David, were in no way intended to throw doubt on the punitive character of natural catastrophes. The early writing prophets emphasize this character very forcibly, and they like to recall in this connection the overthrow of Sodom, as for example Amos, who explains the earthquake, which had occurred some time before, as a chastisement and warning of the people (Am. 4, 11). But the question of the innocent suffering through the punishment of the guilty, the question of the truth of joint expiation, perseveres, it only changes, it embraces all common adversity and finds positive expression in the teaching about the "remnant": those who return to God will be delivered and preserved in the midst of the disaster.

To this idea the prophets held fast, until the fall of Judah begins to show on the historical horizon. As compared with the parallel period in the history of the Northern kingdom we see here a double difference. Firstly, the world political tension between the lands of the ancient East increased in the meantime enormously, and many of the people begin to perceive how fatally Israel is entangled in it; it is true that they do not discern how much this fatality is due to the anti-prophetic covenant politics of the kings. Secondly, many of the people think that in the reform of the cult God was given what belonged to Him, and they find it hard to understand why just at that time the punishment advances without restraint. The prophets hold before their eyes their social iniquity, their misdeeds and misbehavior. But the increasing influence of the prophetical word and the movement of repentance does not avert the disaster. Those who return in penitence see themselves caught up in the whirlpool of destruction. And the prophet has no answer to their questions other than to refer to the guilt of the people and that of the fathers. But in the atmosphere of the catastrophe the old idea of solidarity has broken down; men rise up against the very suggestion that they should suffer and perish for the guilt of others. The prophet declares—in a saying, which perhaps was not spoken by Jeremiah, but which is characteristic of his generation (Jer. 31, 28f, EV 29f)—that in the days of the redemption from the evil lot now commencing, the rebellious saying, that the children's teeth are set on edge because the fathers have eaten sour grapes, will be annulled, for each man will suffer only for his own iniquity. The reference here is not to the individual, but to generations: in the realm of human justice it was long ago ordained (Deut. 24, 16, cf. 2 Kgs. 14, 6) that children should not be put to death for the fathers, whereas in the realm of God's dealings with generations of the people it is announced only now.

But such a promise can no longer calm the opposition in the souls that cannot acknowledge the righteousness of the faithless Manasseh's success and the faithful Josiah's disaster. Jeremiah himself asks (12, 1) why the way of the wicked prospers, and receives nothing but a reproving answer from God. Ezekiel (18, cf. 33, 10–20) returns to the popular proverb, but for him it is no longer enough to prophesy that in the future this saying will be done away with. He denounces the whole religious tradition of collective responsibility, a tradition the result of which is the bitter irony of the proverb. The righteous "will live" (Habakkuk's saying about the righteous appears here recoined), the violent "will die," but he too will live if he returns to God (18, 21); for God's way may be "meted out" (v. 25, 29)—in contrast to Israel's ways, it is right and recognizable for its rightness. This, however, is not meant as a general article of faith, but refers to the approaching catastrophe only,[1] even though elsewhere in Ezekiel (21, 8f) God's word announces the coming disaster for "righteous and wicked" alike. Ezekiel individualizes the prophetic alternative; it may be said that he individualizes the idea of "the holy remnant"; the remnant no longer appears as a preserved life-community of the faithful who are saved, but as a sum of individuals: pious ones and penitents. For the "remnant," in the sense of the people, there is at first no room in the thought of a prophet, who sees in his vision YHVH's departure from Jerusalem (11, 23). Because God again wanders as in former days, although not as then with the people but over the "beasts" (1, 5, 26), from place to place, each place capable of being the place of His revelation, as "His place" (3, 12; this is the prophet's exclamation, not the beasts' cry) [2]—because of this the continuity of the people's unity is rent asunder, and it is consistent that Ezekiel sees the future restoration in the form of a resurrection of the people from dry bones (ch. 37). If at first he hoped that the renewal would come from the return to God of the "house of Israel" making for themselves "a new heart and a new spirit" (18, 31), he learns in the exile to look for salvation only from God, Who after He had eliminated out of them in the exile the rebels and the disloyal (20, 38) purifies for His name's sake those brought back by Him, establishing them as God's people by giving them a new heart and a new spirit (36, 24–8). It may also be said that Ezekiel in his Messianic prophecy sees Israel as a community, but in his vision and reproof of the present he sees it as a multitude of individuals, each one of whom is responsible before God for himself alone. This personal responsibility, however, is full and entire. No one has to bear an inherited sin, no one shares in accumulating new guilt, no one has to answer for his fellow, but each one has to answer fully for himself, and

---

[1] Cf. J. Hermann, Ezechiel (1913), 113; Bertholet, Hesekiel (1936), 69.

[2] Buber, Zu Jecheskel 3, 12, Monatschrift fuer Geschichte und Wissenschaft des Judentums, LXXVIII (1934), 471ff.

even the grace, of which the prophet will expect to receive everything for Israel, does not limit this duty. This is the special character of the time of the great transition, the time that has begun
even now. In days to come a new cult will unite the members of
the people (this hope of a new order of worship is more important
and real to Ezekiel, the Jerusalem priest, than to all the prophets
before him); but now each one stands for himself over against his
God, that is to say, each one in the religious solitude of the prophet.
And God stands over against each individual with demand, zeal,
and avenging power just as before He stood over against the
people. The people no longer exists as covenant partner, until
God will make for it the "eternal covenant"; but in the time of
transition there is opened to *every man* of Israel a covenant relationship to God, each one, as formerly the people, being set at
the crossroads between life and death. This is in force especially
at the hour before the catastrophe, the hour that is, in which and
for which Ezekiel, sent to the "house of Israel" as "watchman"
and warner of *persons* (3, 17–21), speaks his message of personal
responsibility. For this hour and in reply to the doubts of the
despondent, he establishes the concept of a God in Whose justice
it is possible to believe, a God Whose recompense of the individual
is *objectively comprehensible*. Those deserving salvation are saved.

This image of the godhead, traces of which can be seen in the
teaching of Judaism up to a late generation, and against which
Jewish religion repeatedly protested that it set up man as a creature serving in the world "for the sake of receiving a reward," is
problematic in itself, as is the case with all divine images which
come not from an overwhelming experience, but from an attempt
to overcome a questionable situation. This does not mean to say
that the man situated on the borderland of prophecy, between
prophecy and priesthood, between prophecy and theological construction, between prophecy and apocalypse, had no real personal
experience. He was a true seer of visions even though he inclines
to speculation—but he lacked the simple, peculiar experience that
gives meaning to life. For this reason the subsequent generations,
the generations of the Babylonian exile, did not accept his message
and his image of God as an answer to their new questions. These
questions were—or it is better to say, this question was: *why do we
suffer what we suffer?* The question did not deny the belief in in-

dividual recompense, it merely denied the objective comprehensibility of the recompense. Over against the dogmatic principle of Ezekiel, that in this hour the punishment for sin without repentance *was to be recognized* as "death" while the reward for striving after purity and an effort of repentance *was to be recognized* as "life," over against this dogma stood their experience. Be the secret of reward and punishment what it may, in the actual reality of the catastrophe, as in that threatening saying of Ezekiel (21, 8f) about the extirpation of "righteous and wicked," "honest and wicked" (Job 9, 22) are destroyed together by God, and in the outer reality the wicked left alive knew how to assert themselves successfully in spite of all the difficulties, "they lived, became old, and even thrived mightily" (21, 7), whereas the pious, endowed with weaker elbows and more sensitive hearts, their days "were swifter than a weaver's shuttle, and were spent without hope" (7, 6); "the robbers' tents are peaceful, and they that anger God have secure abodes" (12, 6), whereas the upright is "become a brother of jackals" (30, 29). This is the experience out of which the book of Job was born, a book opposed to the dogmatics of Ezekiel, a book of the question which then was new and has persisted ever since.

*   *   *

I cannot ascribe this book—which clearly has only slowly grown to its present form—in its basic kernel to a time later (or earlier) than the beginning of the exile. Its formulations of the question bear the stamp of an intractable directness—the stamp of a first expression. The world, in which they were spoken, had certainly not yet heard the answers of Psalm 73 or Deutero-Isaiah. The author finds before him dogmas in process of formation, he clothes them in grand language, and sets over against them the force of the new question, the question brought into being out of *experience;* in his time these growing dogmas had not yet found their decisive opponents. The book in spite of its thorough rhetoric—the product of a long drawn-out literary process—is one of the special events in world literature, in which we witness the first clothing of a human quest in form of speech.

It has rightly been said [3] that, behind the treatment of Job's fate in this discussion, lie "very bitter experiences of a supra-

[3] Hempel, Die althebraeische Literatur (1930), 179.

individual kind." When the sufferer complains, "He breaks me around, and I am gone" (Job 19, 10), this seems no longer the complaint of a single person. When he cries, "God delivers me to the wicked, and hurls me upon the hands of the evil-doers" (16, 11), we think less of the sufferings of an individual than of the exile of a people. It is true it is a personal fate that is presented here, but the stimulus to speaking out, the incentive to complaint and accusation, bursting the bands of the presentation, are the fruit of supra-personal sufferings. Job's question comes into being as the question of a whole generation about the sense of its historic fate. Behind this "I," made so personal here, there still stands the "I" of Israel.

The question of the generation, "Why do we suffer what we suffer?" had from the beginning a religious character; "why?" here is not a philosophical interrogative asking after the nature of things, but a religious concern with the acting of God. With Job, however, it becomes still clearer; he does not ask, "Why does God *permit* me to suffer these things?" but "Why does God *make* me suffer these things?" That everything comes from God is beyond doubt and question; the question is, How are these sufferings compatible with His godhead?

In order to grasp the great inner dialectic of the poem, we must realize that here not two, but four answers stand over against each other; in other words, we find here four views of God's relationship to man's sufferings.

The first view is that of the Prologue to the book which, in the form in which it has reached us, cannot have come from an ancient popular book about Job, but bears the stamp of a poetic formation. The popular view of God, however, stands here apparently unchanged.[4] It is a God allowing a creature, who wanders about the earth and is subject to Him in some manner, the "Satan," that is the "Hinderer" or "Adversary," to "entice" Him (2, 3)—the verb is the same as is used in the story of David being enticed by God or Satan to sin—to do all manner of evil to a God-fearing man, one who is His "servant" (1, 8; 2, 3), of whose faithfulness God boasts. This creature entices the deity to do all manner of

---

[4] I cannot agree with Torczyner's view, expressed in his later (Hebrew) commentary on the book (I, 27), that "the story of the framework is later than the poem."

evil to this man, only in order to find out if he will break faith, as
Satan argues, or keep it according to God's word. The poet shows
us how he sees the matter, as he repeats in true Biblical style the
phrase "gratuitously." In order to make it clear whether Job serves
him "gratuitously" (1, 9), that is to say, not for the sake of receiving a reward, God smites him and brings suffering upon him, as
He Himself confesses (2, 3), "gratuitously," that is to say, without
sufficient cause. Here God's acts are questioned more critically
than in any of Job's accusations, because here we are informed of
the true motive, which is one not befitting to deity. On the other
hand man proves true as man. Again the point is driven home by
the frequent repetition of the verb *berekh,* which means both real
blessing and also blessing of dismissal, departure (1, 5, 11 ; 2, 5, 9) : [5]
Job's wife tells him, reality itself tells him to "bless" God, to dismiss Him, but he bows down to God and "blesses" Him, Who has
allowed Himself to be enticed against him "gratuitously." This
is a peculiarly dramatic face-to-face meeting, this God and this
man. The dialogue poem that follows contradicts it totally : there
the man is another man, and God another God.

The second view of God is that of the friends. This is the dogmatic view of the cause and effect in the divine system of requital :
sufferings point to sin. God's punishment is manifest and clear to
all. The primitive conception of the zealous God is here robbed
of its meaning : it was YHVH, God of Israel, Who was zealous
for the *covenant* with His *people.* Ezekiel had preserved the covenant faith, and only for the passage of time between covenant and
covenant did he announce the unconditional punishment for those
who refused to return in penitence ; this has changed here, in an
atmosphere no longer basically historical,[6] into the view of the
friends, the assertion of an all-embracing empirical connection
between sin and punishment. In addition to this for Ezekiel, it is
true, punishment followed unrepented sin, but it never occurred
to him to see in all men's sufferings the avenging hand of God ;
and it is just this that the friends now proceed to do : Job's suffer-

---

[5] The explanation that this expression is a euphemism (according to the view
of Abraham Geiger, Urschrift und Uebersetzungen der Bibel, 1857, 267ff, the
language of later emendations, cf. Torczyner, 1, 10) does not fit the facts.

[6] The atmosphere of the poem is not basically historical, even if the chief
characters of the story were historical persons, according to Torczyner's view
(Job 1, 27).

ings testify to his guilt. The inner infinity of the suffering soul is here changed into a formula, and a wrong formula. The first view was that of a small mythological idol, the second is that of a great ideological idol. In the first the faithful sufferer was true to an untrue God, Who permitted his guiltless children to be slain; whereas here man was not asked to be true to an incalculable power, but to recognize and confess a calculation which his knowledge of reality contradicts. There man's faith is attacked by fate, here by religion. The friends are silent seven days before the sufferer, after which they expound to him the account book of sin and punishment. Instead of his God, for Whom he looks in vain, his God, Who had not only put sufferings upon him, but also had "hedged him in" until "His way was hid" from his eyes (3, 23), there now came and sought him on his ash heap *religion*, which uses every art of speech to take away from him the God of his soul. Instead of the "cruel" (30, 21) and living God, to Whom he clings, religion offers him a reasonable and rational God, a deity Whom he, Job, does not perceive either in his own existence or in the world, and Who obviously is not to be found anywhere save only in the very domain of religion. And his complaint becomes a protest against a God Who withdraws Himself, and at the same time against His false representation.

The third view of God is that of Job in his complaint and protest. It is the view of a God Who contradicts His revelation by "hiding His face" (13, 24). He is at one and the same time fearfully noticeable and unperceivable (9, 11), and this hiddenness is particularly sensible in face of the excessive presence of the "friends," who are ostensibly God's advocates. All their attempts to cement the rent in Job's world show him that this is the rent in the heart of the world. Clearly the thought of both Job and the friends proceeds from the question about justice. But unlike his friends, Job knows of justice only as a human activity, willed by God, but opposed by His acts. The truth of being just and the reality caused by the unjust acts of God are irreconcilable. Job cannot forego either his own truth or God. God torments him "gratuitously" (9, 17; it is not without purpose that here the word recurs, which in the Prologue Satan uses and God repeats); He "deals crookedly" with him (19, 6). All man's supplications will avail nothing: "there is no justice" (v. 7). Job does not regard himself as free from sin

(7, 20; 14, 16f), in contradistinction to God's words about him in
the Prologue (1, 8; 2, 3). But his sin and his sufferings are incom-
mensurable. And the men, who call themselves his friends, suppose that on the basis of their dogma of requital they are able to
unmask his life and show it to be a lie. By allowing religion to
occupy the place of the living God, He strips off Job's honor (19,
9). Job had believed God to be just and man's duty to be to walk
in His ways. But it is no longer possible for one who has been
smitten with such sufferings to think God just. "It is one thing,
therefore I spake: honest and wicked He exterminates" (9, 22).
And if it is so, it is not proper to walk in His ways. In spite of this,
Job's faith in justice is not broken down. But he is no longer able
to have a *single faith* in God and in justice. His faith in justice
is no longer covered by God's righteousness. He believes now in
justice in spite of believing in God, and he believes in God in spite
of believing in justice. But he cannot forego his claim that they
will again be united somewhere, sometime, although he has no
idea in his mind how this will be achieved. This is in fact meant
by his claim of his rights, the claim of the solution. This solution
must come, for from the time when he knew God Job *knows* that
God is not a Satan grown into omnipotence. Now, however, Job
is handed over to the pretended justice, the account justice of the
friends, which affects not only his honor, but also his faith in
justice. For Job, justice is not a scheme of compensation. Its
content is simply this, that one must not cause suffering gratuitously. Job feels himself isolated by this feeling, far removed from
God and men. It is true, Job does not forget that God seeks just
such justice as this from man. But he cannot understand how God
Himself violates it, how He inspects His creature every morning
(7, 18), searching after his iniquity (10, 6), and instead of forgiving
his sin (7, 21) snatches at him stormily (9, 17)—how He, being
infinitely superior to man, thinks it good to reject the work of His
hands (10, 3). And in spite of this Job knows that the friends, who
side with God (13, 8), do not contend for the true God. He has
recognized before this the true God as the near and intimate God.
Now he only experiences Him through suffering and contradiction,
but even in this way he does experience God. What Satan designed
for him and his wife in the Prologue, recommended to him more

exactly, that he should "bless" God, dismiss Him, and die in the comfort of his soul, was for him quite impossible. When in his last long utterance he swears the purification oath, he says: "As God lives, Who has withdrawn my right" (27, 2). God lives, and He bends the right. From the burden of this double, yet single, matter Job is able to take away nothing, he cannot lighten his death. He can only ask to be confronted with God. "Oh that one would hear me!" (31, 35)—men do not hear his words, only God can be his hearer. As his motive he declares that he wants to reason with the deity (13, 3); he knows he will carry his point (v. 18). In the last instance, however, he merely means by this that God will again become present to him. "Oh that I knew where I might find Him!" (23, 3). Job struggles against the remoteness of God, against the deity Who rages and *is silent,* rages and "hides His face," that is to say, against the deity Who has changed for him from a near-by person into a sinister power. And even if He draw near to him again only in death, he will again "see" God (19, 26) as His "witness" (16, 19) against God Himself, he will see Him as the avenger of his blood (19, 25) which must not be covered by the earth until it is avenged (16, 18) by God on God. The absurd duality of a truth known to man and a reality sent by God must be swallowed up somewhere, sometime, in a unity of God's presence. How will it take place? Job does not know this, nor does he understand it, he only believes in it. We may certainly say that Job "appeals from God to God," [7] but we cannot say [8] that he rouses himself against a God "Who contradicts His own innermost nature," and seeks a God Who will conduct Himself towards him "as the requital dogma demands." By such an interpretation the sense of the problem is upset. Job cannot renounce justice, but he does not hope to find it, when God will find again "His inner nature" and "His subjection to the norm," but only when God will appear to him again. Job believes now, as later Deutero-Isaiah (Is. 45, 15) did under the influence of Isaiah (8, 17), in "a God that hides Himself." This hiding, the eclipse of the divine light, is the source of his abysmal despair. And the abyss is bridged the

[7] Peake, The Problem of Suffering, (1904), 94f; cf. also Volz, Weisheit (Die Schriften des Alten Testaments III, 1911), 62.

[8] Baumgaertel, Der Hiobdialog (1933), 172.

moment man "sees," is permitted to see again, and this becomes
a new foundation. It has been rightly said,[9] that Job is more deeply
rooted in the primitive Israelite view of life than his dogmatic
friends. There is no true life for him but that of a firmly established
covenant between God and man; formerly he lived in this covenant
and received his righteousness from it, but now God has disturbed
it. It is the dread of the faithful "remnant" in the hour of the
people's catastrophe that here finds its personal expression. But
this dread is suggestive of the terror that struck Isaiah as he stood
on the threshold of the cruel mission laid upon him—"the making
fat and heavy." His words "How long?" are echoed in Job's complaint. How long will God hide His face? When shall we be allowed
to see Him again? Deutero-Isaiah expresses (40, 27) the despairing
complaint of the faithful remnant which thinks that because God
hides Himself, Israel's "way" also "is hid" from Him, and He pays
no more attention to it, and the prophet promises that not only
Israel but all flesh shall see Him (v. 5).

The fourth view of God is that expressed in the speech of God
Himself. The extant text is apparently a late revision, as is the
case with many other sections of this book, and we cannot restore
the original text. But there is no doubt that the speech is intended
for more than the mere demonstration of the mysterious character
of God's rule in nature to a greater and more comprehensive extent
than had already been done by the friends and Job himself; for
more than the mere explanation to Job: "Thou canst not understand the secret of any thing or being in the world, how much less
the secret of man's fate." It is also intended to do more than teach
by examples taken from the world of nature about the "strange
and wonderful" character of the acts of God, which contradict
the whole of teleological wisdom, and point to the "playful riddle
of the eternal creative power" as to an "inexpressible positive
value." [10] The poet does not let his God disregard the fact that
it is a matter of *justice*. The speech declares in the ears of man,
struggling for justice, another justice than his own, a divine
justice. Not *the* divine justice, which remains hidden, but *a* divine

[9] Pedersen, Israel I–II (English Edn. 1926), 371.
[10] Rudolf Otto, Das Heilige, 23–25 edn. (1936), 99f; cf. also Vischer, Hiob ein
Zeuge Jesu Christi (1934), 29ff; Eichrodt, Theologie des Alten Testaments III
(1939), 145f.

justice, namely that manifest in creation. The creation of the world is justice, not a recompensing and compensating justice, but a distributing, a giving justice. God the Creator bestows upon each what belongs to him, upon each thing and being, in so far as He allows it to become entirely itself. Not only for the sea (Job 38, 10), but for every thing and being God "breaks" in the hour of creation "His boundary," that is to say, He cuts the dimension of this thing or being out of "all," giving it its fixed measure, the limit appropriate to this gift. Israel's ancient belief in creation, which matured slowly only in its formulations, has here reached its completion: it is not about a "making" that we are told here, but about a "founding" (v. 4), a "setting" (v. 5, 9f), a "commanding" and "appointing" (v. 12). The creation itself already means communication between Creator and creature. The just Creator gives to all His creatures His boundary, so that each may become fully itself. Designedly man is lacking in this presentation of heaven and earth, in which man is shown the justice that is greater than his, and is shown that he with his justice, which intends to give to everyone what is due to him, is called only to emulate the divine justice, which gives to everyone what he is. In face of such divine teaching as this it would be indeed impossible for the sufferer to do aught else than put "his hand upon his mouth" (40, 4), and to confess (42, 3) that he had erred in speaking of things inconceivable for him. And nothing else could have come of it except this recognition—if he had heard only a voice "from the tempest" (38, 1; 40, 6). But the voice is the voice of *Him Who answers,* the voice of Him that "heard" (31, 35), and appeared so as to be "found" of him (23, 3). In vain Job had tried to penetrate to God through the divine remoteness; now God draws near to him. No more does God hide Himself, only the storm cloud of His sublimity still shrouds Him, and Job's eye "sees" Him (42, 5). The absolute power is for human personality's sake become personality. God offers Himself to the sufferer who, in the depth of his despair, keeps to God with his refractory complaint; He offers Himself to him as an answer. It is true, "the overcoming of the riddle of suffering can only come from the domain of revelation," [11] but it is not the revelation in general which is here decisive, but the particular revelation to the individual: the revelation as an *answer* to the

[11] Eichrodt, *op. cit.,* 146.

individual sufferer concerning the question of his sufferings, the self-limitation of God to a person, answering a person.

The *way* of this poem leads from the first view to the fourth. The God of the first view, the God of the legend borrowed by the poet works on the basis of "enticement"; the second, the God of the friends, works on the basis of purposes apparent to us, purposes of punishment or, especially in the speeches of Elihu which are certainly a later addition, of purification and education; the third, the God of the protesting Job, works against every reason and purpose; and the fourth, the God of revelation, works from His godhead, in which every reason and purpose held by man are at once abolished and fulfilled. It is clear that this God, Who answers from the tempest, is different from the God of the Prologue; the declaration about the secret of divine action would be turned into a mockery if the fact of that "wager" was put over against it. But even the speeches of the friends and of Job cannot be harmonized with it. Presumably the poet, who frequently shows himself to be a master of irony, left the Prologue, which seems completely opposed to his intention, unchanged in content in order to establish the foundation for the multiplicity of views which follows. But in truth the view of the Prologue is meant to be ironical and unreal; the view of the friends is only logically "true" and demonstrates to us that man must not subject God to the rules of logic; Job's view is real, and therefore, so to speak, the negative of truth; and the view of the voice speaking from the tempest is the supra-logical truth of reality. God justifies Job: he has spoken "rightly" (42, 7), unlike the friends. And as the poet often uses words of the Prologue as motive words in different senses, so also here he makes God call Job as there by the name of His "servant," and repeat it by way of emphasis four times. Here this epithet appears in its true light. Job, the faithful rebel, like Abraham, Moses, David, and Isaiah, stands in the succession of men so designated by God, a succession that leads to Deutero-Isaiah's "servant of YHVH," whose sufferings especially link him with Job.

"And my servant Job shall pray for you"—with these words God sends the friends home (v. 8). It is the same phrase as that in which YHVH in the story of Abraham (Gen. 20, 7) certifies the patriarch, that he is His *nabi*. It will be found that in all the pre-exilic passages, in which the verb is used in the sense of intercession (and this apparently was its first meaning), it is only used of men called prophets. The significance of Job's intercession is emphasized by the Epilogue (which, apart from the matter of the prayer, the poet apparently left as it was) in that the turning point in Job's history, the "restoration" (Job 42, 10) and first of all his healing, begins the moment he prays "for his friends." This saying is the last of the reminiscences of prophetic life and language found in this book. As if to stress this connection, Job's first complaint begins (3, 3ff) with the cursing of his birth, reminding us of Jeremiah's words (Jer. 20, 14ff), and the first utterance of the friends is poured out in figures of speech taken from the prophetic world (4, 12ff), the last of which (v. 16) modifies the peculiar form of revelation of Elijah's story (1 Kgs. 19, 12). Job's recollection of divine intimacy, of "the counsel of God upon his tent" (Job 29, 4) is expressed in language derived from Jeremiah (Jer. 23, 18, 22), and his quest, which reaches fulfilment, to "see" God, touches the prophetic experience which only on Mount Sinai were non-prophets allowed to share (Ex. 24, 10, 17). Jeremiah's historical figure, that of the suffering prophet, apparently inspired the poet to compose his song of the man of suffering, who by his suffering attained the vision of God, and in all his revolt was God's witness on earth (cf. Is. 43, 12; 44, 8), as God was his witness in heaven.

* * *

It has been suggested [12] that Psalm 73 was written by the author of the book of Job, and the resemblance (e.g., v. 11 of the Psalm and Job 22, 13) is indeed worthy of attention. But this man of prayer, influenced as he is in his ways of expression by the writer of Job, both of them knowing the great question about the "welfare of the wicked" (Ps. 73, 3, cf. Job 21, 9), has reached a simple certainty and composure, of which we do not find the like in the book of Job. And even if there were not two but one, we would have to suppose that the poet passed beyond the last word of his hero (42, 6), to which would correspond the words of the Psalmist about his former life (v. 22), "I was stupid and knew not"—that he passed beyond and arrived at the simple "yea" of the man of prayer. This Psalmist is a true man of prayer, that is to say, not a

[12] Buttenwieser, The Psalms (1938), 526.

man who composes a speech to God, but one who speaks in truth to God. That the prayer uttered here is not formless, but uses a form shaped by many generations—this fact is connected with the conception that prayer is offered to God in place of sacrifice (Ps. 40, 7) : the one praying brings himself to God as a roll of a book,[13] on which the prayer is written,[14] and does not conceal it in his heart (v. 11, EV 10), but pours it forth publicly, "in a great congregation" (v. 10ff, EV 9ff), because he feels the duty to make known God's "kindness and faithfulness." With this message character peculiar to the type of Psalm to which Psalm 73 belongs, the nature of the prophetic word is introduced into prayer. And again it is not an accident that a song of riddle and instruction closely related to this one in spirit and language (Ps. 49), sung to the accompaniment of the harp, but prophetic in character, opens with the opening words of the prophet Micah (1, 2), words put already in the mouth of Michaiah, the son of Imlah : "Hear this, all ye peoples." It is "a message of God to the whole of mankind together." [15] At the basis of such prophetic prayer, meant to be the expression and transmission of a revelation, there lies hid an overwhelming experience of life, the novelty and strength of which act upon the recipient as a mission. This is not felt so strongly in any other Psalm as in Psalm 73, of which it has rightly been said [16] that the actual experience had almost entirely dissolved the old fixed style and created a special form. The motive in the creation of this form is that it is necessary to make known the most personal matter, to lay bare the secret of the heart, in order that the manifestation be really effected. It is not permissible to translate it from the intimate language of prayer into a more objective manner of speech : the one who prays cannot perform his testimony without preserving the immediacy of the relationship between the "I" and the "thou." The fact that the prophetic

[13] The words "in a roll of a book" mean: as a roll, in the capacity of a roll (cf. 39, 7; Is. 40, 10).

[14] The words "written on me" are to be separated from what preceded and taken with what follows as an introduction to the following verses: written on me—that is to say, on the roll that I am is written what follows.

[15] Volz, Psalm 49, Zeitschrift fuer alttestamentliche Wissenschaft, Neue Folge XIV (1937), 244.

[16] Mowinckel, Psalmenstudien VI (1924), 65.

meaning of his prayer, its message meaning, is perceived by him, turns it into a confession.

The introduction of the Psalm (v. 1, the text of which is not to be altered) marks the situation out of which the whole flows. The one who prays hears around him men complaining that God does not behave towards his people as a good God. Against this complaint he sets his confession: "Verily God is good to Israel." But only those that are pure of heart can experience His goodness, for only a pure heart can grasp that what God does to Israel is goodness: God is good to the children of Israel as far as they are pure of heart. Goodness does not come to them as a reward for purity of heart but, in virtue of this purity, they experience God's act as goodness. And the Psalmist proves that this is so with the example taken from his own inner life. Many days and many experiences passed over him, until he reached the pure heart and the recognition of God's goodness. Indeed, "he cleansed his heart" (v. 13), but this cleansing seemed to him a labor without any blessing attaching to it, no reward fell to his lot, on the contrary, he was tormented without respite, and was compelled to regard his sufferings every morning as "correction" (v. 14). And around him the wicked prospered, free from the trouble with which men are afflicted (v. 5), free from the "fetters" of fate, which constrain and limit [17] (v. 4); not only have they increased their power, but apparently the peace of their souls had never been affected (v. 12, cf. v. 3). If one looked at them one expected to see how the "imaginations" of their lustful and comfortable hearts shine and pass over their eyes, and their careless gaze stands out from their fat faces (v. 7); their violence they set up for show as a collar, on which pride lay like a necklace (v. 6). They declared their oppressing pretensions "from on high" (v. 8), as if their demands were the demands of justice itself, they "set their mouth into heaven" (v. 9). The Psalmist quotes two of their sayings, one (v. 10) in which they mock God's relationship to His people,[18] and one (v. 11) in which they express with the

[17] Here should be read, in accordance with the widely accepted emendation, לָמוֹ תָם.

[18] The word "therefore" is not part of the saying, but introduces it in the sense "Therefore they said." I think that we are here told of the men who were left in the land at the time of the Babylonian exile, and so escaped that situation.

same mouth "set into heaven" the feeling of their assurance
before God Who knows nothing of their behavior, or at all
events does not occupy Himself with it. In vain the speaker
brooded again and again in his heart, and toiled to learn the meaning of this continuous "trouble" (v. 16), the source of the evil
man's inner assurance. Out of lack of knowledge (v. 22) the heart
"effervesces" (v. 21). Finally he comes when he has become pure
of heart "to the sanctuaries of God" (v. 17). This combination of
words "to come to the sanctuaries of God," which is paralleled
by the expression "to understand," is not to be interpreted as referring to the temple, even if the temple was still standing in the
day when the Psalm was written; this "coming" can only be an
inner "coming." When the Psalmist has become pure of heart, he
approaches near to God where alone it is possible to ponder His
spiritual sanctuaries, the structure of His mysteries. Now that he
experiences in himself what the true certainty and composure is,
he recognizes that that assurance of the assured ones was nothing
but an appearance, an attitude assumed to conceal utter unsteadi-
ness. "In slippery places" God set them, there was no firm ground
under their feet, YHVH "made them to fall" into "devastations"
(v. 18) : as soon as they recognize how supportless they are, they
become in an instant "a desolation" and "pass away" "through
horrors" (v. 19), and God, Who now "rouses Himself" to act in
history, disregards their passing "shadow-figure," as men disregard
a nightmare when they awake from their sleep (v. 20). Here, in
this image of the God Who shakes off from Himself the short
slumber, during which the wicked prosper, in order to act again
in history, it becomes clear that the personal experience of the
Psalmist alludes to a common and historical experience. They that
keep away from God dwindle (v. 27). The evil man does not last,
because he has no existence in himself. God does not requite the
evil man, there is no reckoning between God and man, but to be
without God means not to be. He who has been instructed in Job's
school is barred from the paths leading back to the religion of the
three friends; but that part of the living truth of faith, which is

---

"May God restore," they mock, "all His people hither" (that we may exploit
them all), food indeed there will not be, but water they will be able to
drink, "Waters of a full cup will be drained out for them." Perhaps they refer
to prophecy, e.g., Is. 43, 20.

hidden and wrapped up in the teaching of Ezekiel, namely, that sin is not the cause of death, but is death itself, this is covered here on a higher plane, after the hardest sufferings through the way of the world, and is evaluated both for the life of the individual and for that of history. When he has come to the "sanctuaries," the man of prayer will no longer forget that God's justice is His mystery, but even so, in the mystery, he experiences it.

He experiences it as the man who stands in communion with God. As he has become pure of heart, he knows that he remains constantly with God, Who has taken him by the right hand and leads him (v. 23f). "Whom have I in heaven?" he cries; he does not turn his eyes away from the sufferings of earth, persistent as they are, he does not turn to the delights of heaven, it is not heaven with which he is concerned, but *God,* Who is no more in heaven than in earth, but is near him; he does not long to be in heaven, but where he is with God, and if he is with Him, there is nothing on earth which he could desire (v. 25). If his flesh and with it his heart will fail, this heart which formerly effervesced and now experiences the nearness of God, He, Who lives in this perishable heart as the imperishable "rock" and became his "portion" (v. 26), remains forever, and this is enough. Lasting is of God: he lasts who is near to God. Those who keep away from God dwindle; "but as for me, to be near to God is for me the good" (v. 27f). Verily God is good to Israel, to the pure of heart, who are allowed to be near to Him.

After the words, "Thou wilt lead me with Thy counsel" (v. 24), there follows a sentence, the meaning of which has always been disputed, and which may be translated "and afterwards Thou wilt take me in glory." A developed belief in a personal immortality is as little expressed here as in the related verse in Psalm 49 (v. 16, EV 15, "Verily God will redeem my soul from the hand of the nether world, for He will take me"), where also apparently we are told about God "taking" man at his death, but in both places the idea is expressed that in the eyes of the speaker death is already turned into a mystery. This death was in earlier Israelite days only in mythical stories about the ascension to heaven of God's beloved ones during their lifetime, Enoch's (Gen. 5, 24) and Elijah's (2 Kgs. 2, 3, 5, 9, 10), where we are also told of a "taking," and in the case of Elijah it is emphasized by a fourfold repetition. The Psalmist, who gives the idea a new shape, does not mean that he will be taken up to heaven, but he believes that God will care for him in death as in life, that He will be actively present to him also in death. Beyond this certainty that God does not remove His presence from His saints even in death, the Psalmist obviously does not allow his imagination to play. It is indeed true, in my opinion, that the belief in enduring bliss "did not take root in Judaism until a later age and not without the influence of foreign religions" [19]—if by the word "belief" we mean here an orderly religious world view. But there are in Israel, as in other peoples, primordial forms of belief in the power God's nearness exercises over death. Indeed, men leave these forms of the belief—and apparently intentionally—in the mystery of the mythical element, until they are recast in the fire of new and strong experiences of communion with God. The decisive fact is that the conception of God becomes more real and more powerful than that of death: men put their "refuge" in YHVH (Ps. 73, 28)— beyond this they do not go, and obviously this is real enough. It is not the "immortality of the soul" that is the concern of this belief, but the eternity of God. It is not important what dying appears to be in the eyes of man: if he lives in communion with God, he knows that God is eternal and that He is his "portion."

This communion, like Job's vision of God, is acquired through suffering. But only here is this known and expressed: the Psalmist acknowledges just this way that leads to God through suffering. God loves those who suffer willingly. For their sake He performs, in the secrecy of life and history, all His "works" (v. 28, cf. Jer. 50, 25), to tell of which the Psalmist sees his task to be. This is the task laid upon him by this "nearness," this "refuge." The last words of the Psalm, "to tell all Thy works," are not to be deleted, as some maintain: they declare that the prayer is become a message, and why this is so.

C. THE MYSTERY

Isaiah "corded" and "sealed" (Is. 8, 16) in his "apprentices" (*limmudim*) the promise of the people's liberation and redemp-

---

[19] Gunkel, *Psalmen*, 315.

tion, lest in the hour of crisis it should lead the popular mind to trust in a vain security and so the impulse to repentance be kept down. Just as a deed is corded and sealed—the verse in Job (Job 14, 17) may be recalled, where transgression "is sealed up in the cord" like a law-court document—so is it done to the Messianic message, and the place of its preservation is the heart of the living disciples. Only in the hours of extreme distress shall it be their duty to break the seal of their heart and to reveal the message, in order to rescue by the words of salvation those sunk in "anguish and darkness" (Is. 8, 22), to rescue them from despair of the divine leadership.

To this after nearly two centuries the anonymous prophet, usually designated Deutero-Isaiah because his prophecies are collected together in one book with those of Isaiah, refers.

In order to understand the matter aright, it is necessary to realize that the expression *limmud* which Isaiah uses in this verse for his disciples, is found nowhere else in the Bible in this substantival sense except in this book alone, namely in the verse referred to above and three times in the second part of the book, that ascribed to Deutero-Isaiah. The adjectival use of this word in the sense of "trained, accustomed" belongs apparently to popular usage (Jer. 2, 24; 13, 23). From this Isaiah has obviously coined a new and special term. In the memoir, in which he expresses the tragic character of his prophetic mission and prophetic way, he makes a solemn declaration referring to a company of men linked to him. He sees in them the nucleus of the promised "remnant that shall return"; and so he gives this company a name, which expresses the relationship of these men to him, thus introducing a changed meaning for a common word.[1] To this the prophet, who is his heir in the spirit, now returns (Is. 50, 4), again using the word, which possibly had not been used in that sense since Isaiah's time. He returns to it with such emphasis that all who heard it were immediately reminded of the saying of his master, whose memoir was certainly diffused largely among the recipients of the new message, Deutero-Isaiah's message, that is to say, among the Babylonian exiles. It is the prophet's wish to

---

[1] Later a further change of meaning took place, perhaps due to a misunderstanding of the ancient texts; in the Wisdom of Ben Sira (51, 28) the meaning of the word *limmudim* is "teaching."

make it clear that he, a child of a later age, numbered himself with the *limmudim* and wished to be numbered with them. He has received, he says, from YHVH the *limmudim*-tongue, the apprentices' or disciples' tongue, which God wakens each morning, that he may "refresh" the "weary," the people that venture no longer to believe in liberation, with "a word," that is with an exposition of the ancient prophecy. "Disciples' tongue" it was, because his task was to uncover the master's words as a consolation and succour. And so YHVH wakens also his ear, that he may hear in the capacity of a worthy disciple, every morning perceiving anew the message of his master in its true sense. By this the anonymous man tells his hearers that he, born late in time, was called by God Himself to be Isaiah's *limmud,* whose office it was to unseal and to reveal the words handed down by Isaiah to the *limmudim.* Isaiah's message of salvation was not exhausted, we must understand, in the songs and sayings preserved in writing; secret knowledge proceeded from him to be uncovered by God's will before the late disciple. It is often asked why Deutero-Isaiah does not present his word as God's revelation to him after the manner of all the other prophets, seeing that he continually refers to God's word. The reason is that he alone of all the prophets wished to be understood as a disciple, an expositor and continuer of a given message; and therefore he links the "new things," the "coming things," the things designed for the redemption of the world, which only now are proclaimed by his mouth, with the "former things" (41, 22; 42, 9; 48, 3, 6), which were prophesied by the mouth of Isaiah for the liberation of Israel as the *beginning* of the Messianic activity, and so the new things appear as the unfolding of those "former things." It is true, those "former things" reveal themselves in their full sense only now, in the light of the new things. We must conjecture that even the new things were already implied in that same secret, which had not been transmitted in writing but only "corded" in the souls of disciples and now had to be made known to the people. God permits the speaker to hear the words of the sealed message as though he were dwelling in the circle of the disciples, and to transmit them to the weary in exile.

How does he hear them? Here, too, we can only conjecture. In the opening of his book we are witnesses (40, 3, 6) of how the spirits speak in his ears about the meaning of the hour. Often he quotes words of God about what is being prepared, yet not once does he say explicitly that the words spoken by the divine mouth were spoken to him himself. But this singular intermediate position between the full prophetic immediacy of receiving and uttering, and the acquired status of an interpreter who explains words handed down, he sees obviously as a position corresponding to the present intermediate position of Israel that Hosea had already announced (Hos. 3, 4), and even as a position corresponding to the present intermediate position of the whole world. When the days shall be fulfilled all flesh shall see the glory (*kabhod*) of YHVH (Is. 40, 5) which formerly only Isaiah had been permitted to see in a single glimpse, even though the glory fills the whole earth (6, 3, 5); and so then all the children of Israel shall be *limmudim* of YHVH Himself (54, 13), all of them disciples of God: there shall be no more distinction between the man who is teacher and the man taught, no more anything to cord and seal from the eyes of the people—there shall be nothing but the great world publicity of God, in which all shall learn from the mouth of God, their king and their teacher (30, 20), everything there is for them to learn. The request attributed to Moses (Num. 11, 29), and apparently originating from the early prophetic age that all YHVH's people should be prophets through a gift of YHVH's Spirit upon them, has here assumed the form of a promise: "I will pour out my Spirit upon thy seed" (Is. 44, 3).

*   *   *

If we examine the second part of the book of Isaiah from the point of view of form criticism, that is to say not only with regard to the author's use of the words but also with regard to all the details of style and rhythm, we find that chapters 40–55 for the most part belong to one author (some sayings, and in particular chap. 47, and also 49, 14–26, and 50, 1–3, come from another pen), while in the rest of the book, most of which originates from the post-exilic age, only a few fragmentary sayings, e.g., 57, 14–19, or 61, 1, bear the impress of the Deutero-Isaianic stamp. I do not mean by this to say that from the beginning of its existence it was a book. Three stages can be posited. The first was probably oral declarations of the prophet to the circle gathering round him; the second the elaboration of these declarations into pamphlets which were secretly distributed among the exiles; and the third the collection of a number of pamphlets and the making of them into a unity intended to be preserved for future days. The making of this collection cannot have been done at a later date, for the order indicates a definite method that cannot come from any other hand than that of the author himself, for no other hand could possibly make the elaboration requisite to produce this order reaching deeply into the structure of the different sections. The sections are not strung together, as some think, in a merely external way by catchwords recurring in two of them; [2] the root of the matter lies in basic words, and in groups of such words, which recur from section to section, all of them indicating an important inner connection. There is no room to think of poverty of the stock of words; [3] in the midst of a great wealth of language certain forms of expression recur both within each section and from one section to another; they recur in order to form links by which passages may complement and explain each other. It is the way of the author to use the same expressions with different meanings but not at all incidentally; this very difference is designed to draw attention to the inner dialectic of the elements. But in the sequence too, in which these expressions come, there lies an unmistakable intention.

Hence we have also to recognize the manner in which the peculiar relation of the author to Isaiah is expressed. The way in which he returns again and again to Isaiah's way of utterance has been explained as the influence of form and style; but there is more than simply that. Isaiah's images are shaped into an ingenious manifoldness; Isaiah's basic conceptions are modified, elaborated in their innermost potentialities, and, so to speak, made dynamic, and it is done so that a path leads from variation to variation and so on, and the uncovered wealth of the basic conceptions is only on this path made completely perceptible.

One characteristic example will be sufficient to establish this. Deutero-Isaiah adapts Isaiah's fundamental concept, the attribute "the Holy One of Israel." According to this attribute YHVH is

---

[2] This is the opinion of Mowinckel in his treatise, "Die Komposition des deutero-jesajanischen Buches," Zeitschrift fuer alttestamentliche Wissenschaft, Neue Folge VIII (1931), 87ff, 242ff.

[3] As Duhm does.

not only holy, but *the* Holy, that is to say, everything in the world
which is to be named holy is so because it is hallowed by Him and
according as everything is hallowed by Him; but YHVH is in no
such relationship to any being in the world except Israel that He
could be qualified as the Holy One of this being: He is not the
Holy One of the world, nor the Holy One of the human race,
nor of any other people, but the Holy One of Israel only, because
Israel alone was hallowed by Him as a people, and called by Him
as a people to be holy. Since Deutero-Isaiah acquired this fundamental conception, which we do not find at all before Isaiah, and
after him (apart from the legend of Isaiah, 37, 23, 2 Kgs. 19, 22,
which probably preserves a genuine saying of his) only in Jeremiah
and in the Psalms composed in his days and in the exilic age, he
proceeds to combine it with his own conception, with the attribute
"the Redeemer of Israel" (Is. 41, 14; 43, 14; 48, 17; 49, 7; 54,
5). The attribute *goel*, "redeemer," is a term of Israelite family
law and refers to the nearest male relative of the family, his
duty as guarantor being to avenge the blood of the slain, to redeem
the bondservant, to watch over mortgaged property, that is to
say to vindicate in all these cases the right of ownership which the
family had lost.[4] Jacob thanks his God (Gen. 48, 16) for such a
work wrought for him, a work embracing all life's affairs, "redemption from all evil." The story of the Exodus from Egypt takes
the act of liberation as such a redemption from bondage, as is
stated in the song of the people (Ex. 15, 13), and previously in
YHVH's own speech (6, 6). In a similar figure Jeremiah (Jer.
31, 10) and his contemporary, the author of a prophecy inserted
in the book of Micah (Mic. 4, 10), see the future liberation
from Babylon which Deutero-Isaiah announces to be near at hand.
This figure is made possible by YHVH's election of Israel being
taken as adoption, YHVH, so to speak, being both relative and
guarantor of Israel. This figure is now blended in Deutero-Isaiah's
thought with that of "the Holy One of Israel." Israel, destined to
be holy by the Holy One, sold into bondage because of its resistance (Is. 50, 1), refined "in the furnace of affliction" (48, 10),
shall now be redeemed by YHVH from the bond service for debt,
because He, YHVH, in His capacity as Holy, is the Holy One

---

[4] Cf. Procksch in Kittel's Theologisches Woerterbuch IV, 331f; Procksch, Der
Erloesungsedanke im Alten Testament in "Deutsche Theologie" II (1929), 130f.

of Israel, and will not give up being this. What in the mouth of
Isaiah was reproof and warning to the wanton men who "spurn the
Holy One of Israel" (1, 4; 5, 24) becomes in the mouth of his late
disciple comfort for the penitent and despondent: the "worm
Jacob" has not to fear, for YHVH, as the Holy One of Israel, is
his Redeemer (41, 14). This consolation condenses into a historical
proclamation: as the Holy One of Israel and their Redeemer,
YHVH, Who is Israel's Creator and King, sends to Babylon to
bring them out from thence (43, 14). And now He wishes, as the
Holy One and Redeemer of Israel, to teach them the new way,
the new order of their life (48, 17). He, as the Holy One and Redeemer, announces to His servant, to the man who is now still a
"servant of tyrants," that in the new era, when the new order
of life is established, kings seeing him elevated from humiliation
and bondage will rise and worship YHVH Who chose him (49, 7).
And finally, when these fundamental conceptions of the Holy One
of Israel and the Redeemer of Israel appear amalgamated for the
last time (54, 5), Hosea's figure of marriage between YHVH and
Israel returns again after a repetition of "fear not" (v. 4): the
forsaken "wife of youth" (v. 6) is favored again, redemption
comes to her, and she is again received by her husband. The new
betrothal in "kindness and mercy," about which Hosea prophesied
(Hos. 2, 19), is now effected by the "Merciful" in "everlasting
kindness" that "will not depart" (Is. 54, 8, 10). Thereby is the
way of ascent completed, leading with impressive distinctness from
repetition to repetition of the fundamental concepts. But something is added in a fragment, which by its style and content is
proved to be of Deutero-Isaianic milieu (29, 17–23): the redeemed
will hallow God's name, they "will hallow the Holy One of Jacob";
the goal of the election is reached, YHVH's hallowing by Israel,
that is to say, the establishment of His holy kingdom by the people
hallowed by Him. The new "way," which God teaches them to
walk in, is called, as apparently the same author calls it in another
song (chap. 35), "the way of hallowing" (v. 8). The hallowing, as a
reciprocal action in the divine-human relationship, is accomplished.

*   *   *

Deutero-Isaiah is, in spite of the teaching of Amos, Isaiah and
Jeremiah, the originator of a theology of world-history, for he is

the first to base his particular message again and again on declarations about the rule of God over the nations and his works among them, the first to found the particular on this universal, and to deduce it, so to speak, from this. His God is not merely One Who reveals Himself according to His nature—as in all Israelite prophecy—but also a God Who declares His nature theologically. There is no sense at all in calling Deutero-Isaiah "the first monotheist of Israel," but certainly he is the first concerned with a monotheistic theology, because he is concerned with a theology of world-history. And he is concerned with it, because here for the first time the prophet's task is to repel as vain the claims of other gods to the leadership of the world and its destiny; and it is his task, especially because this claim influences the problematic character of this hour of history, namely the problematic character of the political program of the man acting in this hour, Cyrus, lord of the nations. True it was not to him, but about him, the words had to be spoken, proving that the gods, under whose protection Cyrus was inclined to put his program and to let it be sanctioned by them, were powerless in the field of history—this can be proved radically only by showing that they are no gods, but a concoction made by man. Every other kind of criticism would only be liable to produce counter-criticism, every other kind would become entangled in a circle of arguments and answers. No unconditional superiority can appertain to a theology unless it undertakes to demarcate its "all" against a "nothing"; and so that it does not construct this "nothing" dialectically but shows it up perceptibly. In other words, the nonentity of the gods is proved by relegating them into the realm of psychology. The gods, which claim the leadership, have no existence but are "made"; and because of this their so-called claim to leadership and sovereignty over the world is nothing other than the claim of those who "make" them. There are some who ask why Deutero-Isaiah again and again speaks of the gods as images. Did he not know that the religions saw in these images only cases filled with divine life-forces? He needed to speak so, because only so could he express in his concrete language that these gods are not beings but figurations of the human soul; and only so could he set up over against them a god, who is in no sense at all figuration, but thoroughly Being, that is to say God.

From this we must again understand that, in the words of Deutero-Isaiah, God at every stage stands over against the idols of the nations as He Who knows the coming things and announces them from the beginning whereas they, the idols of the nations, know nothing, and therefore are incapable of announcing anything. YHVH appears here as the God Who inspires prophecy, the prophetic God. And Deutero-Isaiah is the first who can see Him in this capacity; because his conception of prophecy is different from that of all the prophets that preceded him. His prophecy has no longer the character of an alternative; his God no longer sets before men two possibilities, in deciding between which they may have a share; He has decided, and man is only the object of His decision. Although Deutero-Isaiah knows deeply the guilt of Israel, and characterizes it stringently, the question concerning the influence of man's repentance upon the divine activity almost fails to stand; it is the presupposition and the beginning of his message that Israel has already atoned for its iniquity (40, 2). His task to prophesy salvation is blended with the fact that his prophecy is in Israel the first prophecy according to the accepted sense, that is to say, he has to foretell things fixed and unchangeable. The sealed announcement of salvation, which his teacher Isaiah had composed against the background of the idea of alternative, Deutero-Isaiah uncovers in a world lacking this background. It is true the prophet knows about the drama between God and man, between YHVH the Holy and His unholy Israel, resisting His hallowing action; but this drama is known to him as a thing of the past only, as a thing overcome by God's forgiveness. And it is clear also that Deutero-Isaiah does not know the mysterious reality of man's resistance that can participate in the determination of his fate. Certainly he knows the mystery of human autonomy in the sight of God, and he knows its importance; but this particular side of the mystery is closed for him: the real opposition of God and man which in its operation touches the utmost depths of history. What man devises against God only occurs, in the eyes of this prophet, upon the surface of world history, whereas the depths are God's alone. The terrible thing, which Isaiah recognizes in his vision, that God inexorably gives to the creature of His hands the power to stand up against Him, is done away for Deutero-Isaiah. The refractoriness against

God spreads in history, because God "bears" it (46, 4), but its activity is composed of movements, which are mere sham, and in fact YHVH did not raise up an opponent for Himself. God foretells the coming things with mathematical precision, because only He appoints them; He announces history, because He makes it. Yet there is no place in Deutero-Isaiah for apocalyptic subjection before a fate entirely independent of man and powerful over him, and no place for an apocalyptic "removing the veil." He sees, as the prophets that were before him, not a sphere on the yonder side of history only arrayed in its likenesses; he beholds the mighty life of the occurring hour. And with all the vigorous proclamations of the divine master, that He knew from the beginning of the world the becoming and coming of this hour—we see Him setting His omnipotence against the sham force, as if this was a true force, and as if he could not conquer it except in hard battle. In this late prophet's book too, and in his book with a new emphasis, it is shown that YHVH is a God living in history. He does not fix history from the sphere on the yonder side and strange to it, He does not allow history to be unrolled as a scroll, but He Himself enters into it, and conquers it in warfare. The "valiant God" of Isaiah (9, 5; 10, 21), which Jeremiah (Jer. 32, 18) and Deuteronomy (Deut. 10, 17) retained only as an attribute among attributes, becomes here a historic reality visible to the eye: as a valiant warrior YHVH goes forth, He stirs up the zealous war (we must recall again the primitive conception of the "zealous" God), raises the battle shout, and prevails over His enemies (Is. 42, 13).

We are probably also entitled to find a connection between this undogmatic historical realism of Deutero-Isaiah's faith and the fact that he points with emphasis to the host of heaven; apparently attacking the Babylonian belief in the power of the star-gods' mastery over earthly life, the prophet points to the countless plurality of the powers, which YHVH, Lord of hosts, brings forth with fixed order, calling them all by name, and none of them missing (40, 26). Not as in an apocalyptic poem of uncertain date but to my mind not very far from the time of Deutero-Isaiah (chap. 24), the army of heaven is seen as opposing the absolute sovereignty of God, that only in the hour of His ascent to the royal throne (here as in Deutero-Isaiah, 52, 7) He "shall visit" and subdue it, until the moon shall become flushed and the sun

pale (24, 21, 23); such an existence of supramundane opposite
powers is not to be endured here, even as a passing affair. The gods
are creatures of the human mind, but the stars and planets are
a living reality: the innumerably vast serving army of the One.
While we are entitled to take the criticism of the astral religion
as a warning to Cyrus, that he should guard himself from the spirit
of Babylon, in another place Deutero-Isaiah appears to deal boldly
and powerfully with the religion of the king of Persia himself. We
read in one of the Gathas (Yasna 44, 5), in the middle of a series
of questions of Zarathustra to the most high God concerning the
formation of the world, "Who created with adroit action light and
darkness? Who created with adroit action sleeping and working?"
The answer "Ahuramazda" is "already given in the manner of the
formulation of the questions." [5] In Deutero-Isaiah's book (45, 6f)
YHVH says in the same message directed straight at Cyrus "His
anointed" (v. 1), where He promises to him "the treasures of
darkness," that is to say the blessings of the time of salvation still
hidden in darkness, He says, "I am YHVH, there is none else;
former of light and creator of darkness, maker of peace and creator
of evil, I YHVH make all these." We do not know when the Gathas
were composed, but there is no reason to doubt that the teaching
about the most high God, Who created light and darkness, was
ancient and widespread in the days of Cyrus.[6] May we therefore
suppose that in contrast to the prophet's handling of the Babylonian astral gods (cf. also 46, 1f), he here identifies the one with
the other, and proclaims that YHVH is this same creator God?
Such an identification would be inconsistent with the severe deci-
siveness of Deutero-Isaiah's belief in the Unity; it is not possible
for him to think of identifying the One with the chief of a world
of gods, even if that world be in the eyes of the Achaemenidae still
only "a princely household of tribal gods." [7] But the truth of the
matter is that the prophet declares of his God something completely different from the Gathas, even though probably the words
used refer to their teaching. Mazda did not by himself create good
and evil, "he brought forth the creators of these oppositions, but
the opposition itself is not his work"; the twin spirits brought

[5] Bartholomae, Die Gathas des Awesta (1905), 65.
[6] Cf. Nyberg, Die Religionen des alten Iran (1938), 101ff.
[7] *Ibid.*, 373.

forth by him produce the opposition of good and evil by choosing each one of them the world opposite to that of the other. YHVH is absolutely different, as He reveals Himself to Cyrus in the words of the prophet. He creates by Himself not only the cosmic opposition pair light-darkness, but also that which constitutes the human sphere, peace-evil. That *shalom,* "peace," "welfare," and not *tov,* "good," is here contrasted with *ra,* "evil," is obviously in order to keep away the notions of ethical opposition. Evil in the sense of wickedness comes into the world only as a result of resistance to God; but evil in the sense of adversity and affliction—here the prophet gives a theological answer to the question of his generation about the origin of evil—is fashioned by God Himself for purposes of His leadership of the world, without gaining thereby the same standing as peace, since in the last resort this rules alone. It should also be noticed that the verb "to create," reserved for the divine activity, is used by the prophet here only in relation to the negative creations, darkness and evil, and it will be found that the expression is emphasized here still more in its content as a theological declaration.

Certainly it would not be right to say that the sentence is directed against the Persian belief in two powers, as was formerly thought. Certainly "verse 7, closely connected as it is with verse 6, is directed against the nations in general." [8] Certainly the prophet sets out "not against a definite religion, but against the religions of the ancient world in general"; [9] but this, as with everything of his, notwithstanding the universalist pathos of the expression, is determined by historical reality; the motive and the direction of the saying are the reality of the hour.

Deutero-Isaiah certainly knew the first chapter of Genesis. Here he found darkness as primal matter which, according to the text, might be regarded as uncreated. In his zeal for the exclusiveness of his God, the prophet could not content himself with regarding darkness as a negative idea, as the mere absence of light; in argument darkness as evil is a polar fixture, and about darkness with its apparently independent power to consume the light it was necessary to know that it is a created thing. But when YHVH says, by the mouth of the prophet, that He creates darkness as He

[8] Haller, Die Kyros-Lieder Deuterojesajas (Gunkel-Festschrift), 268.
[9] Volz, Jesaia II (1932), 64f.

creates evil, there is in this another meaning than simply that both were created in the beginning. In the eyes of Deutero-Isaiah God's creation is something of all ages and times, something happening again and again, something even historical. God created Israel (43, 1, 7, 15), He creates new things in the historical hour for which the prophet speaks (48, 6f), He creates for the sake of His work of redemption a transformation of nature, which is also symbolic of the spiritual transformation (41, 20), He creates salvation and righteousness (45, 8). God creates in history. There is no theological boundary in the eyes of this prophet between creation and history.

Just as in the book of Genesis the story of the formation of the world is only the opening of the story of the formation of the people, and obviously the whole connection is aimed at making us follow the meaning of the origin of Israel back to the meaning of the world's origin, so and still more so all that Deutero-Isaiah has to say about the creation points to history; likewise as all that he has to say about history points to the hope of redemption.[10] In some verses the realms even penetrate one another, and this is most clear when the prophet (51, 9f), in a figurative expression taken from what seems to be a common Semitic myth, calls upon YHVH's arm to "awake," for it is that which in days of old pierced the dragon, and that which dried up the "waters of the great deep" and "made the depths of the sea a way for the redeemed to pass over." The creation of the world and the deliverance of Israel at the Red Sea "coincide for the eye of the prophet into one act of God's universal will to save";[11] and the prophet uses, in order to express as vividly as possible the fusion of both ideas, the same word to describe the depths of the water, *tehom,* as is used both in the beginning of the creation story (Gen. 1, 2), and again in the Song of the Sea (Ex. 15, 5, 8), and the union of the two realms is decided by a third factor, the act of redemption immediately expected. The same thing is expressed in the composition of the book by the repetition of a definite phrase in another sphere; so for example (I only instance here one of many examples) the acknowledgement of the Creator passes over (Is. 40, 12ff) to an

[10] Cf. v. Rad, Das theologische Problem des alttestamentlichen Schoepfungsglaubens (Werden und Wesen des Alten Testaments), 140ff.
[11] *Ibid.,* 142.

acknowledgement of His absolute superiority over the world of of nations, which is as nothing and nought before Him, and afterwards in the promise of redemption (41, 12) the words recur to declare that the enemies of Israel shall be then as nothing and nought. The Biblical mode of expression by repetition the prophet uses in a special way, the same words recurring in different realms, and these being connected by peculiar associations of speech and so explaining and completing each other. So the analogy or even the essential unity of creation, control in history, and redemption imprints itself in the memory of the hearer or reader whose heart is open to receive. Certainly this is no mere artificial means of expression, but the unity of the spheres in the prophet's faith in God transposes itself into a unity of speech and expresses itself in it.

* * *

As Deutero-Isaiah links together creation and redemption, so in the matter of redemption he links the redemption of Israel with that of the nations. The prophet's universalism, however, is still more concrete than is generally assumed.

Amos had proclaimed YHVH to be the liberator of the nations, who in contrast to Israel do not know His name or His nature, and who in His stead beheld the wishes of their heart. Deutero-Isaiah proclaims Him as the future liberator of the subject nations, who do not know Him yet as Cyrus, called by Him to begin the work of liberation, does not know Him (45, 4f, emphasized by repetition): decisive for the things to come is that the nations should know Him as Cyrus should know Him. The call, "Turn ye unto Me and be saved, all the ends of the earth" (v. 22), is by no means only of religious significance—everything announced and everything demanded is here to be understood both as national-historical, and also as religio-suprahistorical—but it is for the same nations, subjugated by Babylon and other ruthless powers, to turn to YHVH, Who wills to bring them into liberty in the great future historical hour. For He is the only Liberator, and there is none else (v. 21). He is "the just God," and justice in the formation of the order of nations (the word *tsedaqah* has assumed this meaning here) proceeds from Him. The close succession of sayings referring to different circles, and the use of similar ideas in different circles, resulted in important verses being improperly understood. If the prophet announces (49, 12) that multitudes should come from far, from the north and from the west, there is no need to see these multitudes as Israel, in spite of a nearby verse where the language does refer to Israel (43, 6): he means all those nations, imprisoned in "darkness" (42, 7; 49, 9), whom God will bring into liberty.[12] They must be made to inherit the desolate heritages upon the restored earth (49, 8), that God's "deliverance" shall be "unto the end of the earth" (v. 6). Israel's comfort, with which the book began, here rises to be the comfort of humanity. As in the aforementioned apocalyptic song (25, 7f) "all peoples" are called YHVH's "people," His people whose reproach shall be removed "from off the whole earth," and as in the psalm (Ps. 47), which is apparently from the same age, the psalm that glorifies the moment in which YHVH shall sit upon the throne to reign over the nations of the whole earth, the princes of the assembled peoples are called by the name of "the people of the God of Abraham," [13] the father of many nations, so here all the afflicted of YHVH are raised up (Is. 49, 13) to the status of "His people," for He has mercy on them. Only from here can we grasp the function of the "servant of YHVH," who is called to be a "light of nations," and a "covenant of the people," that is a covenant of the people made up out of the peoples (vv. 6 and 8; 42, 6; for the word "people" cf. v. 5). He is to establish *mishpat* upon the earth (42, 4), that is to say the new world order, in which that same *tsedaqah* of God materializes. Therefore "the shores await His instruction."

Isaiah prophesied (2, 1ff) the days to come, when all nations will flow to YHVH's mountain, and there receive His "instruction," that will make up matters between them and order the new life of the peoples; he saw in his imagination representatives of the Ethiopians coming up then to Mount Zion, and bringing presents to its God (18, 7). Deutero-Isaiah prophesies that representatives of nations in subjection, whom Egypt made to toil, and whom Ethiopia did sell (so, I think, the difficult verse 45, 14, must be understood), will come when they are freed, albeit of

[12] Only Torrey in his book, The Second Isaiah (1928), 115f, 380, 385, understands these verses aright, but because he assigns the author to a later age, he precludes a historical understanding.

[13] Cf. Staerk, Zum Ebed-Jahwe-Problem, Zeitschrift fuer alttestamentliche Wissenschaft, Neue Folge III (1926), 249.

their own will in chains of iron, to show that they are passing over to YHVH's service, and pray in the direction of Mount Zion, (v. 15 also belongs to the prayer, and perhaps even vv. 16 and 17): "Truly Thou art a God that hides Himself, God of Israel, Savior." YHVH, according to their opinion, had hidden Himself on the other side of history, so to speak, but now He has shone forth as the liberator of Israel and all of them. So, too, Israel had thought their way to be hid from YHVH (40, 27). Over against this stands YHVH's word (45, 19), that not in secret did He declare to the heathen world His message which He handed down to Israel (cf. 48, 16)—and now (45, 20) : "Gather yourselves together and come, draw near together, ye escaped of the nations."

What in Isaiah was only alluded to, is here fully expressed; Israel's redemption and the redemption of the nations are merely different stages in the one great act of redemption which God performs in the world of men. What will happen now to Israel presupposes what will happen to the nations. Israel will prepare for God the proper instrument for His work among mankind. From this may be understood what is meant by the "servant of YHVH."

* * *

The many attempts to explain the figure of the servant of YHVH are essentially of three classes.

Supporters of the first class regard the "servant" corporately: as the actual Israel, or as the "ideal Israel," or as the nucleus or remnant of the people faithful to YHVH; but this interpretation among other things does not agree with the ponderous passage, where at the beginning (49, 5) the original function of the servant is depicted as being to "bring back" Israel to YHVH, and afterwards in a certainly important expansion of this function the restoration of the tribes of Israel is portrayed as a matter "too light" for him. It is certainly right that in the Bible we may see "the corporate personality as a pattern and as an educator," [14] but this does not prove "that this ideal entity can exercise a function upon the real one." The Israel conception living in the people can act educationally, but a real function such as this "to assign desolate heritages" (v. 8) cannot be entrusted to it by God, just as it cannot take upon itself the real suffering of the

[14] Eissfeldt, Der Gottesknecht bei Deuterojesaja (1933), 21.

people. What the prophet says (53, 8–12) about the servant's death and future cannot be connected with a corporate part of the community.

Supporters of the second class see in the servant of YHVH a historic figure. This is either the figure of a well-known person: here a whole line of historical personages has been mentioned, beginning with Moses and proceeding to Deutero-Isaiah himself, and even after his time to one of the martyrs in the Maccabean age (presuming a date of the songs as late as this); or it is a contemporary of the prophet, otherwise unknown to us. This view again is upset principally by the fact that not only is the death of this person related (53, 9), but also a future promised to him after his death (v. 10ff). The language, just here most precise and sober, precludes any thought of a resurrection of the dead.

The third, the Messianic, is also an individualistic interpretation. We find it, as well as the second interpretation, already in the Acts of the Apostles (Acts, 8, 30ff). Although in the essential point this interpretation approximates closely in my view to the prophet's true intention, it is opposed by an unsurmountable difficulty, namely that the servant's testimony about himself, his toil, and his struggles hitherto (Is. 49, 1ff) cannot well be understood as of the future, that is to say as an anticipation of a future utterance of a man not yet existing, or at any rate not yet visible. And so they attempt to attribute the last song to another and later author, and to interpret this song only as Messianic, and to explain the remaining three songs as relating to a historical personage, for example the prophet himself. But this view, that the man of whom it is said (53, 7) that he was led as a sheep to the slaughter and opened not his mouth, is different from the man who says of himself (50, 6), "My back have I given to the smiters," is contrary to a straightforward and plain understanding of the text.

Generally speaking the interpretations are forced either into making omissions or alterations, for which there is no reason as far as the songs themselves are concerned, or into assigning them to different authors. But no statistical analysis of words has been able to uproot the impression of a stylistic unity prevailing in the songs themselves and linking them with the rest of the book. The one thing to which the investigation points again and again, is that the songs may be from another period in the life of the prophet than the rest of the book, and apparently from a later period.

For a more exact understanding of the personality of the servant of YHVH the following things should be taken into consideration:

1. In the book of Deutero-Isaiah the changing proclamations come to three recipients, Israel, Cyrus, and the servant. Between these recipients different orders of relationship prevail; expressions recur here and there in due proportion, and their recurrence cannot be regarded as accidental. This connection in the choice of words is greatest between Israel and the servant: both are "chosen" by God (cf. on the one hand 41, 8f; 44, 1f; 48, 10; and on the other hand 42, 1; 49, 7), both are fashioned by Him "from the womb" (44, 2; 49, 5), both are "preserved" (49, 6; 42, 6; 49, 8), both are "upheld" (41, 10; 42, 1), both are "honored" (43, 4; 49, 5) and in both YHVH "glorifies Himself" (44, 23; 49, 3), both are to act according to the divine "instruction" (42, 21; 42, 4), on both God's Spirit is bestowed or poured (44, 3; 42, 1). But we also find linguistic connections between Israel and Cyrus: both "are called by name" by YHVH (43, 1; 45, 1, 4), and both are ignorant of what God is preparing for them, or who it is that is preparing (48, 8; 45, 4f). Furthermore there are some expressions that connect the three of them; the most characteristic of them is this, that it is YHVH's "desire," His purpose, which it is Israel's task to execute (42, 21), which Cyrus is considered to accomplish (44, 28; 46, 10; cf. also 48, 14), and finally which will prosper in the hand of "the servant" (53, 10). Over against this there is no special connection between Cyrus and the servant, apart from the fact (if we take together here the fragment, 61, 1, which has become fused with later parts) that both are "anointed," as Elijah was bidden (1 Kgs. 19, 15) to anoint an alien king and also his own successor; only the king of Israel is missing, characteristically, among those anointed in Deutero-Isaiah's words. This fact, that there is no connection between Cyrus and the servant, apart from the personal divine charge symbolized in the act of anointing, is significant; these two, acting to a certain extent in the same age, have nothing common to both of them alone; apart from the general concept of

divine charge (this is common to both of them, as also to Israel and others) they differ quite essentially in their character, their destiny, and their acts. To Israel and Cyrus there is nothing common, except that both of them are called by God, though neither of them know it. It is different with Israel and the servant; here the servant succeeds and replaces Israel, so that being and activity belonging to Israel pass over onto him. To Cyrus the servant is related as the charge of the one is related to the charge of the other; to Israel he is related as the charge conceived in accomplishment is related to the unaccomplished one.

2. Many times in the book of Deutero-Isaiah the "coming" things or the "new" things are set over against the "former" things. These latter are prophecies of former times, prophecies which now have been, or are being, fulfilled, whereas the former are prophecies now uttered, or hinted at, which will be fulfilled with the same certitude as are now the others. Often the nations or their idols, the products of the nations' desires, are asked whether they have made known or have known aforetime anything of the things now being fulfilled, whereas Israel is witness of the prophecy spoken aforetime; or the nations and their idols are asked whether they understand the course of things, and whether they can interpret the announcement now proceeding forth into the world. In connection with the confrontation of the two (that sometimes is only hinted at) always one of them, the former or the new things, or both of them, are elucidated by means of present or future events. So the call of Cyrus, recorded in 41, 25, which has already taken place, belongs to the confrontation in vv. 22f, 26; 42, 9, in connection with the "new things" looks back to the proclamation of the servant's mission, vv. 1–8; the "former things" of 43, 9, are elucidated by the once announced and now approaching return of the exiles, vv. 5f, whereas the "new things" of 43, 19, are only revealed in the prophecy of the outpouring of the Spirit, 44, 3, which is again summarized in v. 7 as the "coming things"; the "former things" of 46, 9 refer again to the "hawk" from the east, v. 11; and finally the contrast of the "new things" and the "former things" of 48, 3–6, is expanded in the following: the former things are God's imminent work in Babylon by Cyrus (v. 14f), whereas the new things express themselves in a saying that clearly interrupts the sense (v. 16), but that at all events cannot

be said to be a later interpolation, but only an addition of the author himself, and obviously is to be understood as a saying of the servant of YHVH: "And now my Lord YHVH has sent me and His Spirit."

If we now examine all the "former things" together, we see that they are definitely related to the verses in Isaiah's song of the child (9, 3f) about the redemption from the oppressor's rod, that is to say, to the prophecy of the people's liberation, which the *limmud* Deutero-Isaiah understands as the liberation from the Babylonian exile. Over against this Isaiah's prophecy concerning the future ruler is interpreted of Cyrus, the "anointed one" (the "man of my counsel," 46, 11, compare the "counsellor of the valiant God" of 9, 5, EV 6). David's throne (9, 6, EV 7) man shall no more sit upon; the "faithful graces (promised) to David" (53, 3) pass over to Israel ("to you"); the king of Israel, in accordance with the primal covenant, is now none other than YHVH Himself (52, 7; cf. 41, 21; 43, 15; 44, 6). The "shoot" that comes out of "Jesse's stump" (11, 1) is no offspring of David; this is no natural seed, but a "holy seed" (6, 13). This is the man, on whom YHVH's Spirit rests (11, 2), as it is "put upon him" (42, 1; cf. 61, 1) and sent together with him (48, 16), the man who "vindicates with equity the weak of the earth" (11, 4), just as he is sent "to bring good tidings to the weak" (61, 1), the man who "judges" (11, 3f), and "sets justice in the earth" (42, 3f), the man who does not smite except with the rod of his mouth, and does not slay the wicked except with the breath of his lips (11, 4), who does not cry, nor make his voice to be heard in the street, who does not break the crushed reed, nor quench the smoking flax (42, 2f), that is to say the servant.

3. It has been, I think, rightly observed,[15] that in the second half of the book of Deutero-Isaiah the person of Cyrus withdraws, as the prophet becomes disappointed with the lord of the nations. Perhaps Deutero-Isaiah, who apparently handed on his message to Cyrus either from his proximity to the court or by another way, had received "a clear and definite rejection of his suggestions," even before the overthrow of Babylon. But the text itself leads us farther than this explanation. Not only did Cyrus not call upon YHVH's name at all (41, 25), but after the conquest

[15] Haller, *op. cit.*, 273f.

he venerated the former gods of Babylon. By this act he explicitly stated that he, Cyrus, "did not know" YHVH, nor wished to know Him, at all events as the One. In the first servant song, which apparently was the first composed as well as the first in order, the prophet supplies the answer to this. Here his God says (42, 8): "I am YHVH, that is my name (this means, my name testifies to me as the One Who, in contrast to all the idols, is really there), and my glory (*kabhod*) I will not give to another, nor my praise to graven images" (cf. 48, 11). Bel and Nebo, idols of Babylon (46, 1), that are carried on the shoulder (v. 7), must not boast themselves, as Cyrus glorifies them, that they are those who called and empowered him to go forth in punitive battle against Babylon. The whole of this world historical spectacle, which YHVH devised for the hour of turning, and which Cyrus imperfectly executed, was only a prelude. "Behold the former things are come to pass, and new things do I declare, before they spring forth I tell you" (42, 9). The hour of the king of Persia, who has liberated Israel from the yoke of Babylon, passes away and the hour of the "servant" begins, he who attends to YHVH's "desire" to redeem the world of the nations from the yoke of its guilt.

4. From this point it becomes clear not only that in the second half of the book the figure of the servant ousts that of Cyrus, but also that the first song is placed so much earlier than the rest; the song (42, 1ff) follows immediately the first declaration of the deeds of Cyrus (41, 25). In the days when the book was being composed out of the speeches and pamphlets, there must certainly have been everywhere a feeling of disappointment, and therefore it was necessary to connect with the recognition of the unsatisfactory character of the work of Cyrus the announcement of the future satisfactory work of the servant. This, and one further point. In 41, 8ff, God addresses Israel as His servant, whom He has chosen and held. Here in the first part of the book Israel receives only comfort and encouragement, but soon, perhaps on account of certain negative experiences of the people, the dispute with Israel begins (42, 18ff). In order to guard the hearer and reader against errors liable to arise from restricted horizon, and to enlarge his vision in the revealed ways of God, it was necessary to set up over against the inadequate servant, Israel, the anony-

mous servant, who has been "chosen" and "held" as Israel but unlike Israel was one in whom YHVH also delighted, and upon whom
He put His Spirit (42, 1). This contrast recurs again and again
during the course of the book. The stubborn is contrasted with
the submissive, the timid with the bold, the blind with the en-
lightening, and for all this God calls both of them without distinction "my servant" (for Cyrus the prophet avoids this epithet,
although Nebuchadrezzar is so called by Jeremiah, 25, 9), and
promises to both of them His protection, His assistance, and the
future gift of His bliss. This contrast is a strong paradox of the
book, and again it is not surprising that often the attempt has
been made to identify them. There are also those who try to overcome the difficulty by means of positing a later fusion of different
elements, and further that the verses among them which speak of
the personality of the servant have been adapted to refer to Israel.
Especially have they stressed the verse (49, 3) in which the servant
tells that YHVH said to him: "My servant art thou, Israel in
whom I glorify myself." These words are not to be regarded as
proof of the truth of the corporate interpretation, nor is the word
"Israel" to be omitted as a later insertion. If the saying really was
directed to Israel, there was no need to say: "Thou art Israel."
If, however, what is meant by the servant is a person, but a person
standing in a quite peculiarly close relationship to Israel, it is
fairly evident that God speaks to him: "*Thou* art the Israel in
whom I glorify myself." The paradox of the two "servants" cannot be solved or dispelled. It is intended to be a paradox. In it
we recognize the supposition necessary in order that Isaiah's
Messianic prophecy should be transformed into the Messianic
mystery of Deutero-Isaiah.

*   *   *

Two nearby songs of the servant, 49, 1ff and 50, 4ff, are spoken
in the first person: the servant speaks of his lot, and his work,
and of God's dealing with him. The second song is closely connected with the first both by content and language; there is hardly
any doubt that the "I" of the second too is the "I" of the servant,
even though it is also clear that it is the prophet himself speaking.
Like Jeremiah he speaks about the vocation and suffering of the
prophet, but Jeremiah's complaint is not heard from his mouth.
He speaks as a prophet's disciple, as one who stands in the line

of the prophetic tradition, who expounds an ancient tradition that had reached him and reveals its true meaning. And it is YHVH Who enables him to expound it so, and to express its meaning. What YHVH works on him is not so powerfully primal as what He worked on his master, whose *limmud* he calls himself. "In my ears is YHVH of hosts," so the young Isaiah described his experience (5, 9), whereas the disciple says (50, 4), "Morning by morning He awakens me an ear." The recipient of the revelation is no more overcome again and again by the revealer; in a gentle contact with Him he feels the steady influence of His might, and he regards this influence not as a penetration, but as a removal of the seal, as an "opening" (v. 5). He says that he did not "rebel" like Jeremiah; every affliction and ignominy that happen to him in the fulfilment of his duty, he not only received heartily, he "gave his cheeks" (v. 6). The ignominy did not cause him shame, he cannot be put to shame, for "his justifier is near" (v. 8). Because his lord helps him (v. 9), his adversary will not be able to condemn him; let him do what he will do, but he will not be able to make him a condemned one.

Shall we then say that the servant is none other than the prophet himself? If so, it would follow that the last song must be separated from the preceding songs with which it is intimately bound up— the last song, which cannot be understood at all as spoken of himself. We must for the time being stand by the fact that he is entitled to speak as "servant," without being the servant; that he can identify himself with the present of the servant, without by this identifying himself with him. The servant is not a corporate, but a personal being; and in spite of this the prophet is included in him. We touch here upon the second paradox of this book.

The first of the songs in the first person also begins in prophetic language. The speaker does not address Israel, as in the preceding or following section, but the "shores"; he requires the distant peoples to attend to his word, for what he has to say, to say about himself, concerns them. He says first what we know from the prophecy of Jeremiah (Jer. 1, 5), that YHVH has called him from the womb. But now a new matter arises, that does not remind us of any prophet's tale about himself: God, Who has set His mouth like a sharp sword, and even has made him altogether like a polished arrow, has hidden him in the shadow of His hand, He has concealed him, the arrow, in His quiver. The saying does not mean that he, who is called to be servant, was first preserved, and afterwards "worked in Israel as sword and arrow." [16] Nothing at all is told of a moment in which the sword kept in the hand has been brandished, and in which the arrow hidden in the quiver has been brought forth and shot. Only because the servant feels himself to be an arrow in God's quiver, which God has not used really according to the forces placed in him, an arrow that has not been shot, and is not apparently likely to be shot any longer, can he say (49, 4) that he has toiled in vain, that he has consumed his strength for nought and vanity. A great might was put in his soul in the hour he was called, but this might was never allowed to act. He felt that he was fashioned and trained for a special service (v. 5f): it was laid upon him to "bring back" to YHVH, and to set up anew, Israel which had sinned and gone into exile, but which was "preserved" in its core; and just for this he had toiled in vain. Now, however, he hears (v. 4) that his right and his "work," that is the success of his work as it is due to him, are "with his God," they are reserved for him by God. For YHVH honors him with a far superior task to that which he conceived as his own. That is the hour (v. 7), in which the vanity of his work stood out most, in which he—called to be YHVH's servant—is forced to be a despised servant of earthly rulers (perhaps this saying hints at a small and unblessed office held by the prophet in the court of Cyrus). And in this very hour YHVH addresses him directly, and hands over to him the task for the new world of men, the task for the sake of which the peoples from afar must listen to this message of his, and at the fulfilment of which kings shall arise and worship the Holy One of Israel (v. 7). YHVH wishes to set him as a "light of the nations" (v. 6), and as a "covenant of the people" (v. 8)—it is his part to cause light to shine for the nations in this hour of darkness, and to link them together to be a human people of God. With the "time of favor," in which God thus makes answer concerning his affliction, there dawns the "day of salvation" (v. 8), in which God's salvation shall be to the end of the earth (v. 6). And for this work, which he must perform in this day, YHVH wills to "preserve" him (v. 8).

In the song "My Lord YHVH has given me a *limmudim*-tongue"

[16] Volz, *op. cit.*, 157.

the prophetic situation as it is comes before us; the song "Hearken, ye shores, unto me" departs from this situation, and overflows its bounds. The former is easily understood from the life conscience of the man who is speaking; whereas the latter draws a large circle, which may appear to the person as belonging to him by its nature, but in the reality of the fulfilment spreads far beyond this peculiar being. The servant's personality encompasses and covers the personality of the prophet, going out and beyond his bounds. For the duration of the "preservation" extends beyond the domain of a human life.

The afflictions related in the song of the *limmud,* the toil told of in the message to the shores, are transformed in the last song (52, 13–53, 12) into the whole existence of a man of sorrows. In this life there is nothing to be found of the promised fulfilment of the great task. In a different likeness, in an appearance "marred more than that of man" (52, 14), the servant stands before us, and yet things are perfected here, which we have already met there. His affliction has here become the disfigurement of the whole resemblance, like leprosy ("as one that hides the face from us," 53, 3; that is to say, one that has to hide his face from us, cf. Lev. 13, 45), his state as one despised has become as one whom all creatures shun, seeing in him one smitten of God (v. 4), and his willing patience has become a self-sacrificing going to death. And as finally the truth of his being and life is revealed, we again hear of the "kings" (52, 15), how they are amazed at that which they had not divined as occurring before them in the garb of the mystery, as they had been amazed before over the fulfilment of the task among the nations.

The song is related to a prophecy—"a report" (53, 1; cf. 28, 9, 19)—that was sent aforetime to the rulers of the nations; this is to be seen as textually, or at all events essentially, identical with the first two songs. In this later stage of the message, in which YHVH reveals also the amazing way to its materialization, he declares that when the fulfilment takes place before the eyes of all in a way of which the kings had not heard before (52, 15), they will in their memory come up to the same hour, in which the prophecy was sent to them: who could believe, then, such an unbelievable thing? (53, 1). Only in their mouth are the following verses understandable in direct connection with the rest, that is the insight born and nourished by the new unexpected facts, the insight into the meaning of the servant's afflictions as a bearing of iniquities. These iniquities, which he has borne, are not those of Israel, concerning which it was publicly announced (40, 2) that they were already atoned for by their affliction. It was already known since the prophecy of Amos (Am. 3, 2), that among all the peoples Israel are the people which God Himself visits for their offences, and when they return in repentance He Himself redeems them; no one can interfere in the matter. The people receive correction from God's own hand; but again it is God Himself Who "bears" Israel's offenses (cf. for example Hos. 14, 3, EV 2; Is. 33, 24; this verb must not be weakened to mean forgiveness only); yes, He Himself bears the people themselves "from the womb" (46, 3), loads them upon Himself, and carries them unto its old age, He will punish them and will save them (v. 4). The gods of the nations are not so: certainly the nations think that the gods can bear them, they load themselves upon them as upon a beast, but the gods merely bow down under the burden and cannot bear nor save (v. 2). How will the sinful nations be saved? Here the servant, experienced in affliction, offers (50, 6) his back. Certainly he does not know what it is that he wills to load upon himself, but this readiness of his to carry affliction for God's sake is limitless. And from heaven his offer is accepted. Upon him there now falls the "chastisement of our peace" (53, 5); he bears all the sicknesses and the griefs of the sins of the people (v. 4)—"of my people" (v. 8) every king says for his people—the sins pierce and crush him (v. 5), his appearance is unhumanly marred (52, 14), he appears as a leper, despised and shunned (53, 3). This is no mere symbolic, ecstatic carrying, like that of Ezekiel (Ezek. 4, 5f), who had to lie on his side and to bear the iniquity of Israel and Judah as a burden laden upon him, but a quite real carrying. And it is not meant that the servant takes upon himself the penalty for all this wickedness: he bears the iniquities themselves, which indeed are not from the first—as men are inclined to regard such a matter today—diseases, but become such, dreadful decompositions and disfigurements. The fact that this awful fusion of all the evil in the servant's body-soul experience manifests itself in leprosy, is surely connected with the view, which I recalled above in relation to Isaiah's vision, that in this disease there breaks out a disturbance of the relationship between heaven and earth. Perhaps we may see in this also some connection with the beginning of that same vision, with the mention of the leprous king near to death, with the prophet's confession of impurity, when he identified himself with the guilty people. What is there hinted at is here completed. But it seems to me that by the picture of the leprosy a much discussed saying in this song is explained. In one of the most difficult verses in the difficult text (Is. 53, 10), YHVH states as a condition of the future life and work of the servant: "if his soul makes a guilt-offering." Some scholars see in this a "clear and definite" expression of "vicarious expiation." [17] But the wording does not allow such an interpretation. *Asham,* "guilt-offering," means compensation and not expiation. It is the name of the gift which the leper had to bring on the day of his purification (Lev. 4, 11ff). We have no indication as to how we should picture in our minds the future purification of him stricken with the leprosy of the world; but we are told that he must purify himself before he enters upon his duty of bringing to the nations the order of righteousness, and of linking them together to a people of peoples in his capacity as a "covenant." All of them have erred like sheep, every one has become separated from the others and turned to his own way (Is. 53, 6); and he, who lets himself be brought as a sheep to the slaughter, shall now arrange anew the re-united flock.

After the speech of the rulers, the prophet announces at first in his own name, and afterwards in YHVH's name, about the servant's future, about the future that fits God's "desire," His plan (v. 10), which will prosper in the servant's hand. This closing saying links on to the opening one: the servant must now accomplish his active work after the passive, he must exalt himself highly, enjoy the new blessings among the "many" (v. 12), whose iniquities he bare, and see a succession ("seed") which shall prolong his work (so we are certainly entitled to complete what is said). But how can all this come to pass, since we have been told of his death and burial (v. 9)? One is inclined to think that here a resurrection of the dead is spoken of; but in such a case a direct exposition would necessarily have been given of this supernatural conception, for individual resurrection was utterly unfa-

---

[17] R. Kittel in his edition of Dilmann's Commentary on Isaiah, 456.

miliar to the thought of the Israelite hearer or reader of the prophet. We can only understand the real meaning, if we conjure up in our minds what we have already discovered in the second song and which we can here recognize even more clearly—that is, that the substance of the servant is more than a single human person without, however, having a corporate character. Here we infer that this person takes shape in many likenesses and life-ways, the bearers of which are identical in their innermost essence, but no supernatural event, no resurrection of the dead leads from one of these figures to the next. It seems to me that we are permitted to take the remarkable phrase "in his deaths" (v. 9) quite literally: it is not a single death that comes upon the servant on his way, he goes from death to death, and to new life again.

There are three stages on this way. The first is the prophetic stage. In the futile labor of the Israelite prophet in Israel, he sees himself as an arrow which, it is decreed, is to remain in its quiver; but he is promised that a great work will be preserved for him in the future, reaching far beyond the confines of Israel, and compared with which all that he now does and endures is mere preparation. The prophet does not know when and how this will take place; but because God offers him to bear an immense affliction, he who is accustomed and willing to suffer, loads it upon himself not asking how and why, for he knows that he has to bear it for God's sake. The second stage is the *acting* of the affliction. Since the servant not only endures the affliction loaded upon him without kicking against it but also, as it were, accomplishes it, it becomes as though changed into an *act*. Job recognized that affliction is a mystery of God, and the Psalmist recognized that God loves those who suffer willingly; YHVH's servant recognizes the mystery of affliction in this that it is affliction for God's sake and for the sake of His "desire." And the third stage is the "success" of the desire: the work born out of affliction, the liberation of the subject peoples, laid upon the servant, the divine order of the expiated world of the nations, which the purified servant as its "light" has to bring in, the covenant of the people of the human beings with God, the human center of which is the servant. Only now the sharp arrow is expelled from the darkness of the quiver and hurled forth. The Spirit of his Lord is on the "anointed" servant and reveals him. It is still laid upon him, who was a

prophet from the foundation on, to proclaim a message (61, 1);
but this message ends in the inauguration of God's new order
of justice for the world (42, 3).

These three stages are not to be comprehended in the life span
of a single man. They are the way of the one servant, passing
through all the different likenesses and life cycles. We do not know
how many of them the prophet himself saw in his vision; it is
to be supposed that it was not given him to know very much
about what he saw. Neither can we presume what historical figures
he included in the servant's way; it was laid upon the anonymous
prophet to announce a mystery, not to interpret it. But one thing is
clear to us, that he saw himself at one point on the way. It can
never be proved that these two, the servant and his announcer,
are one; but many sayings in the two songs written in the first
person tell us that "Deutero-Isaiah" felt himself as one of the
figurations of the servant, and that he felt himself as the one
among them before whom was uncovered the mystery of the servant's being concealed and of his future being revealed. We may
assume that, after he had despaired of Cyrus, he recognized his
own being as one of the temporal elements in the way of the person
for whom the very work of the redemption of world history was
reserved. He was able to recognize it because he was in truth a
prophet, a *nabi*, and in so far as he was such.

                              *   *   *

The Israelite *nabi* was in former days a leader, a prophetic
leader; it was as a *nabi* that the first liberator lived in the memory
of the people. According to the book of Deuteronomy (Deut. 18,
15, 18), Moses received God's word and transmitted it to the
people, that in time of necessity there would be raised up for them
again and again a *nabi* "like him," that is, there would again and
and again appear a prophetic leader. Certainly in the time of the
Judges we do not generally find the *nabi* as leader, but in order
to lead it was necessary to receive the divine Spirit, and therefore
it was laid upon the "judge" to pass through the *nabi* stage. After
the kingdom had been firmly established, the *nabi* was pushed
from his place if he was not willing to be paid court minister of
spiritual affairs, and instead he became a powerless opposition to
the powerful; instead of leading, he had to expound what true
leadership is and what it is not. And from the nature of things this

meant for the *nabi* an increasingly dangerous venture. God's truth, which he had to prophesy, is opposed to all that the court and princes wish to hear, and in the sphere of foreign affairs also opposed to what the people wish to hear. The *nabi* has more and more to be prepared not only for scornful rejection of his message, but also for ill treatment, imprisonment, and even death. The Messianic promise of a king, who will fulfill his task, hints at things beyond this state. Nothing is said about prophets in the Messianic days, possibly because it seemed that in future there would be no need of them. But at the time of the catastrophe, the disappointment with kings grew into disappointment with the kingdom in Israel. In Ezekiel's plan for a temple theocracy, God's vicegerent, the prince, becomes a figure without other meaning than external representation. But the *nabi* begins anew to acquire in prophetic thought the vocation to lead, the same vocation of which tradition told in former days. Certainly the *nebiim* now too frequently fail to find an attentive ear, now too they are reviled and tormented, but now they see the state of martyrdom as a transition to a new leadership; not the king but the *nabi* is appointed to be deputy of God's kingdom, and this kingdom now signifies in reality all the human world. Now there is no more need, as there was in his former prophetic career, to make his voice heard in his cry over the transgressors. Neither is there any need to break the bruised reeds from among the nations nor to quench the smoking flax, as the men of Cyrus' sort were used to do; the order which he "brings forth" sets up everything in its true place. He himself, unquenched and unbruised, establishes the order in the earth, and the most distant shores wait for his instruction. But the realization of this new vocation is laid upon the prophet himself to achieve—by making an act of the enduring of his sufferings. The suffering *nabi* is the antecedent type of the acting Messiah.

Perhaps we may see here the explanation of the enigmatical epithet of the servant, *meshullam* (Is. 42, 19). *Meshullam,* that is to say "the perfected one," [18] he is called after the maturity of his vocation, inasmuch as he is sent by God as His "messenger" to the world of nations. The fact that he is called in this place "blind" and "deaf" is apparently to be explained by the fact that at the moment God speaks he, the *nabi,* has not yet proved able

[18] So Torrey rightly interprets, *op. cit.,* 331.

to grasp fully his own destiny and the way to its accomplishment in spite of his many experiences and of the fact that his ears are open to receive God's word. His readiness to serve in his appointment is in advance of his "knowledge" (53, 11; a colon must be put after this word: the servant recognizes and knows the intention of God concerning him that is expressed in the following verses). Deutero-Isaiah sees himself as the figure the servant assumes in the hour of knowledge, the hour when the great connection of things is made known.

Admittedly the aforementioned verse about *meshullam* belongs to the verses which speak of the servant of Israel and of the personal servant in the same expressions, and the dividing line between them appears somewhat blurred. So there are passages before this (42, 16, 18) speaking of the people as blind and deaf, as this passage speaks of the blind and deaf servant. But just as we must nevertheless distinguish between them, so on the other hand we cannot overcome the difficulty by the supposition of later additions or alterations. The prophet wishes us never to forget the special tie between the personal servant and the servant Israel. They are closely fastened one to the other. The personal servant is that Israel in whom YHVH glorifies Himself as in His faithful one (49, 3), but just because he is that, YHVH can glorify Himself in Israel generally as in that which is redeemed by Him (44, 23). YHVH's love for faithless Israel, a hurt and suffering love, renews itself from the prophet's love of God, a love hurt and suffering for God's sake. There is a nucleus of Israel, preserved through the generations, that does not betray the election, that belongs to God and remains His. Through this nucleus the living connection between God and the people is upheld, in spite of the very great guilt: not alone by interposing on behalf of Israel, but far more by being the true Israel. God's purpose for Israel has put on skin and flesh in these powerless combatants. They are the small beginning of the kingdom of God before Israel becomes a beginning of it; they are the beginning before the beginning. The anointing of the kings was unfulfilled, and Deutero-Isaiah no longer awaits a king in whom this anointing should be fulfilled; the anointing of the *nebiim* has been fulfilled, and therefore it is from their midst that the figure of the perfected one will arise. All that the *nabi* in this his ultimate form shall establish in the world of the nations, Israel shall establish by him. For through him, through his word and life, Israel turns to God, and becomes God's people. No more will these two, Israel and the prophet, be opposed one to the other, and there will not even be any more distinction between them. Now not only, as up to this time, the truth of Israel, but the reality of Israel in its purity, will be embodied in the *nabi*, the reality of *Jeshurun* (44, 2), the upright people, in the reality of *Meshullam*, the perfected one. At the same hour when this man is allowed to go up, after persevering again and again in the hiddenness and migrating through afflictions and deaths unto true life; when he is allowed to go up and be a light for the nations, at that hour the servant Israel and the personal servant will have become one.

Time and again, when God addresses Israel as his servant, He speaks to one chosen by Him. The servant here denotes a person—individual or corporate—whom God chose to fulfil a special function, as anointing denotes the empowering to fulfil permanently a special function. We do not find in any other prophet in the same way as in Deutero-Isaiah the belief in the election as the basis of all his declarations. Israel was chosen from of old, and it is as a "chosen one" that the personal servant too appears in the first saying addressed to him (42, 1). The two elections mean designation to service and action. But the work to which Israel had been elected aforetime was a work complete in itself: the establishment of Israel as God's people, that is to say as a people building its whole common life under God's order and rule; it was laid upon Israel to work not on others but on itself, this work, however, was to shine in the midst of the world of nations, to win souls for God and thus to become the beginning of His kingdom, "the first of His harvest" (this conception of Jeremiah's is taken for granted by Deutero-Isaiah). This work, which Israel was called upon to do for itself and thereby for mankind, it did not do. For this reason the *nabi* was now called, who in former generations had worked continually not for himself but for Israel, to fulfil a work that had to be done directly for the world of nations, first the "bearing" of affliction, afterwards the setting up of the order of the kingdom. But the people of Israel, redeemed from the sovereignty of strangers, and cleansed from iniquity, this people has now been set up by YHVH as His kingdom (52, 7); it will establish God's sovereignty upon itself and serve as the beginning of His kingdom in the world. The suffering and acting servant acts now no more, as in his earlier form as *nabi,* from opposition to Israel, and he suffers no more because of this opposition : he suffers and acts in the name of Israel initiating the kingdom, yes, he suffers and acts as Israel. And rightly the kings speak of him and of Israel in one breath, in one utterance. He is Israel as servant. When the nations look at him, they look at the truth of Israel, the truth chosen from the very beginning.

*   *   *

The *nabi* as an early form of the Messiah we find as late as a Christian apocryphal fragment, in which the Spirit says to the Christ that It has been waiting for Him "in all the prophets" (*in omnibus prophetis*) that He should come and It should rest in Him (*requiescerem in te ;* cf. Is. 11, 2 ; and 42, 1). But the figure of the suffering Messiah that appears from generation to generation, and goes from martyrdom and death to martyrdom and death, has recognizable traces up to the latest popular tradition of Judaism : still in Hasidism the tale is told of this or that *tsaddiq,* dying a violent death, that he was Messiah, son of Joseph.

But the unity between the personal servant and the servant Israel passes over to their unity in suffering. As far as the great suffering of Israel's dispersion was not compulsory suffering only, but suffering in truth willingly borne, not passive but active, it is interpreted in the image of the servant. Whosoever accomplishes in Israel the active suffering of Israel, he is the servant, and he is Israel, in whom YHVH "glorifies Himself." The mystery of history is the mystery of a representation which at bottom is identity. The arrow, which is still concealed in the quiver, is people and man as one.

The anonymous prophet's hope that his Messianic message might be realized in his age, was not fulfilled. In the building of the Jewish state in the days of the Second Temple, in the life of the community that returned from Babylon, there was little evidence of it, in spite of all the honest attempts made by Israel to take upon itself YHVH's commandments. But the great scattering, which followed the splitting up of the state and became the essential form of the people, is endowed with the mystery of suffering as with the promise of the God of sufferers

The God, Who in the days of old caused the first father to

"stray" from his father's house and went before him in his wanderings of set purpose as a faithful shepherd, is acknowledged by suffering generations in their way, the way of exile, to be their Shepherd (40, 11). They do this in the strength of the prophetic faith: "YHVH goes before them" (52, 12). He Whom the *nabi* Abraham had recognized in days of old as the God of the way, remained the leader in the way in the anonymous prophet's message (48, 17), which the suffering generations have carried with them on their wanderings.

(The order of the books is that of the Hebrew Bible. Where references vary in the English Versions, this is noted in the text, the English reference marked EV following the Hebrew).